Praise for *I*

'*Intrinsic* enables us all to learn f
effort that inspired tens of thousan┌
to find their inner

WENDY KOPP, founder of Teach ̶ ̶ ̶ ̶ ̶ ̶ ̶ ̶, co-founder and
CEO of Teach for All

⚡

'A powerful call to arms, to live differently and better at home and
at work. This is a book which might just change how you live and
work, for the better.'

JO OWEN, bestselling and award-winning leadership
and management author

⚡

'Based on his rich observations of organizations and leaders and
the latest in motivational sciences, Jeevan points to practical
solutions to re-ignite excitement and engagement in the workplace
and beyond.'

RICHARD RYAN, co-developer of Self-Determination Theory

⚡

'*Intrinsic*'s insights are invaluable for any entrepreneur building
a successful business.'

NICK JENKINS, founder of Moonpig.com and former 'dragon'
on BBC's *Dragons' Den*

⚡

'Ground-breaking, and thought provoking. *Intrinsic* is a must read
for all parents about how we can all live more motivated lives.'

ESTHER WOJCICKI, author of *How to Raise Successful People*,
co-founder of Tract.app

⚡

'*Intrinsic* inspires optimism for a better future.
It's both a great read and a stimulus for change.'

BARONESS SALLY MORGAN, Master of Fitzwilliam College,
Cambridge University; former Chair, OFSTED

⚡

'Using stories of the impact of intrinsic motivation, purpose and autonomy, Jeevan provides a profoundly optimistic book about how to tackle the big challenges of our world, workplaces, and lives.'

HILARY PENNINGTON, Executive Vice President, Ford Foundation

'*Intrinsic* delivers an impassioned plea, backed by powerful examples from around the world, for reconstructing work, school, family, and politics to make them more worthwhile and to make our lives more fulfilling.'

DANIEL MARKOVITS, Guido Calabresi Professor of Law, Yale Law School and author of *The Meritocracy Trap*

'Built on cutting-edge research and practice, *Intrinsic* helps both employees and organizations improve engagement and impact from within – in a truly authentic and sustainable way.'

PAULO PISANO, Chief People Officer at booking.com

'In an age of anxiety, comes a fresh voice asking us to reflect, and critically to act. Rarely have we heard from an expert with a track record of reigniting the motivation of hundreds of thousands of teachers. He takes the lessons from that success to help us look into ourselves and others, to find that spark of change in our lives.'

ANTHONY PAINTER, Chief Research and Impact Officer, The Royal Society of Arts (RSA)

'*Intrinsic* is a remarkable manifesto for life. Jeevan uses his observation and instincts to develop a compelling argument for the re-focussing of individual and family life as well as communities in the world of work. He shows us how to ignite a beacon and keep the flame burning.'

ANTHONY LITTLE, former Head Master, Eton College

Intrinsic

A manifesto to

Reignite your inner drive

SHARATH JEEVAN

ENDEAVOUR

For Aida, Eashan & Sayan

Amma & Appa

My colleagues, partners & friends at Intrinsic Labs

& STiR Education

For your love, companionship and support on the road so far;

and in anticipation of the miles still to travel

First published in Great Britain in 2021 by Endeavour, an imprint of
Octopus Publishing Group Ltd
Carmelite House
50 Victoria Embankment
London EC4Y 0DZ
www.octopusbooks.co.uk

An Hachette UK Company
www.hachette.co.uk

This edition published in 2022

Copyright © Sharath Jeevan 2021, 2022

All rights reserved. No part of this work may be reproduced or utilized in any form or by any
means, electronic or mechanical, including photocopying, recording or by any information
storage and retrieval system, without the prior written permission of the publisher.

Sharath Jeevan asserts the moral right to be identified as the author of this work.

ISBN 978 1 91306 839 4

A CIP catalogue record for this book is available from the British Library.

Printed and bound in UK

1 3 5 7 9 10 8 6 4 2

This FSC® label means that materials used for the
product have been responsibly sourced

In order to protect the privacy of certain individuals, a few names and identifying
characteristics have been changed.

Contents

1. An Intrinsic Journey: From Jaded to Reignited   1

2. Intrinsic Work: From Balancing to Engaging   29

3. Intrinsic Success: From the Few to the Many   93

4. Intrinsic Relationships: From High Stakes to High Safety   143

5. Intrinsic Parenting: From Straight Lines to Zig-zags   183

6. Intrinsic Citizenship: From Divided to United   231

7. An Intrinsic Life: From Resignation to Revolution   277

Acknowledgements   304

References   307

Index   335

About the Author   344

'People are like stained-glass windows.
They sparkle and shine when the sun is out, but
when the darkness sets in, their true beauty is
revealed only if there is light from within.'

Elisabeth Kubler-Ross[1]

1

An Intrinsic Journey: From Jaded to Reignited

I love India when it rains. For those brief moments, the pure smell of water and earth wipes out the noxious fumes that make Delhi one of the most polluted places on the earth. The pitter-patter of raindrops masks the incessant honk-honk of the traffic – the auto-rickshaws, cars and motorbikes that clog the city's mostly narrow streets.

James, Sid and I were sitting on the roof of our makeshift apartment-turned-office in Kailash Colony, a pleasant South Delhi neighbourhood. All of us stripped down to our boxer shorts; we looked like roosters awaiting our fate in a factory farm. A solitary clothes peg hung in the office, and underneath a puddle created by our soaked clothes. Fortunately, Neha – our female colleague – had possessed the smarts to leave the apartment much earlier, saving herself from this spectacle.

London was my theoretical home, but in 2012 Delhi had become my makeshift one. I was the father of a 14-month-old son, so you can imagine that this was not a source of delight for my wife. It had been a brutal first few weeks kick-starting the non-government organization (NGO) I'd founded, STiR Education, in East Delhi's poorest slums, all in 40°-plus heat. We'd visited more than a hundred schools, and had spoken to more than 400 teachers, in search of the most promising teaching ideas. Selecting, publishing and spreading the most inspiring of these 'micro-innovations', we believed, would benefit teachers and children around the globe. India – the world's largest school system – was the obvious place to begin our quest.

We'd asked for directions from cycle-rickshaw-*wallahs* and ear-wax-remover-*wallahs*, and dodged ever clear and present danger from unexpected potholes to cow dung that often caught our feet.

Google Maps had not been a reliable friend: it's amazing how even the accuracy of maps is linked to a community's income. The mosquitoes, to their credit, were much more reliable. They nibbled at our ankles and arms for tasty morning or late-afternoon snacks. So much so that Sid would be diagnosed with dengue fever just a few weeks later.

This should have been a jubilant evening – an evening of celebration. That morning we'd completed our final school visit –

to congratulate the last of the 25 teachers whose ideas we'd selected to be published. This week I'd even been quoted in *The Economist* – what bigger stamp of credibility could you want?[2]

After those long, hot, treacherous months, we'd made it, goddammit. Yet, that evening I felt a sense of foreboding. The reason: the phone in our office in Delhi had not stopped ringing for eight consecutive days. The calls were all from teachers. We only had three staff in Delhi then, and so phone-answering had suddenly become a big part of everyone's job.

'Look,' one teacher told us, 'I'm not disputing why my idea wasn't selected. I know it was a fair process…But you've awoken something in me I've not felt for a long time. You made me remember why I became a teacher in the first place.'

The calls from teachers kept coming. I felt sceptical. Of course, teachers would say all these warm and glowing things, wouldn't they? My training as an economist had always led me to believe that 'extrinsic' motivators – money, rewards, status, incentives – make the world go around. All this positive intent was great, but where was the hard proof that the teachers would actually commit to changing their behaviour?

On that rainy evening, like any self-respecting economist, I decided to run an experiment. I asked Sid and Neha to hire the largest venue we could find: a rickety but colourful wedding hall on the outskirts of Delhi. And we called the four hundred teachers we'd been interacting with over the past months and invited them to the beginnings of what we called a teacher network.

The meeting was booked for a Sunday morning. It was a modest 45° Celsius that day. It was also the final day of a cricket test match between India and England – a nail-biting climax.

I remember taking bets among our team over how many teachers each of us thought would show up.

Sid said 250.

I laughed and said too high.

Neha said 180.

I laughed again.

I put in my own wager at 80.

In the end, almost 340 teachers attended – not all right on time, but they came.

Many of them were young women who brought their children with them, as their husbands were unaccustomed to childcare (though, in far too many cases, acquiring a husband meant they were expected to stop teaching in the first place). We quickly had to set up a makeshift crèche on the side. Others brought sceptical-looking brothers, and in a few cases husbands.

We did serious stuff in the meeting – supporting teachers to share dozens of new teaching practices between themselves – but also games to help them get to know each other and feel a sense of connection. The energy was palpable all the way through the morning. I still remember the smiling faces and the sense of possibility – and most of all the sound of laughter.

The teachers came from far and wide, from all over the city, and I was fascinated by their stories. 'Priya' was a primary teacher in her 20s from a school in Shahadra, one of the poorest communities in East Delhi. She'd relocated to Delhi, and to this job, from her home state in the north. She had the most infectious of smiles. She didn't hide that her life in Delhi made her feel lonely at times. She felt isolated and had no friends or family in the city; with the new husband came a new adopted family and, that most Indian of mixed blessings, a mother-in-law. She'd enjoyed a relatively high level of education before – much more than her new teaching peers – which often caused them to resent her. She loved trying out and mastering new teaching techniques.

Immediately Priya noticed that her kids found it hard to learn the English poetry that was required in their English curriculum. Think Rudyard Kipling's 'If' – or, even more common, Wordsworth's 'I Wandered Lonely as a Cloud'. So she started applying Bollywood tunes to old English poems as a way to hook children into learning them. After applying this technique, 100 per cent of children in her class were now able to recite the poetry required by the English curriculum.

Here's the bit that floored me: there was no extra money for the teachers who joined us that morning in Delhi. Most had battled significant obstacles: weather, transport and in these conservative communities often the wrath of their husbands or fathers or brothers. There were no direct career incentives either – we certainly weren't promising this would help them with a promotion or a higher salary.

Nothing had explained what I was seeing in one of the world's poorest and most challenging places.

In my conversations with hundreds of teachers over that period, I'd heard the glimpses of three concepts that would occupy many of my waking thoughts and nocturnal dreams for the next nine years: Purpose. Autonomy. Mastery.

Here are some potted definitions: Purpose, as I define it, is about knowing how what you do helps and serves others. Autonomy is believing in your ability and agency to actually change things for the better. Mastery is the sense of being on a continual, almost infinite journey of improvement towards being the best version of yourself you can be.

I had seen all three concepts play out through those scorching weeks. Our interactions with teachers had reminded them of their Purpose – of the critical difference they could make to a child's life, particularly a child whose parents had usually never been to school before. That sadly was the norm in these forgotten parts of Delhi. Meanwhile the discussion and sharing of new teaching ideas seemed to have rekindled the teachers' sense of Autonomy. Although many still felt like small cogs in a big administrative wheel, their time together had stirred a profound realization: they actually had a lot of control over how they taught in their own classrooms. And the sharing of practices with other teachers was inspiring them to develop true Mastery in their craft – and to want to become the best teachers they could be.

How had we accidentally rekindled the energy and passion of so many teachers? It became my life's work and quest to find out.

Intrinsic is a book about how we can reignite our inner drive – and fall back in love with our lives and world. Those three words – Purpose, Autonomy, Mastery – are the three keys to unlocking how to do it. As you read on, they'll form the core framework that we'll use to analyse the most important areas of our lives – as individuals, in the organizations that we are part of and in our societies at large.

Think of life like a long Indian car journey, complete with the belting Bollywood beats on the radio and samosa crumbs all over the back seat: Purpose is the destination you've entered into your GPS. Autonomy is you firmly at the wheel (no matter how many people, especially in India, are chattering away behind you and telling you how to drive). Mastery is becoming an ever better and more patient driver as you navigate fumes, motorbikes, cycles, auto-rickshaws and (still) the occasional cow – especially when they're reversing at full speed right into you.

Think of motivation as being like the type of fuel you put into your car.[3] Extrinsic rewards are like diesel – they get you to where you want to go, but it's rarely a pleasant ride – you might be choking everyone with your fumes along the way. Incentives, status, bonuses and financial rewards, and at the extreme end, outright bribes – they're all examples of what motivation thinking calls extrinsic motivators. You're doing something basically because something else is promised at the end.

Intrinsic motivation, by contrast, is about going on a journey because it's inherently satisfying, rewarding and enjoyable in its own right.

In this book I'm not going to pull any punches about the motivational mess – indeed, crisis – we are in. We are deeply confused about what matters in our lives and about the state our world is in. As we'll see in the coming chapters, that holds true whether we are millennials, silver-surfers or somewhere in between, whether we live in London or New York, Delhi or Shanghai, São Paulo or Kampala (or in smaller cities or villages anywhere), and whether we are rich or poor, female or male, black or white, heterosexual or gay.

Many of us feel like we are going through the motions – as individuals, organizations and society at large. We feel empty, jaded and unhappy with the organizations we are part of, whether that's the company we work for or our child's school. And we feel deeply alienated from the wider societies in which we live. Just look at the massive social problems in front of us that don't have easy or obvious solutions. Sometimes we feel that all we can do is despair.

The promise of this book is that it doesn't need to be this way. We *can* make major breakthroughs: as individuals, for sure – but also through inspiring the wider organizations and societies that we are part of.

Developments in motivation thinking provide the basis for this promise. Motivation started being studied in the 1940s and 1950s, particularly through American psychologist Abraham Maslow's theory of a 'hierarchy of needs'. Maslow's work has been pivotal in our thinking on this topic. His core insight: after basic food and security we all crave higher things to motivate us. And as we climb the pyramid we eventually get to self-actualization – the discovery of our true selves, our true potential.[4] Harry Harlow famously tested some of these tenets in studies with monkeys in the 1950s.[5]

Frederick Herzberg, a US business professor of Lithuanian descent, built on this thinking with his 'two factor' motivation theory.[6] His key insight: what demotivates someone is *not* the opposite of what motivates someone. For example, in the world of work (where motivation thinking mostly focused in its early days), he found that extrinsic factors like pay, good working conditions and formal career structures were of course important – and their absence could lead to demotivation. But once you have these in place as 'hygiene factors' (basic factors that need to be present to stop demotivating us, but which don't deeply motivate us), intrinsic factors (the concepts of Purpose, Autonomy and Mastery) are what's needed to keep our motivation sustained. And 'carrots and sticks' (contingent rewards) can actually undermine intrinsic motivation in the longer term.

Herzberg's work was then developed and turbocharged by two brilliant academics, Richard Ryan and Edward Deci, who devoted over 30 years to understanding the role of intrinsic motivation in a diverse range of fields. Their work inspired hundreds of other researchers around the world, giving us a substantial, robust evidence base that clearly demonstrates that the concept of intrinsic motivation (including the concepts of Purpose, Autonomy and Mastery) strongly applies to a wide range of life domains.[7] In 2009, writer Daniel H Pink masterfully popularized many of the earlier insights from this body of research on motivation, particularly focused on the domain of work, in his bestselling book *Drive*.[8]

But while the robust evidence base behind intrinsic motivation now exists, there have been relatively few attempts to practically apply it to our own lives, organizations and societies – at least at any true substance and scale. STiR Education, the NGO I founded, ended up arguably becoming the world's largest intrinsic motivation initiative, focused on reigniting the inner drive of teachers. And reignite it we did. I watched STiR grow from those hundreds of teachers that morning in Delhi to involve over 200,000 teachers by 2020, in over 35,000 schools. Eight years after that fateful Delhi morning, almost 7 million children were being impacted by the initiative. STiR's work spread across three states in India, to a quarter of all schools in Uganda and into East Indonesia. It also saw interest from countries as far afield as Ethiopia, Egypt and Brazil.

That morning in Delhi, we had run our first ever network meeting where we developed teachers' Purpose, Autonomy and Mastery: their intrinsic motivation to teach. Now 8,000 such meetings take place each month – today they're smaller, typically with about 20 to 30 teachers each.

Many of the world's leading foundations, such as Mastercard, Ikea and UBS, funded our work, as did the British and US governments. I met people like Bill Clinton, and had legendary investors like Bill Ackman and Bill Draper invest in our efforts. I was awarded an honorary doctorate by Roehampton University for my contribution to the field, and was invited to join the high-level steering group of the Education Commission, the pre-eminent body founded by former British Prime Minister Gordon Brown.

Like any expert, I learned as much as I taught. Most of all, I learned that everything about intrinsic motivation is ultimately interlinked. I learned that for teachers to develop their love of teaching – and with it their Purpose, Autonomy and Mastery – school principals and education officials at all levels needed to role-model the same Purpose, Autonomy and Mastery in what they do. Based on all this learning, STiR now has partnerships with national governments to ensure that its approach reignites the motivation of every official and teacher in an education system. Because it can use existing government resources and people to run and manage the teacher networks, its approach to reigniting intrinsic motivation costs less than 40 pence per child per year – and that will fall even further in years to come.

I felt very privileged to have been able to go on this journey, but they were the most challenging years of my life. Really because I had to rely on the University of Life – as another former British Prime Minister, John Major, famously called it – to practically teach me how to reignite Purpose, Autonomy and Mastery in teachers. I learned a great deal, but it was almost always painful learning.

Why has it been so difficult to apply intrinsic motivation thinking in practice as individuals, organizations and societies?

I believe there are five fundamental reasons.

The first is that most of us think of motivation as something we are either born with or not. 'I know exactly which kids in my class are really motivated,' a teacher in India or Uganda would often tell me. That teacher didn't see it as her job to help ignite the children's motivation to learn. And, to add insult to injury, she would put the already 'motivated' kids at the front of the class, where they got the most time and attention – and would almost entirely ignore the rest.

But in fact intrinsic motivation can be nurtured in all of us. Some years ago leading Stanford University psychologist Carol Dweck kick-started a revolution with her notion of a 'growth mindset'.[9] She helped us see ability and intelligence as malleable – something that can be developed, like a muscle. We now need a similar revolution with intrinsic motivation. As we'll see in the upcoming chapters, there is a lot we can do individually to reignite our inner drive – and, by working with others, reignite motivation in the organizations, communities and societies we are part of.

The second reason is that we have been brainwashed into thinking of human nature and motivation from an entirely economic lens. 'Practical men, who believe themselves to be quite exempt from any intellectual influence, are usually the slaves of some defunct economist,'[10] wrote prominent economist John Maynard Keynes in the 1930s. And the way that economics primarily sees us is as selfish, ruthless 'maximizers' of our own interests and welfare. As a result, we've been conditioned to think that the world operates by rewards and incentives (or carrots and sticks). If you want someone in your team to do a better job, for example, just promise them a bonus if they achieve it – even in the 21st century, that's all too often the prevailing mantra.

But in so many areas of our lives we don't act like rational economic robots at all. Huge leaps in our understanding of human nature – from happiness to mindset to 'grit' – have come through advances in positive psychology. And that's no bad thing. Yes, rewards and incentives can be effective in a small number of contexts (though their impact often rapidly fades away). But take rewards and incentives to their extreme – which is pretty much what we have done in recent years – and all kinds of collateral damage emerges, from demotivation and unhappiness as individuals, to spiralling wealth and income inequality, to the existential threat of climate change. Applying intrinsic motivation to our lives requires us to throw much of this economic baggage out and to replace it with a new way of thinking – a replacement exercise that I hope this book will help with.

The third reason it's been difficult is that motivation can feel a little intangible and hard to measure. So the approach we'll take throughout this book is resolutely practical. We'll reference research and academic studies from motivation thinking, for sure, but we'll focus our time on how we can tangibly and practically apply its insights to how we think and behave in the key areas of our lives – from work, success and talent, to relationships, parenting and citizenship.

The fourth – and perhaps most important – reason is that this kind of journey can feel deeply scary, even terrifying. And that's because in whatever area of life we are looking at, there is a difficult question to answer: what are we reigniting intrinsic motivation *for*? The biggest challenge we faced at STiR, for example, was that education systems, particularly in emerging countries like India, were all geared ultimately to produce rote learning – kids able to memorize facts and then regurgitate them back in exams. It was no wonder that teachers felt demotivated: nothing in their current Purpose was actually about helping kids develop the love of lifelong learning, and the ability to 'learn to learn', that a fast-changing country and world called for. So we had to start working with governments to redefine the purpose of education in the first place.

It's an incredible irony: India built a million free-to-access government schools, one for almost every kilometre of the country[11] – by any standards, a remarkable achievement. But, years later, the country has yet to decide what the purpose of education is. What are those million-plus schools truly for? It took until 2020 for the Indian government to publish a coherent (and extremely good) National Education Policy to address this.[12] India, I should stress, is far from alone: most countries, even in the rich developed world, struggle with exactly the same question, and have largely shirked from answering it. These are inherently 'wicked' questions – questions with no easy technical solutions.

We can only harness intrinsic motivation if we know what we are motivating ourselves for. Yet in so many of our most important areas of life, as we'll see in this book, we are confused about our ultimate Purpose. The good news is that motivation thinking can provide a helpful 'double whammy': it can help us define this Purpose – and then also find the best way to realize it.

The fifth and final reason it's been hard is that everything about motivation is inherently interconnected. The effect of poor motivation at work can all too easily spill over into how we treat our children, as we'll explore in later chapters. And how we individually behave has huge knock-on effects for the communities, organizations and societies we are part of too.

These are the five reasons why applying the insights from motivation thinking – despite the decades of robust evidence on its importance – has been so challenging. The core purpose of this book is to overcome these difficulties and help us find a way to practically incorporate its insights – deeply and in the most important areas of our lives.

We'll look at the most important domains in our lives: work, success and talent, relationships, parenting and citizenship.

To start with, we are deeply confused about work. We've fundamentally misunderstood the Purpose of work in our lives and societies, and see work entirely from the lens of providing income. That income, of course, is a critical 'hygiene factor' for most of us to survive, but work has to be so much more if it is to truly reignite our intrinsic motivation. The gleam of our offices and the quality of the free coffee are (for white-collar workers at least) other examples of hygiene factors we've let morph into motivators. As a result, we've allowed our Autonomy to be sapped away by controls, targets and incentives – and with it our intrinsic motivation and even our fundamental humanity. Just as worryingly, we have become even more susceptible to trends like automation and artificial intelligence that are threatening the already precarious 'deal' between employers and employees today. Finally, we have misunderstood Mastery at work, leading to employees and workers not developing the broader skills – or 'smart essentials' – that are the most critical if individuals and our organizations are to survive and thrive.

While of course there is a need for work-life balance to reduce stress and burnout, we'll see that alienation and emptiness at work can be just as important – if not more important – contributors to our current work malaise. Meanwhile, the majority of us are forced to wear a 'mask' of inauthenticity at work – where we have to show up, but in a way that feels artificial, even false. Our need to feel constantly connected to the office outside work means this malaise seeps further into our wider lives. According to a Gallup survey, 85 per cent of employees globally are either not engaged or actively disengaged in their work – costing our global economy $7 trillion in lost annual productivity.[13] Modern work is a fundamentally cynical and jaded place. In the next chapter we'll ask what it would take to see our motivation at work reignited.

Our second confusion is around success and talent. We all want a world where our individual and collective talents – whether it's in the labour market, on the sports field, in the classroom or concert hall – can be recognized and truly nurtured. Instead we are hurtling towards a 'winner takes all' world where the spoils of any field accrue only to a few. We are following this crazy success and talent path on the false promise of 'meritocracy'. In its name (though rarely in its reality), we have created increasingly formal structures for managing our collective talent, from new armies of admissions officers, talent scouts and performance managers, to entrance exams, rankings and structured 'talent development programmes'. These systems have fundamentally confused true Mastery with competition – and virtually everyone has been left the poorer for this confusion.

What's happened as a result? The already most proficient and fortunate among us increasingly have access to the best teachers, coaches, training and facilities – and that creates what Malcolm Gladwell calls 'accumulated advantage'.[14] These trends hold true whether it's a talented student or worker, fledgling artist or athlete, writer or chef, or a budding entrepreneur with a big idea to solve an important business or social problem. This 'winner takes all' world has led many of us to fall out of love with the activity we are pursuing (whether in school, sports or work) and to lose our inner drive, particularly when tough times hit. Collectively, we are in danger of losing our broader love of learning itself. It's also led to a lack of uniqueness and diversity in our talent base in so many fields, from sports to publishing – and makes us unable to stand out in increasingly crowded sectors or marketplaces.

But most troubling of all, it's leading to a world where whole swathes of our society – particularly women, minority groups and the less affluent, but also many others – see no ways for their talents to be recognized, let alone celebrated and nurtured. It's leading to increasing protests about unemployment in our emerging countries, and movements like Black Lives Matter in our richer ones. Management consultants McKinsey estimate that our current inequality in income by gender costs our global economy $12 trillion each year – and the black-white income gap costs the US alone $1.5 trillion dollars annually.[15]

Our third mess is around our relationships. We are increasingly dependent on our key romantic relationships to achieve our overall motivation in life, but we aren't being honest with ourselves about what we really want. We see the Purpose of our core relationships as ever more intrinsic – as helping us discover our true selves. Yet (though we rarely want to admit it to ourselves), we also see hygiene factors such as looks and socio-economic status, for men and women respectively, as important too. So we feel despondent when the ways in which we search for our romantic partners – such as online dating – fall short of what we want and need.

Once we are in a relationship, however, things don't seem to get much better. We often sacrifice too much of our personal Autonomy to our relationship, and women in particular may experience a double bind in Purpose between the demands of the relationship and those of work. Finally, we don't have effective ways to develop true Mastery in relationships – and have less and less time to develop together as couples, due to the pressures of social media and modern parenting (for those of us who have kids). As a result, we can often feel demotivated in one of the most important areas of our lives. That's leading either to break-ups or divorce, or increasingly to couples not getting together in the first place because of the fear of both.

To compound matters, we're even more confused as parents about the core Purpose of parenting. Our instinct to act like helicopters – flying in at any sign of trouble – is well-meaning, and ostensibly done to protect our children from harm. But instead an increasing body of evidence suggests that it's leading to anxiety, depression, self-harm and even suicide among our children. According to a 2020 survey by The Children's Society, British young people have the lowest levels of life-satisfaction in Europe, due to a 'particularly British fear of failure'.[16] It's created transactional parenting relationships where attaining good grades or getting into a top university are the Purpose – the ultimate be-all and end-all. And it's led to unusually direct warnings from even the Dalai Lama that 'The problem is that our world and our education remain focused exclusively on external, materialistic values.'[17]

Most of all, this has led to a crisis of Autonomy among many of our young people. 'The son of a duck is a floater' is a well-worn

Arab saying, meaning that a new generation expects their parents to swim (do everything) for them. There's nothing particularly unique about that saying now. The most affluent parents, as the 2019 US college admissions bribery scandal showed, see their Purpose like 'snowploughs' – removing all obstacles so that their kids live as 'straight line' a life as possible. This is destroying the Autonomy of our children. We often lack Mastery as parents, too. The onslaught of extra-curricular activities and tutoring we subject our children to distracts them from engaging deeply in school. And it stops parents and teachers truly working together to ensure our children's academic success and personal development.

Our fifth confusion has been about citizenship. We know that to live more fulfilling and motivating lives we need great leaders in our countries, and we need to engage as active citizens ourselves. But with the really big issues that face us – climate change, inequality, issues around identity and sovereignty – we look at our current politicians, our so-called national 'leaders', and despair. We don't trust their motivation and Purpose. Even more tellingly, we don't trust their ability to create a true national Purpose that unites us all – particularly our haves and our have-nots. Due to this distrust, we've hemmed in our leaders' Autonomy further and further through absurd levels of scrutiny on TV and social media. And we've created more and more accountability systems, ranging from hospital 'patient charters' to school league tables.

Rather than helping, these attempts have led to grandstanding and political tribalism among leaders. We do little to encourage our leaders to develop true Mastery in what they do as political figures, legislators, leaders and managers. And by not sorting out key hygiene factors – such as how our political leaders and their campaigns are funded – we've ended up with leaders coming from a tiny subsection of our society, beholden to the very special interests and factions that create this tribalism in the first place.

These are the five profound motivational crises that we're in. After the end of the Cold War, American political theorist Francis Fukuyama propagated the idea that capitalism and democracy would lead us on a journey of constantly improving living standards, happiness and quality of life[18] – this now reads like a cruel joke. Where Fukuyama's prediction went wrong was in not recognizing that capitalism and democracy are like macro (or larger) hygiene factors. Both are ultimately just structures. How we all behave in these structures – whether as employees or citizens – is what really matters, and that requires us all to feel motivated.

But this is a profoundly optimistic book. We'll use motivation thinking not just to accurately diagnose these problems, but also to find emerging solutions. Indeed, it's the practical *how* that we'll explore in this book. We'll look at the stories of many inspiring people I've been fortunate to encounter these past years – from an editor of *The Economist* to an auditor based in China, young Ugandan and

Indonesian parents to British divorce lawyers, Indian talent scouts to Ethiopian leaders and American political hopefuls. And we'll harness ground-breaking research and insights in realms ranging from psychology to economics to philosophy and behavioural science.

We'll close the book by looking at how we can transition our own lives and the world we live into a more intrinsic way of being – and establish some key principles to achieve that transition. To ensure we truly have lives worth living.

There really is no better time to look at intrinsic motivation with a new practical lens – and apply it to our lives, personally and holistically, and to our world's most pressing problems. There truly is a way out of the motivational mess we find ourselves in, but to realize it we need to be honest and upfront.

External shocks, such as the Covid-19 outbreak, have already catalysed a more honest thought process in many of us. In our heart of hearts, we know that our lives and our world need to profoundly change.

Unlike most 'big ideas' today, this one – as we've seen – didn't emerge from the quads of Cambridge or Harvard. Nor did it come from a politician's speech or a podium at Davos. (Though we will certainly travel together to these places later in the book.)

There is something especially fitting about the story behind

Intrinsic, starting in the slums and gullies of a capital city of a country that will soon cradle the largest share of our common humanity. And especially fitting that it came from teachers. Because through the voices of teachers, I could hear the voices of parents: parents who had almost nothing to their names, but who were willing to bet whatever little they had – every rupee, dream and sinew – in the hope-beyond-hope of a better future for their children.

We all play important roles as workers, mentors, partners, parents and citizens – and it's so important that we find motivation in each of these roles, both for ourselves and the other key people in our lives. This book hopes to be a catalyst, friend and inspiration on that journey. We owe that journey to ourselves. We owe it to our planet. And most of all we owe it to our children, the next generation, for whom we act as custodians.

Intrinsic is, at its heart, a love story. A story about how we can fall back in love with our lives and our world, and live the lives we want.

'Career success rarely begins with finding the right solutions to problems. It starts by finding the right problems to solve.'

Adam Grant[1]

2

Intrinsic Work:
From Balancing
to Engaging

Many of us can remember the dramatic Saharan backdrop to the film *The English Patient*, the adaptation of Michael Ondaatje's quietly breathtaking book. Ralph Fiennes plays the dying man, bandaged from head to toe, tended to in his last days by a beautiful, dutiful nurse in Juliette Binoche. During his final few days there are flashbacks to his colourful working life, where he has been mapping the African landscape. And of his equally colourful personal life, which included an affair with a married Englishwoman.

But what about the London Patient?

When one of my closest friends for the last 25 years – from school, university and many hours on the tennis court – appeared on the cover of *The New York Times*, I was completely gobsmacked.

'HIV Is Reported Cured in a Second Patient,' declared the *New York Times* headline in March 2019.[2]

The 'London Patient' was the second patient in the world to have been cured of HIV, following the first 'Berlin Patient' a few years earlier. My friend Dr Ravindra Gupta – the researcher from University College London – is quoted in the article. He calls it a cautiously optimistic step forward in the global search for an HIV/AIDS cure. His magic method: the London Patient was treated with stem-cell transplants that carried a genetic mutation. It was this mutation that was key to preventing HIV receptors from being expressed.

But Ravi's work up to this point had been entirely focused on developing countries. How and why on earth was he treating the London Patient in the first place?

'Well, I was lucky, to be honest,' Ravi admits. 'The London Patient registered himself at University College London, where I'm on the faculty. The hospital told me about him. And my research funding is flexible – I'm fortunate to be a Wellcome fellow. It wasn't hugely expensive to do the treatment, but the flexibility was critical. Wellcome are happy to fund whatever I do, as long as it's roughly in the broad direction we agreed. With other research funders it's so much harder to be this flexible.'

His ability to treat the London Patient goes against where academia is moving. The stereotype of the mad professor pursuing whatever obscure interest takes his or her fancy is now very far from reality. 'There's huge pressure to ensure consistent publication in the mainstream journals, and so we feel pressure to play it safe,' Ravi shares.

We saw in the opening chapter that Purpose is the destination we put into our proverbial GPS. Autonomy is our ability to fully and convincingly take the wheel. Mastery is our ability to be a better and more patient driver along the journey.

Ravi was able to see a broader Purpose in his work. He was then able to enjoy enough Autonomy to seize the opportunity in what he saw. Fortunately, his training and experience meant he had developed a broad enough Mastery to quickly but effectively adapt his techniques to the context of a developed country's health system.

But there's no doubt, as he admits, that he has been lucky. And our world luckier still. Imagine if those three elements hadn't been in place – if he hadn't been able to treat the London Patient? We might have lost a major step forward in the search for a global HIV cure.

Sadly for us and our world, Ravi's story flies in the face of where modern work is going. What we have collectively conspired to create, as employers and employees, is nothing short of a car wreck.

We have fundamentally misunderstood the Purpose of work in our lives. We have compensated for a deeper lack of Purpose in work through constantly ratcheting up what in the last chapter we called hygiene factors – things that stop demotivating us but which don't deeply motivate us. These include ever more gleaming office towers and (for the luckier ones) ever-increasing pay. Instead of genuinely harnessing Purpose, we have reduced employee Autonomy through increasingly elaborate targets, incentives, competitive rewards and outright management controls – which almost always end up being 'gamed' by smart managers, who devote their waking hours to finding the most effective shortcuts to achieving these targets. And which destroy any sense of authenticity at work. Rather than promote broad Mastery of skills, we've sliced and diced work into such specialized roles, and put in so many barriers and silos, that employees can no longer see more broadly the ultimate Purpose and impact of what they do on customers, stakeholders and society.

'What motivates me at work is that I can pay the bills each month,' a fellow cricket dad told me, as we were waiting for our sons' practice session to end. But it doesn't need to be this way. Reigniting intrinsic motivation at work costs very little for employers, and sometimes can even save them money. And for employees and leaders, it can make the 90,000 working hours we're likely to face over our lives [3] feel fulfilling rather than a marathon endurance test.

Reigniting our inner drive at work is a big prize – and it can be done. It simply takes commitment and leadership.

In this chapter we'll use our Purpose, Autonomy and Mastery framework to diagnose the current malaise in work, and then to suggest some emerging solutions. Let's journey into the wild world of modern work.

*

Today, our work often destroys – rather than augments – the underlying Purpose we had coming into our jobs in the first place. The medical profession vividly illustrates this trend. 'Most of my medical-school friends have become hospital doctors and general practitioners. And in most cases, the frustrations of the NHS have gotten to them...Before it was the hospital consultant's word that was always the last word. Now it's the NHS manager's, who is accountable to the hospital's chief executive and governing trust,' says Ravi.

'The more paper you put in front of doctors, the less motivated they are,' he adds. 'We live in a world where we want counting, numbers, transparency. That's what makes us tick. But what it also means is that medicine is now being seen as a routine job, and much less like a vocation.'

Does Ravi think the numbers and targets have helped anything? In a word, no.

In 2015–16 there were the (in)famous doctor strikes over working conditions in the UK. There was genuine dissatisfaction from doctors about work on Saturdays and evenings being treated as standard and not being eligible for overtime pay. These looked like hygiene-factor concerns.

However, when I talked informally to dozens of doctors, I found that underlying these concerns and the strikes was a more fundamental unease. The National Health Service has been increasingly run on the lines of traditional managerial thinking – thinking that is well past its sell-by date. You can see it in so many ways in how the modern NHS is designed – from how 'internal competition' between hospitals is supposed to bring about efficiency, right down to the 'patient charter' that's at the heart of the NHS constitution. In the face of this long-term managerial drift, the insistence by then Health Secretary Jeremy Hunt that we needed a '24-hour NHS' sounded – to the ears of many committed doctors – as if we were equating it to a 24-hour supermarket. It felt like the ultimate affront to an increasingly cynical, demotivated and angry professional workforce.

Of course, it's hard in principle to argue against any national service – particularly one as critical and cherished as the NHS – putting patient needs first. But in practice it has led to a sharply increasing 'bureaucratization' of the NHS – to byzantine systems and processes, and thousands of managers who exist mainly to collect data to show progress against these patient targets. These take up valuable resources that could instead be used to hire more doctors and nurses in the first place, and to support existing doctors and nurses in their increasingly stretched roles.

This bureaucracy has fundamentally severed the human connection between the doctor and the patient. Increasingly, doctors feel like a helpless cog in a larger wheel. We could not have dismantled the sense of Purpose more successfully if we had actively tried: we've managed to prevent doctors – whose *raison d'etre* is serving patients – from seeing how their work helps and serves others. How on earth can that possibly be considered 'putting patient needs first'?

A similar trend appears to have hit nursing. A 2020 report from the highly respected King's Fund in the UK concluded: 'The workforce had been struggling to cope even before the pandemic took hold. Staff stress, absenteeism, turnover and intentions to quit had reached alarmingly high levels in 2019, with large numbers of nurse and midwife vacancies across the health and care system.'[4]

Yes, the public recognition of doctors, nurses and other key workers during the Covid-19 crisis – including the weekly ritual of 'clapping for key workers' – might have provided some short-term cheer, but the fundamental motivational challenges remain in place.

This is not just a UK problem; the equally complex scheme of insurers and health-care providers has led to similar pressures all over the US. It's even led to TV shows like *New Amsterdam* gaining immense popularity. The drama sees Dr Max Godwin setting out to reform one of the US's oldest public hospitals, rooting out bureaucracy in order to provide better care for patients, and its tagline is 'Fight the System': so different from the somewhat saccharine (albeit addictive) medical shows like *Grey's Anatomy*. Adina Kalet, director of the Kern Institute for the Transformation of Medical Education in Wisconsin, tells me that these issues around

Purpose are as severe in the US – if not more so – as they are for UK doctors.

It's not just frontline professionals who are suffering a dwindling sense of Purpose – it's a trend that's now terminal in the business world. Business education is generally a pretty good bellwether of how business thinks about itself. US business schools were founded in the early 20th century with the explicit Purpose of helping the American economy, and American society more broadly, prosper through stronger management practices. But now business schools often feel like deeply cynical places, aimed to advance the personal goals – and salaries – of their participants. Indeed, the percentage salary jump on graduation for MBA students is one of the most important measures used to rank business schools in annual rankings conducted by the likes of *Businessweek* or the *Financial Times*.

The effect of this has been nothing short of cataclysmic. The late Clayton Christensen was a humble but highly illustrious Harvard Business School (HBS) professor. In *How Do You Measure your Life?*[5] he reflected on the generations of HBS MBA students he'd taught over the years. They came to the school to change the world in some way – from fielding a big entrepreneurial idea to wanting to solve an important social problem once they graduated. But he found that, more often than not, HBS graduates select their first jobs almost entirely based on the hygiene factors of salary, status and perks. They end up in places like McKinsey and Goldman Sachs.

A few of them genuinely love what they do. But in many cases it's an arranged marriage of money and status that finds many of our brightest people leaving jobs early and gaining a reputation for being 'good time' leaders – jumping ship as soon as harder times come. Those who do stay often feel increasingly empty, and sometimes completely lost.

Richard Ryan – one of the co-fathers of modern thinking on motivation, whom we met in the opening chapter – cites a study looking at the careers of 500 Canadian business-school alumni. Their sense of Purpose (or, in some cases, lack of it) was highly predictive of whether they would leave an organization they entered or stay.[6]

Purpose in work – the sense of how your work helps and serves others – really matters, in whatever job you do. This applies equally to blue-collar workers. In her epic book *The Job*,[7] Ellen Ruppel Shell talks to a wide variety of Americans at work. Talking to a group of firefighters, for example, she finds a highly passionate band where the social bond with each other matters a lot. It's the connection between them and their link to helping others that seem to drive them the most; human relationships are central to the idea of Purpose. But isn't this just a fancy fad for pampered Westerners? Not necessarily. 'Charles' works as an auditor in a global professional services firm, based in China. The bread and butter of his work is fraud: how to detect it, and how to deal with it. One of his roles has been helping Western companies conduct due diligence when looking to acquire or partner with their Chinese counterparts in the world's second largest economy.

As the son of Chinese immigrants to the UK, it was only years later after moving to China that he fully understood the depth of the parental sacrifice that was involved in his upbringing. Since he was five his parents had grafted without complaint to send him and his siblings to prestigious private schools, apparently out of keeping with his family's social status as Chinese restaurant owners. Only later he learned that often the restaurant simply didn't bring in enough cash to pay the school fees on time, so his father sometimes borrowed on his credit card to make ends meet. Recently, when helping his parents to move house, Charles discovered not only his old school reports, but also all the invoices for school fees with the dates of payment in his father's handwriting. Charles realized that his parents' Purpose had been to give their children the best education they could afford, having had only a very basic education themselves when growing up. Their Purpose was founded on providing a better future for their children, and also motivated by pride in their children's academic achievements, which they themselves had missed out on.

Now, having emigrated back to China to the total bemusement of his parents, Charles is dealing with the complicated side-effects of this kind of parental obsession. His next-generation Chinese recruits join the firm with informal subtitles like 'son of wealthy businessman' or 'daughter of prominent official'. *Guanxi* (connections) matter as much as they ever did in modern China, perhaps even more. These new recruits tend to be somewhat pampered and not always willing to undertake the hard graft. But even recruits who come from less wealthy backgrounds tend not to be motivated. Often they have managed to get the job due to the sacrifices of their middle-class parents, and they tend to hop from job to job like dragonflies, attracted to whatever looks interesting at the time.

What used to create a sense of Purpose at work even in countries like China – building enough wealth to provide security for your children – has actually often ended up causing today's new generation of workers to be spoiled and demotivated.

Purpose has to be, as we've seen, front and centre at work. But that's not to say that pay and other hygiene factors don't matter. Remember Herzberg from chapter 1 and his 'two factor' lens on motivation. Low pay, or pay that feels unfair relative to other jobs of similar demands, can demotivate you.

This insight applies to the question of teacher pay. 'The data is pretty clear that the pay of teachers relative to other professions does matter,' says Sam Sims, who is one of the UK's leading education experts.

There is some irony in the location of our conversation. Sam and I are meeting in a swanky hotel on the fringes of the Global Teacher Prize summit in the Atlantis Hotel in Dubai. Peter Tabichi – a Kenyan teacher – has just won a million dollars from The Varkey

Foundation. Peter has been selected by a prestigious committee, among thousands of potential applicants, as the best teacher in the world. But setting aside the prize money, low teacher pay is actually a global challenge. In the US, for example, many Democrat presidential contenders over the years – including most recently Vice-President Kamala Harris – have wanted to lift teacher pay as a key plank of their nomination platforms.[8]

It's a moral travesty that many teachers in Africa – such as in Uganda, where I had the opportunity to work – often can't put bread on the table with what they are paid, so they have to drive a *boda* (motorbike taxi) or toil in their family farms to supplement their incomes. And, to add insult to injury, they are often paid months late.

But equally the evidence is clear that pay alone is rarely a silver bullet – it's not a true motivator. In India, public-sector teachers have had several successive pay increases over the past 15 years, to the point where teachers in some Indian states are now among the best paid in the world relative to average national income. And yet a quarter of Indian teachers remain absent on a given school day, a metric hasn't moved a bit over the last 20 years. The role of pay in the overall attractiveness of teaching is much more nuanced than we might think, as a World Bank report by Tara Béteille and David Evans points out.[9]

All of the above validates Herzberg's core hypothesis about hygiene factors: sharp increases in pay might stop demotivating teachers, but they won't truly motivate them either.

What about pay and conditions in the army? Surely that's where a heroic sense of Purpose is most important? For Lieutenant Colonel Steve Turnock, stationed at the prestigious British army base at Abbeywood, one of the toughest challenges he faces is ensuring that pay and conditions – the 'army offer', as it's called – doesn't become the main motivator for officers wanting to stay on, particularly if their sense of Purpose declines as they advance in their careers.

This army offer was until recently a guaranteed final-salary pension from the age of 55, and perks like subsidized boarding school for their children (given how often army kids would be otherwise asked to move). Although the offer has become less attractive over time, you still have what Steve calls the 'pension effect': officers a few years away from the end of their service don't want to leave at any cost. 'Fear of losing the army offer can be the reason why officers stay on, and that's never a good thing,' he explains. A lot of the time, Steve's role is to counsel them to overcome this inertia and help those who might have lost their drive for service to move on.

But, Steve stresses, that doesn't mean you can ignore the hygiene factors, either. 'A soldier's family is living in cold quarters somewhere and it takes three weeks to get the radiator fixed – that's not great. You've got to get the pay and housing right.'

Richard Ryan summarizes the academic research on this topic: 'Positive motivation to work, especially motivation to achieve quality work, is more a function of psychological incentives than financial incentives, so pay arrangements should support rather than undermine the psychological incentives.' Ryan also notes how so many studies re-emphasize that pay needs to be fair and just. These findings hold true in diverse work contexts from workers in shoe factories, US banks, volunteers in non-profit organizations and even the United Nations.[10]

Performance-based pay has emerged as one of the most popular mechanisms for short-term motivation – paying people (often substantial) bonuses for strong performance. It's now standard practice for top executives in most industries, even though it's widely acknowledged in the corporate world to have contributed to some of capitalism's worst excesses, including the 2008 financial crisis.

When lecturer and author Alfie Kohn conducted a review of dozens of US studies of performance-based pay in the 1990s, he found that most of the claims of a positive relationship with actual performance were hugely overblown and complicated by methodological issues.[11] For example, few such studies looked at the quality (as opposed to just quantity) of worker productivity, and few were able to track the effects beyond a relatively short-time horizon.

At STiR we conducted a review of 18 randomized control trials of pay per performance for teachers in developing countries (cases in which teachers were paid bonuses for achieving better academic results for their kids). We found equally mixed results. Even in the small number of cases where pay per performance 'worked', the schemes were very expensive (often over 10 per cent of a teacher's annual salary). And very few studies looked at the long-term effects of such pay schemes – more than say a couple of years out.

Shwetlena Sabarwal, an economist at the World Bank, likens pay for performance schemes to paracetamol. Sure, they can dull some short-term pain, she tells me, but rarely are they a long-term medicine for the underlying problem of work motivation in teaching.

This backs up our broader learning around the use (or, rather, misuse) of incentives as motivators. Recently economists Jean Tirole and Roland Bénabou have shown that the use of incentives will almost always undermine intrinsic motivation in the long term.[12] Psychologists Marianne Promberger and Theresa Marteau show that intrinsic motivation leads to much more favourable long-term behaviour compared to the use of incentives: in other words, it's much more sustainable.[13] The problem is that the more we believe in incentives, the more they become our mental models – and the more they make our world go around.

Richard Ryan looked at the evidence on pay for performance and concluded that 'they often fuel motivation to take the shortest possible route to the end, often with considerable collateral damage'.[14]

Covid-19 has shown how overinvestment in hygiene factors, as opposed to things that drive true Purpose, can be counter-productive – and hugely expensive. Tech giants as far afield as

Silicon Valley and Bangalore built gleaming work 'campuses' with state-of-the-art facilities – air-conditioned offices with top-of-the-range broadband, the obligatory indoor *foosball* tables, outdoor netball and basketball courts, and cafes with free-flowing multiregional menus. And then they even paid for employee coaches (powered with strong wi-fi, of course) to shuttle their employees to and from these campuses and their homes.

Yet many employees in these same companies now seem to prefer the opportunity to work from home that Covid-19 lockdown presented, even when (as in parts of India) they've had to work out of bedrooms in cramped city apartments.[15] Now the same tech giants are scratching their heads, wondering what to do with these campuses – and the billions of dollars that have been sunk into creating them.

Prithwiraj Choudhury from Harvard Business School is one of the biggest cheerleaders behind what he calls a 'work from anywhere' movement. He believes in a world where a physical office is no longer a reality, at least for the majority of employees most of the time. When I interviewed him for my podcast episode on the trends in remote working he was seeing, he pointed out that since Covid-19 many of the tech giants have now created ambitious plans to move towards 'work from anywhere' arrangements. He's also witnessing new start-ups creating workforce apps like 'virtual water coolers', where employees can still meet and talk – a software algorithm randomly assigns people to the water coolers during their virtual breaks. (Yes, pretty Orwellian, right?)

At that point – with no logo on the door, no company 'uniform' (formal or informal), no boss with his hovering eye over you – you're left with only one thing that holds you and your employer together: Purpose. To that end, Prithwiraj believes the ability of organizational leaders to consistently and continually reinstil a deep sense of Purpose in employees, and role-model living this Purpose themselves, will become indispensable in this new work age.

This may seem like a scary future – but let's remember it's the reality for the majority of global workers today. More than 60 per cent of the world's employed workforce already works in the informal sector – in shops or small-scale enterprises, neither taxed nor monitored by the government – according to the International Labour Organization.[16] And that's likely to be even more pronounced in emerging countries going forward: 90 per cent of all new jobs in fast-growing Ethiopia are predicted to be informal jobs, for example, advisers from the former British Department for International Development told me. In the informal sector, there are already no corporate trappings to speak of. Sustaining Purpose throughout all the shocks of being an informal-sector entrepreneur – from rapacious moneylenders to the arrival of big retail chains encroaching on your turf – is, and will be even more, paramount.

It's amazing what can be achieved at work even without the fancy corporate trappings – provided Purpose is intact. Ollie Dabbous is one of the UK's most innovative chefs, and his first restaurant, Dabbous, achieved a rare feat: it gained a Michelin star within eight months of opening. When he told me about his graduation through the restaurant 'food chain' – climbing the rungs from under-sous-chef to sous-chef, for example – there were few such trappings to speak of, even in places as fancy as Le Manoir aux Quat'Saisons. He had much of his classical culinary training there – and describes it as a 'make-or-break' kitchen. Yet he kept going, inspired by an ultimate Purpose – to create a food that he truly wanted to eat himself, and that was equally distinctive for those he served.

As we've seen, Purpose should be the destination we put into our inner-GPS in our work. And here I'm going to say something controversial: I think we have been willing to compromise too much on the Purpose front. And that's because of the current obsession with 'work-life balance' in our discussion of work, which may have actually distracted us from the core question of Purpose.

France has been one of the most aggressive countries when it comes to cutting down working hours. Any overtime over the prescribed hours – at least for professionals other than the managerial class – is religiously totted up and then counts towards additional annual leave. It sounds great on paper, but – talking to many Parisians – the reality is that having so much vacation is actually extremely expensive (as any parents with school-age children will attest). And you end up in situations where you have theoretical holiday that you can't take if you want to get any real work done. Or with Parisian offices in a permanent 'skeletal' state because there are so few days when everyone is in the office at the same time.

The company Saga – whose client base is almost entirely composed of older customers – found an interesting trend in a 2018 survey. A large majority of people surveyed in their late 50s wanted to continue working rather than retiring. Saga's Karen Caddick concluded: 'For many older workers, staying in work has profound physical and mental benefits, with many reporting that working longer helps improve their overall wellbeing.'[17]

Much of the stress and burnout that we are now seeing in modern work reflects this absence of Purpose in the hours we do work, as much as it does the number of hours worked per se.

Sweden, often held up as a paragon of work-life balance, provides an interesting example of this trend. Less than 1 per cent of Swedes work more than 50 hours per week, and almost all jobs provide more than five weeks paid holiday.[18] Parental leave and subsidized childcare are also close to universal – a fantastic achievement in terms of the hygiene factors we've discussed. Yet employee burnout in Sweden has been climbing alarmingly. The incidence of chronic stress-related illnesses at work, for example, has doubled among younger age groups. 'Clinical burnout' now accounts for one in five cases of long-term absence from work across all age groups, according to the Swedish Social Insurance Agency. Swedes are working fewer hours, but if these hours are devoid of Purpose they cause stress and burnout nonetheless.

We are all living longer. Professor Lynda Gratton of London Business School even talks about 'the hundred-year life'[19] needing to become our new reference point. That inevitably means we'll be working longer too – and certainly the pressures on our pension systems and retirement age will only reinforce that.

Our time working from our living rooms and bedrooms has shown us that work need not be this partitioned, hermetically sealed thing we've often believed it to be. It's true that not everyone is able to follow their true calling at work, but I hope some of the ideas in this chapter will help work to feel at least immediately more engaging – and that may encourage us to find our calling in the longer term.

Of course, working hours and flexible hours do matter. Because of the crazy hours my parents worked as young doctors in the British NHS of the 1980s, I spent the first three years of my life being looked after by grandparents in India. When I finally could move to Britain to join my parents, childcare came from an eclectic coterie of neighbours, nurses and taxi-drivers at Barking Hospital in east London, all of whom I'll be forever grateful to. Yes, we need to have enough time with our partners and families (more on this in subsequent chapters), and no one should be exploited at work. And yes, it's true that more flexible working models and hours may help keep the talents of our most experienced employees in the workforce, as the Saga survey itself noted. But just like pay and working conditions, working hours and flexibility are at their heart just another hygiene factor. And as the Swedish example shows, simply increasing hygiene factors won't solve the core challenge of Purpose. We have to tackle the Purpose challenge head on.

Work truly is part and parcel of our lives. Let's make it as Purposeful a part as we can.

We've seen how a lack of Purpose has been endemic in many of our workplaces. Rather than try to address this problem head on, employers have responded with an alternative strategy – undermining Autonomy and trying to control employees instead.

The irony is that several studies show that Autonomy is highly linked to employees' intention to stay in jobs. A study in Taiwanese health-centre workers, for example, found that increased job Autonomy contributed to a reduced intention to leave.[20] Similar results were seen among the same type of workers in Australia.[21]

Policing provides an interesting example of this trend. Many of us have read Malcom Gladwell's story of the celebrated William Bratton and how he revolutionized New York policing through using data to target smaller crimes. This includes the famous 'broken windows theory': by targeting smaller but visible crimes – of which broken windows are a great example – the police can help create an aura of order, which in turn can prevent the risk of more serious crimes subsequently occurring. [22]

Although unintended, these developments sometimes contributed to an implicit narrative: in days of old, we left too much to an individual police officer's judgement and discretion – to their Autonomy. Closer, tighter and, of course, data-driven, management was the key.

Since then, however, economists have studied the reasons for the fall in crime much more closely. Many now believe that while data-driven policing approaches may have played some role, the fall in crime may have had much more to do with the then booming economy that reduced the incidence of crime in the first place. Steven Levitt has gone a step further to suggest that the most important driver of lower crime was a reduction in unplanned pregnancies in the couple of preceding decades. This, according to Levitt in his book *Freakonomics*,[23] reduced the incidence of children growing up in vulnerable contexts and therefore led to a reduction in young people subsequently entering the criminal-justice system.

Many of us who have suffered a crime recently in the UK can see what data and targets, mixed with frontline cuts, have done. A west London resident I spoke to had a car stolen from his driveway and had to deal with his local police entirely through an online portal;

not a single iota of investigation was done. The portal appeared to have been set up just to provide the relevant details for his insurance company. The local police service then had the cheek to ask for a 'victim satisfaction survey' – also only online, of course.[24]

In response to the trends above, many respected police leaders have joined the call to re-examine the lack of Autonomy in their profession. That's the thrust of the book *Intelligent Policing* by Simon Guilfoyle.[25] In a nutshell: the cascade of targets, 'management by objectives' and cost reductions has led to profound demotivation among many police officers.

It would be wrong to think that public services – because of the unending budget pressure – are the only fields to see Autonomy declining. Steve Drummond is a senior editor at National Public Radio in the US. He tells me that even journalists are now under enormous pressure to meet numerical targets – and are feeling a real squeeze in Autonomy as a result.

'We're constantly challenged by our funders, many of them foundations, to show the metrics of *how many*. How many people read our articles. How many have read all the way through to the end – that's possible to measure with technology now, given most people read online.

'The problem is that often crowds out attention from the articles that really change things. For example, we wrote an investigative piece – it took months – into how thousands of our young people lost college scholarships because of a small administrative error they made on their financial forms. As a result of our investigation, many of these young people regained their chance to stay in college. But it's so hard to focus on stories like these when we are under numerical pressure to keep churning things out.'

In a related profession, publishing, there is a similar trend towards reducing Autonomy. Some years ago, I completed a short but fascinating work stint in the non-fiction department of a major global publishing house. The editor I worked for was clearly motivated – passionate, dynamic and full of energy and ideas.

On my second day, however, I saw her come into the office looking crestfallen.

'Have you heard of this man?' she asked me, tossing a manuscript on my desk.

I admitted that I hadn't.

'Lots of people in America seem to be talking about him. And the UK rights for his first book are up for sale. I just went into an acquisition meeting with our sales people, but they think the starting price is far too high. I keep pushing back, but they won't budge... They won't even let me enter the negotiations.'

What was frustrating her so much was that the refusal appeared to be based on a limit – imposed by head office – on how much the publishing house could pay for a new, particularly American, author. She could see – even smell – the potential the book could have. But even as a senior editor she didn't have the Autonomy to override this centralized decision.

That was a year after the gentleman concerned addressed the Democratic National Congress for the first time and created quite a stir.

As you can probably guess, the author was Barack Obama. And the manuscript was *Dreams from My Father*.[26] The UK rights for *Dreams from My Father* were snapped up by an independent publisher, Canongate, who perhaps had more trust in the Autonomy of their editors at the time. That book and Obama's subsequent *The Audacity of Hope*[27] (which they also got the rights to) sold nearly five million UK copies. Obama's two books on top of a fiction title they had also betted on earlier, the Booker-winning *Life of Pi*,[28] propelled Canongate to become one of the fastest growing publishers in the world.

As I watched Obama's inauguration speech in 2008 – having spent a lot of time in Washington around the election campaign – my thoughts went to my former boss, and how haunted she must have felt at the thought of what might have been.

Previously, editors were hired by publishers – based on their experience and ability – to make good choices on books. The job of the sales team was to basically then sell what an editor chose. Nowadays, most publishers buy 'by committee', and sales, finance and marketing colleagues all have a say in what books are acquired.

It's ostensibly a good way to mitigate risk, and at one level it feels more democratic. But it's led to a sense of lost Autonomy among the very professionals whose job it is to actually buy the book – and who will ultimately have to cheerlead and project-manage it. The stereotype of the editor who can jump on any whim, if she has the conviction, is becoming a rarer and rarer species.

Ever-reduced Autonomy is a key feature in teachers' working lives, too. At one end of the scale is Bridge International Academies. A high-profile for-profit chain of schools that operates in Africa and India, which has been funded by the likes of Bill Gates and Mark Zuckerberg, Bridge uses an interesting (and controversial) 'school in the box' model that creates school buildings from tin shacks. Teachers come from the community and are often not previously professionally trained. Instead, they're unabashedly 'scripted' – teachers follow real-time instruction through an electronic tablet that dictates exactly what they teach and when. The analytics in the tablets allow Bridge to monitor what happens in every second of every classroom in their schools.

To no surprise, Bridge has been hammered by the teaching unions: if you switched on the TV in Kenya a couple of years ago, you'd usually see a union statement against Bridge in the headlines. But Shannon May, Bridge's co-founder, argues that providing scripting this way liberates teachers from worrying about lesson content and helps them think about engaging children.[29]

What is happening at Bridge is only the (admittedly extreme) tip of the Autonomy iceberg.

In all societies there seems to be a gradual, often subversive, trend towards limited Autonomy. I remember speaking to one east London teacher about how her school had started prescribing everything about what should be happening in the classroom, in minute detail. Even including how you should hang work up on the classroom wall (where, how high, how much, were all strictly defined). The deputy head – who was responsible for managing OFSTED inspections – would come in each week to inspect (rather than observe) each classroom. The more the teacher's practice deviated, the bigger the deputy head's frown. It got to a point where she felt physically sick when the deputy head came in.

A shocking 40 per cent of English teachers expect to leave the profession by 2024, according to the National Education Union.[30] The reason? More than 60 per cent blamed workload and 40 per cent blamed the accountability regime, amid complaints around the pressures of OFSTED inspections and school performance tables. All of these factors, as we'll see shortly, are inextricably linked.

If you're based in the UK, you may have seen the dreamy teacher-recruitment advertising proclaiming that 'Every lesson shapes a life' and showing vignettes of happy teachers turning children's lives around, *à la* Michelle Pfeiffer in *Dangerous Minds*. Unfortunately, it doesn't quite square with the reality.

'My job is no longer about children,' one teacher responding to the 2019 National Education Union survey said. 'It's about a 60-hour week with pressure to push children's achievement through.'

That teacher wanted to make an impact, but not in the ways that OFSTED and school league tables seem to care about – and seem to demand. Most teachers join teaching hoping to inspire and educate young people, and to convey the passion of their subjects – not to spend large percentages of their time entering data into spreadsheets.

How viable is it to try to prescribe or script teaching like this in the first place? Lant Pritchett, one of international development's big thinkers, distinguishes between jobs that require discretion and those that are mostly logistics. It's impossible, he argues, to try to prescribe or script the jobs that can't be reduced to logistics.[31]

The truth is that no matter how much we try to pretend otherwise, teaching is a complicated profession. It can't be reduced to logistics and it's extremely hard to capture in standardized processes. Just ask the Bill and Melinda Gates Foundation, which spent nearly $250 million trying to codify and specify what US public-school teachers should be doing in the classroom. It was a failed attempt at precision, which (to its huge credit) the foundation publicly admitted.[32]

Teaching is a classic example of a job where there are millions of potential permutations in front of the teacher every minute, every day: a different child, a different topic, a different context. Even if you can automate some of the sharing of content, the critical role of the teacher will always be linked to building a deep human connection with the child.

In the US, well-meaning but less well-designed national initiatives like President George W Bush's No Child Left Behind – and somewhat better designed successors such as President Obama's Race to the Top – have tried to exert federal influence and funding on the notoriously decentralized US education system, where individual states have the real power over implementation. Both schemes, linked to efforts to have a more consistent national curriculum (called the 'Common Core'), tried to shift the holy grail – changing what teachers focused their time and efforts on.

The desire to focus more on the basics (such as reading and maths) was laudable and hard to argue with. But both were done in ways that undermined the Autonomy of teachers and led to the phenomenon of 'gaming', as fierce critics like Diane Ravitch point out.[33] Ravitch is a research professor at New York University and a former US Assistant Secretary of Education. Her own research and analysis of dozens of other research studies show a persistent trend: towards 'teaching to the test'. She also shows a trend towards 'narrowing down' what success looks like in the first place, through reducing – if not eliminating – other important aspects of the curriculum such as the arts and physical education. All in order to hit these test-score targets.

But isn't this all a worthwhile sacrifice for the larger goal of improving academic performance? Ravitch's killer punch: most of the apparently impressive test-score gains in states like New York may be illusory. Her analysis shows that the gains are linked to easing testing requirements, direct teaching to the test – and, most alarmingly, teachers themselves cheating when moderating the tests: for example, by changing students' answers. She also uncovered disturbingly strong correlations between the level of teacher cheating and the level of test scores across schools. These trends came to a dramatic head in 2015, when a racketeering charge brought by the Atlanta public schools system led to arrests of teachers. After a number of unsuccessful appeals, a few of these teachers ended up serving prison sentences.[34]

Not only are teachers being robbed of their professionalism, but in these extreme cases they're even being robbed of the bedrock of their profession – their moral integrity. Around the world, it's hard to deny that teachers are falling out of love with teaching.

When we think about Mastery, we often instinctively think of Malcolm Gladwell's 10,000-hour rule propounded in *Outliers*: the idea that dedication and deliberate practice over something like 10,000 hours are what's required to achieve true Mastery in a field.[35]

There's certainly a strong kernel of truth in that, but it belies something much more complicated. Mastery – at least in its purest form – is much more a crooked path than a straight line. And

Mastery over any work domain is also much broader, more complex and multifaceted than we think.

David Epstein's book *Range: How Generalists Triumph in a Specialized World*[36] talks about the need to combine and synthesize different experiences, and how that can really help people integrate a broader Mastery. He argues that in everything from tennis to science we have undervalued the role of broad and generalized expertise. Epstein talked to Roger Federer's mother and found that Federer played many sports – football, badminton and not just tennis – for years before he committed to one.

Epstein's point can be applied to organizational life, too. Often in companies, what look like kind problems (simple, straightforward and largely technical and defined in scope) are in fact wicked problems. And this 'wickedness' comes not from the technical demands of the role but from its broader aspects – in particular working with and influencing others.

That's certainly true of the challenges 'Charles' (whom we met earlier in this chapter) is facing in China. His profession as an auditor seems dry, numbers-focused and detail-oriented, you might think. But when you talk to Charles, it is clear that his role has multifaceted demands, well beyond sheer execution. This includes keeping young team members motivated and feeling recognized and appreciated, despite the sometimes repetitive and highly precision-oriented nature of the work. He also had to learn to understand the different perceptions and cultural mindsets behind acceptable business conduct in different countries, and to deal with the cultural expectations of Chinese clients and counterparties, as compared to Western clients and other stakeholders.

We've fundamentally confused Mastery in work with specialization and order. The complex – even wicked – world we now live in means we need to take a much broader approach.

In short, we've seen that Purpose, Autonomy and Mastery are being systematically undermined, even dismantled, in our modern working world. Clearly it's detrimental to our own working lives; but it's also an existential risk to the organizations that we work for.

Management gurus around the world tell us that in an increasingly competitive world (more on this in the next chapter), the secret for organizational success will be around distinct 'positioning' – offering something that others can't in the crowded sectors and marketplaces that organizations operate in.

Play Bigger[37] is the latest of such positioning books, and has galvanized attention in Silicon Valley and the start-up world more generally. Its thesis: given the explosion in venture-capital money now available, far too many start-ups have been following undifferentiated 'me-too' strategies. Instead, the book's co-authors argue, the winners of tomorrow's markets will create entirely new categories. Chrysler's minivan is an example they cite of a category that was created in the car industry. By producing a smaller 'magic wagon', Chrysler created an entirely new vehicle segment that hadn't existed before.

But to achieve a different positioning, employees need to be deeply engaged in an organization's Purpose. How employees represent their organizations in their day-to-day behaviour, whether attending a meeting in a shiny corporate office or Zooming in from their bedrooms, matters so much. Especially when the options of just hiring more staff, or promoting people faster, are not available to organizations when economic times are tough.

The link between our individual Purpose and the Purpose of the organizations we work for and represent is going to matter much more in the future. It can't be just the tenuous connection that it's often been in the past, propped up by hygiene factors like the fancy office or the coffee machine.

The good news is that reigniting intrinsic motivation at work doesn't cost a lot – and sometimes can even save organizations money – but it does take leadership and commitment. We can turn these trends around.

Surely this is the time to forge a 'New Deal' at work?

Let's look at how we could.

We *can* rebuild Purpose, in almost any job or profession. One of the best ways is what I call *reframing*: for all of us as employees, simply but deeply understanding and articulating how our work contributes to the overall Purpose of the organization we are in – and, in turn, how our organization's Purpose contributes to helping and serving others.

As I was writing this section of the book, I was at the Conduit, a members' club in London that was built on the idea of Purpose and a common interest in social impact. There I witnessed a conversation between the bartender and two guests that made me sit up. The guests were a middle-aged man and his 13-year-old daughter.

Eblis, a bartender from Ecuador, was talking to the father and daughter about various non-alcoholic spirits for almost an hour, and asking them to taste and smell what they saw.

Afterwards I asked Eblis why he had put so much effort in. 'The daughter was spending precious time with her father,' he explained. 'I helped the father do something cool for his daughter. So the daughter will think her father is cool, and she will want to go back and spend time with him.'

'This is what bartenders do,' he concluded. 'We bring people together.'

As he moved seamlessly from lamenting the world tequila shortage to letting me taste his new range of non-alcoholic spirits (it was certainly one of the most fun interviews in writing this book), Eblis told me about his earlier training at the bar of the Connaught Hotel. There he met legendary bar-industry figures Walter Pintus and Cameron Moncaster. After a lot of back and forth, they persuaded him to join the Conduit team with them. It's clear the social Purpose of the Conduit resonated with his own Purpose, and that's what encouraged him to come on board.

It's all about how you make the sense of Purpose come to life, which reminds me of the famous story of John F Kennedy visiting the NASA Space Center in the heyday of the US–USSR space rivalry. He noticed a janitor carrying a broom. Kennedy went over to the man and said, 'Hi, I'm Jack Kennedy. What are you doing?' 'Well, Mr President,' the janitor replied, 'I'm helping put a man on the moon.'[38] Reframing can happen with staff at any level in an organization.

Emma Judge consults to consumer-goods giant Unilever, where – she tells me – every manager has to be able to find and articulate a personal Purpose statement. And that goes beyond selling more soup or soap. Each manager has to articulate clearly and personally what's important to them in the work they do and how that work in turn benefits society more broadly. This is an exercise that all of us at work might want to consider emulating.

Sometimes the working environments around us can help reframe Purpose for us. Second Home is a co-working space trying to do things differently:[39] rather than just house companies, it wants to actively nurture the Mastery of the companies and employees it houses. It makes a bold claim that companies based there grow significantly faster than companies of a similar size elsewhere. You can always debate the chicken-and-egg question (did they just select more promising companies?), but Second Home's Breakthrough Programme draws an amazing range of speakers talking about all aspects of company growth, as well as work and life more generally, including 'lessons learned' talks from the co-founders of Deliveroo and Mumsnet. Second Home also has its own bookshop, Libreria, which draws its own broader group of literary speakers and thinkers. 'Be better' sessions further encourage members to share their experience – from how to pitch your brand to financial planning.

What about reframing Purpose in one of our most demanding professions: policing? Reuben Abraham runs the prestigious IDFC Institute in India and is one of the country's leading experts on public-sector reform. He is trying – against many odds – to reframe the role of police in India. He believes there is an opportunity to move from a mindset of fear, intimidation, and command and control, to one of genuine community policing in the way that Robert Peel, the founding father of modern policing, espoused.

The long-term reputation of the Indian police force is rather bleak in the national imagination – something that even manifests itself in popular Netflix series *Sacred Games*, based on Vikram Chandra's bestselling novel.[40] One scene sees a senior police officer interrogating a witness in custody in a Mumbai jail cell. The witness is hoisted from a rope and swings towards the senior officer like a human cricket ball. The officer is standing, in perfect batting-ready position, with his cricket bat at hand for the interrogation. Screams of 'Four!' and 'Six!' ricochet off the jail cell as the officer goes into batting mode, each drive and *thwack* more ferocious as he realizes the witness isn't cooperating in his responses. It's chilling stuff.

Reuben doesn't deny that behaviour like this might still exist in small parts of the police force, but he believes that we can get to a point where this is the exception rather than the norm.

The good news is that the Indian police seem to be making progress towards this goal. A recent, fully anonymous survey by the IDFC Institute among thousands of Indian citizens showed that the police, through their day-to-day actions, are trusted a great deal by a large majority of the population in cities like Mumbai and Chennai.[41] This is in a country where trust of anyone is generally not in abundant supply.

Reuben tells me a story to illustrate the point. One of his senior female colleagues, Pritika Hingorani, recently slipped accidentally in the bathtub in her Mumbai home. It was a nasty fall and left her with bruises all over her body, including all over her face. Shortly after the accident Pritika returned to work. (That part was no surprise to me – I've met Pritika and she's a human dynamo.) She was driving home from the office on her first day back, with her mother in the passenger seat, and crossed a traffic light only to see a police car immediately follow her and signal her to pull over.

Oh god, she thought. What had she done? Had she jumped the lights by mistake?

When the police officer came to talk to her, he simply asked her what happened to her face. Was there a husband or father he should talk to? After a lot of sceptical looks and probing, Pritika and her mother were able assure him that it really had been an accident.

If it ever happens to you, the police officer told her, please don't hesitate to report it. Please call me. And then he gave her his personal cell-phone number for that purpose.

The jury is still out on whether such an ambitious reframing of Indian policing towards community policing, so that the police work in genuine partnership with the communities they serve, is possible – but the potential feels promising. Through the Institute I spoke to many dynamic Indian police leaders from states like Punjab, who espouse this way of reframing police work and who believe that it could become a reality. The Institute is now supporting state police forces to move towards this ambitious vision, through leadership development of police leaders and officers.

The citizen surveys that IDFC continually run will help keep Indian police forces honest in this regard. If the effort is successful, we'll hopefully see an end to the behaviour referenced in shows such as *Sacred Games*.

Nowhere is reframing Purpose more important than in the modern army: as our military technology and bureaucracy increase, fewer lives need to be risked on the frontline. But there is a risk in the process that Purpose for officers begins to feel more distant and removed. Lieutenant Colonel Steve Turnock, whom we met earlier in the chapter, is fervently trying to offset this.

The army has a deliberately structured scheme of progression that means that you are strongly encouraged, and often required, to change roles and locations every couple of years. 'The challenge,' Steve says, 'is that most military projects are really eight to ten years in ambition. So the person running that project can change four or five times over the length of the project.' Steve's current role focuses on acquiring the new breed of equipment the army needs to stay competitive. 'I'm effectively developing training plans for equipment that my successor's successor's successor will actually implement.'

That's a significant hurdle in the gaining of Purpose – the distance between what an officer does and when they know it will save lives. He says the army is working on that, both by trying to make placements longer and by ensuring people move roles at significant 'milestones' rather than arbitrary cut-off dates.

Steve constantly helps himself and his team see the bigger picture in what they do – including in his most recent role, which focuses on army equipment. 'We'd used the Snatch Land Rover in Northern Ireland and then tried to use them in Iraq and Afghanistan. It didn't protect enough, so there were casualties and fatalities.' He uses this fact to remind his team why their search to procure and develop the very best army equipment is so important in saving the lives of countless soldiers in the future, even if they may never directly see or meet those soldiers themselves. 'The chances of me going out to war are now slim,' he adds, 'but I know the work I'm doing now will make a big difference to the lives of the future 18-year-olds out there in battle.'

We've created such complex organizations that we've often severed the link between our individual work and our wider Purpose. Reframing involves bringing to the forefront voices of people our work ultimately serves – voices who otherwise would go unheard.

What about reigniting Autonomy in the workplace? When I talk to employers and employees about this, I often hear a deep sigh. There is a fundamental concern that Autonomy will mean anarchy.

It doesn't have to be that way. Autonomy doesn't necessarily mean you can't have alignment and coherence across an organization, nor does it mean that everyone in an organization will start pulling in completely different directions.

Of course, you can have different ranges on the Autonomy scale. In Frederic Laloux's thought-provoking book *Reinventing Organizations*,[42] he describes what he calls Teal organizations – organizations that are driven by the principles of self-management. Teal organizations are decentralized and adaptive, and sense and respond rather than predict and control.

Laloux cites as an example a successful Dutch social-care organization, Buurtzorg, working with thousands of elderly clients, while having almost no formal management structure, no CEO and no centrally planned targets or even budgets. Instead it's all driven by teams of frontline nurses sensing local trends and needs, and acting accordingly. Targets and budgets get built up from there. Laloux argues that it's possible for Teal organizations to have strong financial results and also achieve goals like low staff turnover.

Adapting to a Teal-type organization, while right for some, is really tough for others. There were attempts to expand the Buurtzorg model to the UK's NHS and social-care professions, but the Autonomy requirements of the approach hit too many roadblocks to be fully adopted, particularly in how it flew in the face of traditional targets and controls.

The concept of 'guided Autonomy' might help here. For example, when we started running our monthly teacher network meetings at STiR, we made the mistake of thinking that it was really critical for teachers to focus straightaway on the teaching topics they felt were most important to them. The problem was teachers often naturally focused on topics that were outside their own direct control – a classic example was parental engagement. It followed teachers' (correct) instincts that parents weren't engaging in their children's education as much as they had hoped. It's not that parental engagement isn't important; it critically is, and we'll talk more about this in a subsequent chapter. But it's something that teachers have limited direct control over, and therefore efforts to improve this area can take a long time to bear fruit.

While we were seeing strong signs of increased motivation and effort from teachers in our early years of working, we weren't seeing as much change in how they actually taught. This flummoxed us until we spoke to management writer Dan Heath, who has written extensively about behaviour change, along with his brother Chip, in bestselling books like *Switch*.[43]

Dan stressed to us the importance of sequencing behaviour change – that it's best to start with quick, visible wins that then build the possibility of success in people's minds, and then to build further on that momentum.

Following his advice, we started to focus teachers on the most tangible aspects of classroom practice first – for example, the routines they use to organize the classroom. We explained to teachers why focusing on routines is so important: lots of studies show that up to half of all learning time in classrooms can be lost due to poor classroom management. When routines change, both the teacher and the child feel that something different is now happening. That creates a wider belief that change is possible, and so the teacher is willing to try longer-term things they can influence, like engaging parents.

Now, the network meetings organized for teachers are deliberately structured to promote Autonomy: teachers are given examples of what good routines can look like, but they aren't told what to do. They have to decide – working closely with the other 20 or so teachers in their network – what types of routine make most sense to work on for their specific classroom contexts.

It's still strongly about Autonomy, but it's guided. As a result of these changes, STiR's data is suggesting that well over three-quarters of the 200,000 teachers it works with are now tangibly and positively changing how they teach each month.

The notion of guided Autonomy provides a ray of hope: you can still have Autonomy without dispensing with the priorities or values an organization feels are important – whether it's a focus on a key product or an important organizational value like diversity. And it can actually help rather than hinder the connection that we've just discussed, between an employee's Purpose and that of the organization they represent.

Richard Ryan writes about the notion of 'autonomy support'. For example, a study has shown that employees' sense of Autonomy is actually stronger when its reinforced and supported by line managers in an organization.[44] If managers can role-model a supportive 'cocktail' of trust, feedback and coaching, they can build confidence in their staff and encourage them to be increasingly autonomous. The positive relationships this engenders – particularly between different levels of an organization – can further enhance Purpose – something we observed in government education systems at STiR.

Increased Autonomy at work doesn't need to feel like a mad, chaotic dash. It can be guided and supported, as individual employees and our organizations work together to create a deeper sense of Autonomy – one that we both feel comfortable with.

We've talked earlier about the profound hyper-specialization and de-skilling trends around the world, which undermine a true sense of Mastery at work. What can be done to reverse them?

Often I am asked the same question by organizational leaders across different sectors: 'Why invest in more development when my professionals can't even do the basics right?'

There's a deeper issue here: often the 'basics' aren't done right because we as individual employees spend too much time on the wrong things – things that take up significant time at work but add little value. The honest truth is that we sometimes don't raise these 'wrong things' with our employers.

One key change we can all make immediately is to identify and remove the elements of a job that get in the way of our core Purpose. It's been fascinating serving on the high-level steering group of the Education Commission, the global body founded by former British Prime Minister Gordon Brown. One of the steering group's key questions is: how can we help teachers in developing countries actually focus on teaching? In many communities, teachers are among the most educated people and therefore tend to be tasked with many other things, from conducting censuses and vaccination drives to collecting large amounts of administrative data. We need to find other people in and around schools to do these tasks, important as they are, in order to free more time for teachers to teach. Harnessing the power of teams of people with varied skillsets in schools is vital to achieving this.[45] That's the one of the key ways teachers will find the time and focus to develop true Mastery in their core teaching skills, and in building deep and authentic connections with their students.

As individual employees, we should be able to raise these 'distractions' with our employers, and remind them of the huge cost and toll they take on us and the organization. If you're a teacher, for example, remind your headteacher that every hour you spend entering data into a spreadsheet is an hour you could be better occupied preparing a lesson, or following up individually with a child who may be struggling. And if you can, suggest alternatives of people or resources who could do that job better and faster. Is there a better software package whose cost would quickly break even in terms of hours it would save you and your colleagues? Or are there people around the school – parent volunteers or school leavers who could be part-time apprentices – who could help with this instead? Even if there isn't an immediate 'magic wand' answer, making your manager or employer aware of the 'cost of inaction' (something we'll return to in the final chapter) can at least spark their awareness of the issue and build longer-term commitment to change things.

A helpful tactic is to create a 'time diary', where you can show your employer how your time has been spent over the past few weeks. The first time I did this myself, I was horrified. For the first time I could see clearly how much of my time was being misused: spent on small administrative tasks, mostly around the scheduling back-and-forths for the many meetings I have, rather than the really important leadership and management duties I was truly being paid for. It led me to trial new calendaring software and to get a few hours of admin support each week to help manage my diary, which together gave me back a day a week to reinvest for the things that were really important in my role.

The second strategy, once we've taken these 'distractions' out, is to invest in smart Mastery essentials – things that at first glance may seem like niceties, but are actually critical to achieving broader Mastery in the role in question. Daniel Franklin is executive and diplomatic editor at *The Economist*. One of the things the paper does as an employer is accept that people can develop different interests and specialisms over time. Bearing this in mind, *The Economist* deliberately tries to move its journalists around. With rare exceptions in fields that require deep specialism (such as science), journalists at *The Economist* have forged their own unique and interesting paths.

In Daniel's case, he's been one of the longest serving staff members at the newspaper, joining them right after his PhD in Post-Soviet Studies to cover Russian policy and staying on for 35 years. Daniel says that, when he first joined, the older editors were incredibly forgiving of him as a young journalist and gave him a lot of slack to make mistakes. Since then he's done everything from writing the paper's quarterly reports and several branded books to focusing on US foreign policy, to the point where he now splits his time evenly between London and Washington.

One of the things that really helps the development of Mastery at work, Daniel argues, is putting in processes that at face value can seem like luxuries, but are in fact smart essentials. For example, every single member of the *The Economist*'s journalistic team attends the weekly Monday editorial meeting. 'You could be a person writing about biology but weigh in on an article on China,' Daniel says. 'It's an ideas culture most of all – most people are attracted to writing here because they are excited about truly great ideas. It doesn't matter where great ideas come from.'

And – in an irony of ironies – contrary to its typical (though gradually softening) editorial line of advocating competition and extrinsic incentives, *The Economist*'s own work culture feels highly collaborative, even intrinsic. 'The fact that our individual names aren't published on articles means personal egos are less of a factor... That doesn't suit everyone – for example, Andrew Marr moved on because he felt he needed to make more of a personal name for himself. But it means we all muck in and help with everything – even senior editors help with proofreading.'

I'm an avid reader of *The Economist* myself because it's truly distinctive among all the other publications in the world, in both breadth of coverage and strength of its editorial perspective. That must surely be due to the culture Daniel describes.

Mastery is not the same as competition. Jack Welch became famous (or infamous) for automatically firing the 'bottom 10 per cent' of his workforce at General Electric each year – and 'Neutron Jack' was lauded and emulated for this practice all over the corporate world. But who constitutes the top or bottom 10 per cent is actually itself a highly subjective issue. Personality, politics and patronage – how closely you are aligned to your manager – play a critical role. The amount of sheer stress, angst and politicking that this kind of approach creates is much less discussed. And often, diversity expert Selena Rezvani told me, these brutally competitive processes end up discriminating against women and minorities the hardest. Now, owing to pressure from millennial workers who've been far less enamoured of this competitive culture, General Electric has scrapped performance reviews and moved to collecting more immediate peer feedback on employees' Mastery, including through apps – and has even introduced initiatives like mindfulness training for its staff.[46]

One of the best investments we can make in developing the smart essentials is giving ourselves as employees sufficient time to gain Mastery – both over our careers and also within our working weeks.

A few years ago Unilever was wondering why it was struggling to achieve truly 'breakthrough' innovations – products that built new categories in the way that *Play Bigger* advocates. Then they looked at how they developed Mastery in their top managers, and realized why. Managers were being rotated every two years, which created enormous incentives to do things that had shorter time frames – such as incremental changes or quick-acting product promotions. Anyone who has worked with the Indian civil service – and other civil services in emerging countries – might have a similar experience: you're lucky if a senior civil servant stays even two years in a role. Unilever has since increased the required length of time in each role in its rotation policy (the Indian civil service, sadly, hasn't).

During an episode of my podcast, Selena Rezvani stressed to me the importance of 'stretch opportunities' in developing broader Mastery. For example, there may be a chance to contribute to an organization's broader strategy development, or a part-time project in a different organizational unit to the one you normally work in. These are key additional projects or assignments that provide a person with exposure to other ways of working and networks – particularly for women and those who might otherwise be overlooked at work. They can be 'make or break', in her experience, in developing a long-term path to Mastery and, with it, career success.

But often (just as in promotions) the process for deciding who gets these stretch opportunities is far from transparent. Selena talks about insisting on open application processes for these opportunities, so that anyone in an organization can apply for them, but she also believes those who are usually overlooked, particularly minorities and women, need to develop a personal Mastery in what she calls 'self-advocacy'. In essence, they need to learn how to champion themselves and negotiate these stretch opportunities with the leaders of their organizations.

In research conducted in partnership with LinkedIn,[47] Selena has discovered a fascinating insight: women are much less likely to 'self-advocate' than men overall. But women are much more likely to self-advocate *if it's on someone else's behalf.*

That's where Purpose can be such a useful friend. If we can self-advocate, but frame our advocacy in how these opportunities can better serve our organizations and others, it can feel a lot less daunting for us to make the case to our employers – and particularly less daunting for women.

Selena rates corporate America's response to the Black Lives protests as not more than a 'three out of ten'. Few companies, she tells me, have genuinely increased their budgets on diversity, and fewer still have C-suite (top-level) heads of diversity reporting directly to the CEO. She's talking about corporate America, but I think her perspective would extend to many countries.

An important start, Selena believes, would be for corporate leaders to be more open to us as employees self-advocating in this way, provided it's done with the best intentions of the organization in mind. She thinks this would lead to a much deeper dialogue around 'job-crafting' – designing or crafting a job based on our unique skills, talents and even the nuances of our individual Purpose as employees. This is something she finds millennials particularly crave.

Cynthia Hansen is a senior leader at Adecco, the global staffing group that places hundreds of thousands of people into jobs each day. She tells me that the frontier of diversity in organizations is going to move beyond just gender and ethnic diversity (critical as these dimensions are). It will move towards 'cognitive diversity' – different ways of thinking and seeing the world – and towards putting different skills and experiences into an organization's overall mix of talent.

There's another important strategy to boost Mastery within our working week: the 20 per cent principle – the idea that 20 per cent of someone's time should be freed to develop a broader Mastery. This was pioneered in the corporate world by companies like Google – and described extensively in Dan Pink's wonderful *Drive* – and is an idea that we should hold dear in whatever field we do.

Lucy Crehan's book *Cleverlands*[48] looks at what truly makes the education super-powers – such as Finland and Singapore, who regularly top the global education league tables – as successful as they are. What she learned about these high-performing systems is that they give teachers the equivalent of 20 per cent of their time to plan lessons together, try out new practices and establish broader areas of research interest. In other words, to develop broader Mastery in their craft. The trade-off is class sizes that may be 20 per cent larger than if the teacher was teaching at nearly 100 per cent of their time – but Lucy believes it's a worthwhile trade-off.

This resonates with my previous experience, when I founded a leadership programme for heads of department and heads of year in the UK's most challenging inner-city schools. The piece of evidence that inspired the intervention was finding out that there was four times more variation in teaching quality within schools as between schools.[49] In other words, you could have a great history lesson happening in one classroom with one teacher, and next door the same content was being delivered but much less effectively by another colleague. Meanwhile, the head of history didn't see it as their role to step in and intervene. They felt uncomfortable leading and (positively) challenging other peers.

We filled these department leaders' minds with all kinds of leadership and management tools, often using cutting-edge ideas from business – the scheme we eventually created, Teaching Leaders (now called Ambition), was a bit like an INSEAD or Harvard Business School for inner-city schools.

But there was a fundamental problem. These department leaders – who were managing often as many as eight full-time staff and responsible for overseeing the teaching of hundreds of children – were given *one and a half hours* (the equivalent of two lessons) for all their management and leadership responsibilities each week.

You heard me right. Just two lessons per week. And it should help underscore a fundamental lesson. In complicated professions like teaching or medicine – professions that can't be reduced to logistics or the proverbial 'paint by numbers' – we need to give professionals the proper time and space to develop Mastery. We ignore that lesson at our peril, and more importantly at the peril of our children and citizens.

Providing time for people to transition properly into new roles and develop the Mastery requirements of those new roles matters equally. My sons go to Loyola, a Catholic boys' school on the London/Essex border that had the same headteacher for over 30 years. He was a truly inspirational and hands-on figure, and I suspect many parents (my wife and I included) initially enrolled our sons into the school because of our belief in him.

Two years ago, Mr Nicholson announced he was going to retire – a completely justifiable ambition given he was well past any formal retirement age.

Initially parents panicked. Then it was announced that a senior teacher in the school had been selected by the governors to be his successor. That successor happened to be my son's form teacher that year, Mrs Anthony, and it meant she had to be out of his class a considerable amount over the next six months to ensure a good handover and induction. It worried my wife and me at times, but now it's hugely paid off: straight into her new role as headteacher Mrs Anthony was able to hit the ground very successfully. And that's because she was given the proper time needed to master the transition to the demanding new role.

Research by McKinsey shows that if leadership transitions were successful, nine out of ten teams went on to meet their performance goals. But when leaders struggled through a transition, the performance of their direct reports was 15 per cent lower than teams with high-performing leaders. Direct reports were 20 per cent more likely to be disengaged or even leave the organization.[50]

We often think of leaders as born, not made. But the evidence from McKinsey shows that the quality of time and effort given to leadership transitions can literally 'make or break' how well leaders perform when they go into a new role. Five years after the executive transition, between 27 and 46 per cent of leadership transitions are regarded as failures or disappointments – mostly due to issues of politics and culture.

When Mrs Anthony came in as head at Loyola, she quickly made some staffing and curriculum changes that marked how she wanted to do things in the school. Some of these changes affected staff that had been at the school a long time, in some cases decades. This also resonated with McKinsey's wider findings: according to the study, most new leaders wished they had dealt with issues of people and culture much earlier.

Employers can also think more about when they schedule time for the development of these smart essentials. They need to be open and accessible for all staff – and particularly for women. For example, many law firms have a guest speaker to address partners on an important new topic, but this almost always happens after work in the evenings. Why not have them at lunch times or in the early afternoons? Or – if feasible – as Zoom sessions later in the evenings, once children are safely tucked in bed?

Mastery is not like a tap we can switch on immediately when we need water. It's like a reservoir that needs to be gradually building over the years, so that the water can gush out reliably and consistently at the time of need.

It's time that all of us as individual employees, workers and leaders had deeper conversations with our organizations about developing our broader Mastery at work. I hope some of the evidence in this chapter will help us make a strong case: a case for how broadening our own Mastery can help our organization achieve its true Purpose.

Don't be afraid of having this conversation, just do it respectfully. If your leaders and managers won't engage, then that itself may provide you with useful information.

*

Where does this lead us overall? What have we learned about reigniting our inner drive at work?

Before we move on to our broader discussions of success and talent – and look at how we can create a world where we all can achieve success, and where all our talents are individually and collectively nurtured – let's briefly recap what we've discovered in the world of work.

Purpose at work is paramount. Remember the quote from Wharton professor Adam Grant, one of modern psychology's big new thinkers, that kicked off this chapter: 'Career success is rarely about finding the right solution to a problem – it's about finding the right problem to solve.'[51]

Find the right problem to solve as an employee or worker, and you're already halfway to intrinsic work. That 'right' problem almost always is right because it clearly shows how your work enables you to help and serve others. See if you can express your personal mission statement in a way that's simple but exciting.

If you immerse yourself in that problem, you'll likely discover the ways in which your work can contribute towards it. And if it's a wicked problem – one where there isn't an easy or obvious technical solution – you'll not only be immersed, but will be submerged and deeply engaged for many years to come, even if the exact way you contribute might change over time (from an employee to an independent consultant, for example). And you're more than likely to find a 'tribe' around you who will support you and sustain your motivation. If you want to move on to another problem, success in this first arena will bring you credibility, experience and networks. But it all starts with finding the right problem to solve.

The gleaming office spaces and employee perks might rapidly become less important, as our future working patterns evolve into more 'hybrid' forms of home and office working. That may not be a bad thing: these hygiene factors were starting to undermine our authenticity at work anyway. Here's the ultimate test of Purpose: see if you can convey it (even pyjama-clad) Zooming in from your bedroom.

Pay matters, but remember it's just a hygiene factor. As an employee, try to find – or craft – the job that will give you the most Purpose, Autonomy and Mastery, subject to the pay you need and which you feel is fair. This will invariably help you become much more versatile in the longer term – and, ironically, this will almost certainly leave you enjoying greater pay growth over time.

As employees, let's remember that targets, management controls and 'incentives' – many of the things that we've been taught are 'organizational best practice' – actually obscure and dilute Purpose at work, not enhance it. Let's not be afraid of telling our employers how downright frustrating – and insulting and counter-productive – treating us either like babies or like Pavlovian dogs truly is. Many of us enjoyed remote working during Covid-19 not because of home working per se (how many trips to the fridge did you make each morning?) but because of the sense for the first time that we could organize our work in the way that best suits our individual preferences and personalities. Let's push further now and use job-crafting – as Selena Rezvani suggested – to organize our roles in the way that best achieves the core Purpose of the role. After all, who's going to know that better than us?

And let's also not be afraid of telling our employers if other secondary tasks and distractions take time away from the core things we want to develop Mastery in – remember the poor teachers spending hours each week entering data into Excel, rather than cultivating the minds and imagination of our next generation. Finally, let's not be afraid to remind our employers how important the smart Mastery essentials are. This means ensuring that stretch opportunities – broader opportunities to grow and learn – are made available to all of us.

As an individual employee, you don't need to wait for your employer to see the light (though it's obviously helpful if they do). There is a lot you can do to self-advocate, to use Selena Rezvani's term. Ask for transparency in decision-making from your employer – it may feel uncomfortable at first, but it will help many others in your organization who aren't as confident or vocal. Don't be afraid to point that aspect out to your employer, either.

Remember that as individual employees this is much easier to do if we're not doing it for our narrow self-interest, but instead because we want to partner with our employers to create the most motivating and Purposeful work possible. That is good for both of us. Most of all, it will be transformational for the people our work ultimately seeks to help and serve.

As an intrinsic employer, your role is to keep that 'right problem' front and centre in the minds of your staff. And to organize work so that it continually focuses on the significance of that problem, rather than distracting from it.

The best thing employers can do is to take pay negotiation off the table: pay well, fairly and transparently, have clear pay policies and levels for different roles, but eliminate entirely the room for it to be negotiated individual by individual. I'm deeply proud of what we've done that at STiR in this regard; each role and level in the organization has a fixed salary that is fully transparent, and that can't be changed, irrespective of an incoming employee's background or previous compensation. This really boosts gender equality: study after study shows men tend to negotiate salaries far more aggressively than women.

Employers also shouldn't be afraid of increasing Autonomy in the workforce, so your employees feel empowered to do what they are truly capable of. Remember, Autonomy doesn't have to mean anarchy; it can be guided. And strategies like job-crafting can be particularly effective with millennials, who want to see more Autonomy in how their roles are defined, rather than have 'cookie-cutter' job descriptions foisted on them.

In place of more traditional perks, employers would do well to invest in allowing employees the time and space to achieve broad Mastery. There is no point trying to utilize 100 per cent of an employee's time if it leaves them devoid of Purpose and the human connection that is so critical to their jobs. And while investing in technical competence – the nuts and bolts of any job – is a first start, investing in the equally critical smart Mastery essentials can make all the difference. Where possible, make learning smart essentials a collective, sociable and ultimately fun experience.

The wonderful thing is you don't need to be a public company or have zillions of venture-capital money to become an intrinsic employer of choice. Yes, creating an intrinsic workplace does take effort, focus and leadership. But the strategies we have discussed around reigniting intrinsic motivation at work rarely cost much – and may even end up saving the organization money.

Overall, we've seen that reigniting our intrinsic motivation at work is critical for three reasons.

First, if we don't reignite it, organizations won't develop the capabilities that are going to be critical for their long-term success – particularly in more challenging economic conditions.

Second, work is one of the main ways we can achieve Purpose in our lives overall; it is a key way we help and serve others.

Third, if we don't as societies fix our approach to work, we may miss our biggest potential breakthroughs – imagine if Dr Ravindra Gupta hadn't possessed the personal Purpose, Autonomy and Mastery that led to his contribution to a global AIDS cure.

As we saw in the opening chapter, 85 per cent of employees globally are either not engaged or are actively disengaged in their work, costing our global economy $7 trillion in lost annual productivity. But it's not the financial cost that should send the collective shivers down our spines. It's the tragic waste of human potential: a waste of the average 90,000 hours each of us will spend working in our lives[52] – hours that could be devoted to achieving Purpose, Autonomy and Mastery.

Work should be, as my former eBay boss Doug McCallum used to say, an adventure. A winding adventure that we figure out over the course of our working lives.

I hope this chapter has shown that work is not something to balance or minimize. It's one of the most important ways we help and serve others and ourselves – and therefore one of the key ways that we need to engage in life overall. Let's embrace intrinsic work as a fundamental, integral part of an intrinsic and deeply engaging life.

'We are told that talent creates its own opportunities.
But it sometimes seems that intense desire creates not only
opportunities but its own talents.'

Eric Hoffer[1]

3

Intrinsic Success: From the Few to the Many

'He's not retiring from life.'

That's how John Jay – the creative genius behind Japanese fashion giant Uniqlo – justified the purported $300 million spent on a ten-year sponsorship deal with Swiss tennis maestro Roger Federer.

Well, perhaps defended more than justified. No one could really quibble with the choice: Federer was widely accepted by tennis commentators and fans alike as tennis's GOAT – Greatest of All Time. At the point of signing, he'd amassed a record-breaking 20 grand-slam titles.

Rather, the controversy was all around the timing. At the time of signing, Federer was in his late thirties and – according to some commentators – surely at the zenith of his career, with only a few professional years ahead. Now the Uniqlo deal had catapulted him into being the highest paid athlete on earth, according to Forbes. Ahead of global peers like basketball player LeBron James and footballer Cristiano Ronaldo.[2]

There's a final twist in the tale of the Federer–Uniqlo partnership. In securing Federer, Uniqlo ended their deal with then world number one, Serbian Novak Djokovic. Djokovic was five years younger than Federer and hot on the heels of Federer's grand-slam record. More pertinently, he had won the majority of their recent encounters. Many of them had been nail-biting classics, but they also included one or two relatively straightforward drubbings – almost always by Djokovic rather than the other way around.

Life is cruel. Life is unfair. To fuel his medal renaissance a few years earlier, Djokovic had taken up a gluten-free diet and eschewed all alcohol. Federer is hardly a slouch either when it comes to physique or physical fitness. But equally he takes Instagram photos with various sizes of Indian naan breads, and unashamedly proclaims a love of ice cream, chocolate and Swiss raclette. In 2017, the morning after his eighth Wimbledon victory, he confessed to a huge hangover at his championship press conference.

And yet he glides around the court with a grace that has inspired hundreds of millions of viewers to fall back in love with the sport. A tennis nut myself, I've watched the pair contest the 2015 US Open

Final in New York, where Djokovic prevailed in a four-set marathon in an atmosphere that felt more like an Argentinian Boca Juniors football match than the genteel contests tennis is more normally known for. And there was absolutely no question about who the crowd was rooting for. In a sport that continually shatters new levels of mental and physical endurance, in his head Djokovic has even learned to convert the crowd's chants of 'Roger' into his own name.[3]

The pair have – along with Rafael Nadal – dominated men's tennis, collectively accumulating (at the time of writing) 57 grand-slam titles. For the last 15 years virtually every grand-slam championship has been claimed by one of this tennis 'holy trinity'.

As perhaps the most globalized of individual sports, tennis has become an uncanny bellwether for the new global rules of success and talent. Because now, in every field – from work to entrepreneurship to music to journalism – success accrues only to a few, not the many.

In this chapter we'll use motivation thinking to diagnose why that is. And ask what it would take to achieve a world where all our talents are collectively nurtured, so success is something that can be realized for us all. We *can* fight back and achieve such a world – and in this chapter we'll explore how.

In tennis, incredibly elaborate 'talent management' systems have been set up by national tennis associations in many countries – including the British Lawn Tennis Association, fuelled by healthy proceeds from Wimbledon. These systems seek and select the best talent at club, county, regional and national levels. And this system is taken incredibly seriously. My son Eashan is aged nine and many players his age play more tournaments a year than Federer and Djokovic combined, all in the race to keep those precious junior ranking points up.

There's a fundamental assumption in all this thinking – what I call the 'scarcity mindset'. There are only a fixed number of top-ranking slots out there, or so the logic goes. The role of 'talent managers' – ranging from coaches at local clubs, to regional talent scouts, to national performance managers – is to provide a fair way to screen the most 'talented' (aka deserving) players out there.

In some ways that makes sense if you extend this logic all the way to the professional level. Given the many options for entertainment available to us now, from live music to Netflix, most of us don't have the attention span to focus on more than a handful of professional tennis players. Two economists, Edward Lazear and Sherwin Rosen, have developed an elaborate 'tournament theory' to explain these dynamics.[4] Here's the gist: a player like Federer commands a huge premium over the next best player, even if the actual performance difference between him and the other player is very small in any objective sense. The latter was brought vividly home when I took my sister-in-law Abla to Wimbledon for the first time. She's not an avid tennis fan, so I had to physically point out the players in the top ten – she literally couldn't discern the difference between them and the others in terms of how they actually played.

Here's the problem with this system: it increasingly leads to an all-pervading 'winner takes all' dynamic, which extends far beyond the tennis court. While Federer can command a purported $300 million deal, tennis economists (yes, there really is such a breed) find that there is limited chance of making a sustainable living if you aren't in the top 150 male singles players in the world. The economic reality for female players is now much the same.

For either gender, the economics are brutal: it can cost well over a thousand dollars a week just to cover the costs of travel and coaching, for example. There are roughly 1,800 ranked male professional tennis players out there, and tens of thousands on the rungs below. Federer can rake in hundreds of millions of dollars, yet a player ranked 170th – who can hit the ball almost as well – finds it hard to survive on the professional tour.

Tennis, as a globalized individual sport, is particularly susceptible to 'winner takes all' dynamics. Like many fields today, most of its rewards accrue to a small few. But how a particular sport chooses to structure and reward itself is surely its own business, isn't it?

Well, to a point.

The problem is that sport has become our mental model for life – literally for how we see the world. And we increasingly see the world as one massive tournament. The 'winner takes all' mentality, and the anxiety it engenders, permeates our view of life so much these days. Talking to children at a school in Pennsylvania, President Obama once told them: 'At a time when countries are competing with us like never before, when students around the world in Beijing, China, or Bangalore, India, are working harder than ever, and doing better than ever, your success in school is not just going to determine your success, it's going to determine America's success in the 21st century.'[5]

Most of us, perhaps even the biggest 'winners' themselves, feel uneasy about a 'winner takes all' economy. Bill Clinton often says that much of his post-presidential time is spent as a translator and mediator between people who have too much money and people who have too little. But actually life *need not be* a tournament – and in fact there are many reasons why that is a very good thing.

Take the case of higher education. Our best universities – institutions like Cambridge or Harvard, or the Indian Institutes of Technology – increasingly market their brands largely on the basis of their academic selectivity. Business thinker Scott Galloway has even gone as far as to call them the educational equivalent of 'luxury bags'[6] – status symbols that we covet precisely because of their exclusivity. Education, as economists would say, has become a positional good: its value arises precisely because it confers on us an advantage in our pecking order over others.

David Deming is a Harvard economist and one of the leading experts on the link between higher education and earnings. The implications of his research are clear: the fastest growing jobs in the United States – and in many other countries of the world – require higher order skills, particularly the highest order social and cognitive skills, as well as specific technical abilities.[7] So it makes sense for our economy and society to increase the number of young people who get into higher education, subject of course to the higher education they receive actually being useful and meaningful.

As any self-respecting economist will tell you, education should not be a 'zero-sum game' – my good education doesn't need to be at the expense of someone else's. Indeed, the economist Paul Romer won his Nobel Prize largely for demonstrating that the more educated people a country has, the greater the positive 'spillover' effects it creates for us all – and the wealthier we become as a society.

Let's think of selectivity in education as a 'hygiene factor'. Yes, we need a certain degree of selection to ensure that people who receive the education or support provided are ready and able to derive real benefit from it. But selectivity should not be what fundamentally motivates people.

I attended Cambridge and it was an incredible experience – one that I'm incredibly fortunate to have benefitted from. I learned so much about life. The range of experiences and ideas it nurtured in me was incredibly rich. But looking back, I wince at how the idea of selectivity was then so core to my own identity as a student, and to my overall identity as a person. The master of my college welcomed me and the rest of my incoming year as the 'intellectual cream of this country'. Here's the irony: even three years prior to that welcome, I wouldn't have been considered 'cream' in this way – nor would I have risen to the top.

Three years prior to that welcome speech, I'd returned to the UK from Saudi Arabia, where – owing to my parents' adventurous stint as doctors in the Saudi national health service – I'd spent the last seven years. Saddam Hussein then chose to invade Kuwait, causing my parents to leave the Middle East out of concern for the disruption it might cause to our lives. And particularly to my education, as I approached my final years of school.

Moving back to the UK was a shock of every conceivable kind: weather, culture, people and academic system. And, honestly, I struggled. I was saved by an English teacher at Brentwood School who saw something in me that perhaps no one else saw and was a Cambridge graduate himself. I didn't think I was the 'right type' for Cambridge, nor did I think I was good enough.

Undeterred, he drove me to Cambridge University and patiently waited outside the college admissions offices while I made the appropriate enquiries. That single act of stubbornness – and those small acts of kindness that came in its wake – changed my life. That teacher – whose name was Paul Henderson – was at his core what every teacher should be: he was a talent nurturer.

There are two other interesting twists to this personal story.

Paul Henderson took me to Cambridge even though I'd left the school he taught at. His nurturing and encouragement during my GCSEs had given me the confidence to apply for a scholarship at Chigwell School for my A levels, which I got and where I subsequently flourished. He even supported my decision to pursue economics rather than English, as he had hoped.

My supportive teacher was a talent nurturer in the truest sense. In today's world, there are talent nurturers and talent managers and they appear in all walks of life: from the coach and the tutor to the literary agent, foundation manager and venture capitalist. What is common to 'nurturers' and 'managers' is that their success is ultimately based on the success of the 'talent owner' they work with, whether that is the student, athlete, writer, non-profit or start-up. But there are four key differences I've found between them in terms of their intrinsic motivation – four motivational differences that reveal whether someone is a true nurturer or a mere manager. What we need more of – to prevent a 'winner takes all' world – are the talent nurturers.

First, nurturers see their Purpose differently. They deploy an 'abundance' – rather than 'scarcity' – mindset. They don't see life as a tournament with a single winner and runner-up. In short, they don't see talent as something that needs to be rationed in the first place.

'Meritocracy' has become – in short – a flimsy and rather lazy excuse for not realizing everyone's talents.

In his lively book *The Meritocracy Trap*,[8] Yale Law School professor Daniel Markovits dismantles key elements of the meritocracy myth. In the business world, for example, he shows that 'superordinate workers' are now creating a huge divide between them and everyone else, 'hollowing out' (in his words) the middle classes. At a tech company like Uber, for example, a handful of elite knowledge and managerial workers run the organization and create its core technology, while the vast majority of 'workers' – a term Uber has often disputed – labour as drivers without benefits. Harvard philosopher Michael J Sandel takes a similarly critical view in his compelling *The Tyranny of Merit* – including quietly berating Barack Obama for hiring so many of his top presidential aides and staff from a narrow selection of elite universities.[9] (Yep, I can see the irony of these biting meritocracy critiques coming from Harvard and Yale professors.)

The 'winner takes all' approach leads to what Malcolm Gladwell calls 'accumulated advantage' – the best (and richest) 'talent owners' get access to the best teachers or coaches, and that makes them even better (and richer). For example, the top 1 per cent of Americans are now collectively wealthier than the entire lowest 50 per cent. That's shocking. A recent analysis by Harvard-based research organization Opportunity Insights showed that in 39 US universities – including 'Ivy League' institutions such as Yale and Princeton – more undergraduates hailed from the top 1 per cent of

American households by income than from the nation's entire lowest 60 per cent.[10] The wealth inequality we're seeing is being almost exactly mirrored by an education inequality that seems hell-bent on perpetuating it. To put it more simply, the process of getting to some illusionary sense of meritocracy may not even be that meritocratic to begin with.

Carol Dweck, whom we met in Chapter 1, defines a 'growth mindset' as when a talent owner (such as a student) understands that their abilities can be developed and grow over time.[11] I define an 'abundance mindset' as taking this logic even further – in other words, seeing talent and potential in everyone.

The very notion of 'winner takes all' would indeed horrify American philosopher John Rawls. Rawls advocated what is now a famous thought experiment: imagine you are floating above the world and realize that the womb you will be born in is a complete feature of fortune. How would you want the world to look in this scenario?

The answer, Rawls pointed out, would be to ensure the least fortunate person lived as well as possible, because that's quite literally where you could end up. Rawls' musings have touched many apparently steely souls, including legendary activist investor Bill Ackman, who has supported STiR's work in the past through his foundation.

Second, true talent nurturers know that the success of talent owners cannot be predicted easily. They realize that any talent journey is bumpy and unreliable, rather than a straight line. Reading between the lines of Chris Bowers' insightful biography, the teenage Federer would hardly have been seen as a 'shoe-in' for tennis's GOAT (Greatest of All Time).[12] He regularly threw rackets, lost matches he should have won, burned through multiple coaches and had a penchant for tantrums. Many tennis observers at the time, Bowers notes, saw Federer as both entitled and with a chip on his shoulder.

Yet there was something in Federer – in his personal sense of Purpose, Autonomy and Mastery – that encouraged others to take the bet on him. And when a talent bet pays off, it truly reaps rewards. Under Federer's example and the renaissance he has inspired, global tennis has boomed. In 2011, total US Open prize money was $23.7 million. In 2019 it was $57.2 million. Federer's intrinsic approach to the sport – centred on a deep love of the game, a respect for its history and traditions, and based most of all on an unparalleled beauty and grace – has significantly contributed to the fuelling of a global boom in tennis talent. A boom that now ironically – as we've seen – needs to be extrinsically 'managed'.

Third, talent nurturers see their Mastery as building new insights, relationships and connections for their talent owners, rather than just imparting technical skills and prowess.

Camila Pereira is a director at the Lemann Foundation, Brazil's largest education foundation, based in São Paulo. She tells me of valiant efforts of the Brazilian government to provide teaching by TV to children across the country during the school disruption caused by Covid-19. Many of the teachers on television were among the best nationally in their subjects, across this vast country. The problem was that children often didn't want to engage because they didn't feel an emotional connection with the teacher on the TV. It wasn't 'their' teacher, many kids told her. No trust or relationship had been built. Teaching is so much more than a mechanism to provide technical content, as we've seen in the previous chapter.

Shripriya Mahesh – the founder of innovative venture-capital fund Spero Ventures – argues that the best talent nurturers, such as venture capitalists or board members, tend to focus on asking the right questions of the entrepreneur they're backing, rather than trying to provide all the answers. They know what questions to ask at the right time, based on patterns they've seen with other people they have worked with. And they can reframe situations, she adds, in a way that helps talent owners see both the reality and their options in a new light.[13]

Fourth and most importantly, talent nurturers take the people they are nurturing to places they wouldn't have gotten to otherwise. That applied quite literally in the case of my teacher Paul Henderson, as we've seen, through that fateful trip to Cambridge.

The Economist recently cited a paper by academics Yifang Ma, Satyam Mukherjee and Brian Uzzi of Northwestern University that showed this point in academia.[14] Based on a rigorously designed study that included a comparison group, the researchers found that the proteges of future Nobel laureates were more than three times morelikely to win the prize than similarly talented counterparts. They also produced more highly rated research. This wasn't because of differences in the innate brilliance of the researchers. Instead, the authors highlighted the difference mentors made in helping mentees produce their most promising ideas, spotting hidden gems in messy results, and suggesting new partnerships and collaborations with other researchers. As the newspaper noted, these nurturing details can individually seem mundane, but collectively they make an enormous difference.

The problem is that talent nurturing is becoming much harder to achieve nowadays. My wife Aida and I often talk about the 'life scripts' we were each meant to play. Mine was to become a doctor and marry a South Indian girl. Hers was to marry into a well-established Moroccan family in Rabat or Casablanca. A chance meeting at a party in Paris changed both our life scripts – something I feel eternally grateful for (though at some points of our marriage, she may not have been as convinced).

Both of us were lucky enough to be able to rewrite our personal life scripts, but many others in the world don't seem to have this luck. Parents from countries as far apart as Uganda and Singapore – which both have brutal systems of Primary School Leaving Examinations

– have told me a unanimous fear: that their children's life scripts (at least in terms of education and therefore jobs and earnings) were decided too early on, through these exams that 'sorted' kids into schools at such a young age.[15]

More than ever before, our life scripts are written not just at 11 or 12, but at birth. We've talked about Malcolm Gladwell's concept of 'accumulated advantage'. Sure enough, the kids that are usually best prepared for the PSLE exams are the most affluent, able to go to the best primary schools based on their postcodes – even in Singapore, which is deemed to be relatively 'meritocratic'.

Black and minority – and many working-class white – women and men are too often typecast, unable to write their own life scripts, and have talents that are entirely ignored, never mind nurtured. Too many of them feel excluded entirely from the Talent Pyramids – the systems of so-called 'meritocracies' which have far too easily been used to justify why only a few of us (not the many) deserve to have our talents nurtured and our potential fulfilled.

Here's the problem: the modern world that is focused heavily on extrinsic rewards has led to the creation of thousands of talent managers but very few genuine talent nurturers. Indeed, talent nurturers are becoming a rarer breed.

In this chapter we'll diagnose why and how the intrinsic motivation, success and talent of so many of us have been eroded, in contrast to the small number of 'winners' who have benefitted.

The idea of 'survival of the fittest' has truly distorted our perspective on the purpose of nurturing talent in ourselves and others. It reflects a deep misunderstanding of evolutionary theory – in particular Darwin's seminal *Origin of the Species*[16] – which has been used as a mental model for so much of how modern society works. Heather Scoville argues in a compelling essay on the website ThoughtCo that Darwin's term 'fittest' has wrongly come to be equated as meaning that the best physical specimens of men – in the best shape and health – will survive in nature. But, she argues, by 'fittest' Darwin actually meant those members of the species best suited for the immediate environment, on the basis of natural selection.[17]

New Scientist writer Michael Le Page builds on Scoville's argument.[18] 'Fittest' may not necessarily mean strongest, he argues. It can mean anything from the best camouflaged to the most fecund to the cleverest or the most aggressive.

A proper reading of Darwin's natural selection theory actually means there must be variations between species – and those variations must be, as Darwin said, 'heritable'. 'By itself, survival of the fittest is a dead end,' Le Page says. He goes on to argue that cooperation is a very sensible biological strategy: for example, when individual cells turn rogue (that is, individualistic and competitive), the result is usually cancer.

The key elements are diversity and cooperation. Margaret Heffernan makes much the same argument in her provocative book

A Bigger Prize.[19] Competition has many side-effects, she argues, both explicit and implicit. At the one extreme are the Olympic Games where for many competitors and some nations 'corruption, cover-up, performance-enhancing drug use' are the norm, she writes.

We are creating ever more elaborate 'talent treadmills' – rankings, entrance exams, selection days, aptitude tests. Treadmills that don't really work. Yes, we now have male tennis players who can hit serves over 140 miles per hour, and women over 120 miles per hour; but who really cares? The difference between a club player and the professional is so night-and-day obvious now that there are now no shades of grey between the amateur and professional sport.

The purpose of talent nurturing has been lost – and lost through the wrong mental models of 'survival of the fittest' and competition. Instead, people see their role in the talent game as simply 'managing' the talent treadmill – their job is merely to ensure that the standards of the treadmill are rigorous and fair.

This leads to a reduction in diversity of talent – the easiest way for a talent owner to acclimatize to a treadmill is to do things the way the talent manager thinks best. And it leads to a huge reduction in Purpose for the talent owner. What is the point of developing their own talent if they just have to jump through the same, standardized hoops as everyone else? It's a lose-lose situation for everyone.

The people whose job it is to nurture talent get stuck on this standardized treadmill. That means they start to lose all sense of their own personal impact, their own Purpose. Equally, the 'talent owners' stuck on the same gruelling treadmill of competition in this zero-sum game of 'winner takes all', start to lose a sense of their own uniqueness, their individual passion and sense of Purpose.

This alarming trend has serious consequences, as Mel Young, the chairman of Sportscotland, points out to me. Professional accolades and medal tallies have motivated national sports associations for a vast amount of time. He points to proud newspaper headlines purporting Britain to be the 'world's best sporting nation' (relative to its size) following the last two Olympic Games. But, he tells me, there's increasing disquiet within the sporting community of what the purpose of sport should really be. There has to be, he argues, a refocusing on 'sport for all' – on its core accessibility. And, by extension, using sport to unlock wider potential, development and talent, and even health in our lives.

Mel is a poster child in this regard: he previously founded the Homeless World Cup, which brings homeless people all over the world to play and celebrate the sport of football – all with the aim of putting a positive spotlight on homeless people's talents and ultimately contributing to ending homelessness.

Just as the Purpose of talent nurturing has been lost, the Autonomy of talent nurturers is being dismantled too.

Three decades ago, economists Michael Jensen and William

Meckling wrote a theory that would make them both famous and extremely popular with corporate America (and eventually corporate anywhere), which lapped it up.[20] It had the potential to make – almost overnight – CEOs and senior managers of the world's largest companies very, very rich. That theory was called 'principal-agent theory'.

The idea starts with the principal (or owner) of a business who wants to make money but does not want to get involved in actually running the business himself. So, he appoints an agent (the manager) to run it for him.

Immediately we run into what economists call asymmetry of information – the manager or agent, because he is so much more deeply involved in the business, is always going to know a lot more about it than the owner. If I am the owner of the business and I want my manager to do what's best for me, then I want to align my manager's incentives with my own. (Yes, the principal-agent theory is all about incentives – it's as extrinsic as it gets.)

Ever since the theory came out, the corporate world has been developing ever more elaborate schemes for this 'incentive alignment' – from cash bonuses to share options to equity to long-term incentive schemes. All of them are based on the same core extrinsic philosophy: you scratch my back, I'll scratch yours. The more profits a company makes, the more handsomely the CEO and his (and sadly it's almost always a 'his') executives are paid.

The theory's success and take-up can now be seen through its side-effects – particularly the ballooning income inequality that it's helped to fuel. As recently as 20 years ago, the pay gap between a CEO and an entry-level worker was typically 20:1 in large corporations. That gap has now reached approximately 300:1.[21] In other words, the average large corporate CEO typically makes almost as much in a single day as the entry-level worker in their organization achieves in a year.

Equivalent dynamics play out in many other sectors, even in the world of charitable foundations. The manager of a charitable foundation has to show his or her competence, and above all give the impression of control. The manager's promise is this: if you trust me to manage this, I'll make sure you get results. The results could range from a valuable or impactful organization – in the case of venture capital or philanthropy – to a new Wimbledon champion in the case of Britain's Sir Andy Murray.

It's a cumbersome and costly system – as Jensen and Meckling would themselves acknowledge – but at least it seems to work, right?

Not really.

Principal-agent theory created a basic problem – a fundamental imbalance of power. No sector brings this to light better than philanthropy. At its best, philanthropy is meant to channel private wealth into an R&D factory to solve the world's most pressing social problems (as opposed to traditional charity, which alleviates the symptoms of social problems). Having worked in this ecosystem for over 13 years, I'm less and less convinced – and I'm far from alone.

Anand Giridharadas' thought-provoking book *Winners Take All: The Elite Charade of Changing the World*[22] is a powerful exposé of the prevailing way of thinking in the philanthropy world. Giridharadas asserts that philanthropic wealth often feels a need to try to reduce complex and complicated social issues, to 'McKinsey-style PowerPoint' simplicity. Remember David Epstein in the last chapter? There are kind and wicked problems. Almost all the important social problems in our world are wicked problems. But most philanthropists behave as if they aren't.

I met Gaurav Singh, the inspirational founder behind the 321 Education Foundation, in a basement bar in Bandra in Mumbai. The foundation partners with schools to provide teacher training and wider support, particularly to low-cost private schools in three Indian cities – schools where parents pay a few pounds a month as school fees.

Gaurav's story is fascinating. Despite having a strong predicted rank for his Indian Institute for Technology entrance exams, he decided – to the consternation of his parents – not to take them. (IIT has a typical applicant acceptance rate of 2 per cent, and requires years of practice and preparation for their achingly tough entrance exams. It makes acceptance into places like Cambridge and Harvard look like a cakewalk.)

During the infamous 'Kota suicides' in Rajasthan, a young woman who was offered an IIT place felt so compelled to go by her parents that she subsequently committed suicide – showing the pressure families put on their kids to get into the institution.[23] It's fortunate that Gaurav's parents' reaction to his refusal to sit the exams was at least a little more balanced.

After completing Teach For India – the Indian equivalent of Teach First in UK or Teach For America in US which places fresh graduates on two-year teaching stints in challenging schools, with leadership development and mentoring support – Gaurav began 321, with a clear education philosophy of how to improve education standards. He's one of the most thoughtful people I've met in the education sector in India and, like so many of us, he finds fundraising through Indian foundations and corporations painful at times. The issue as Gaurav sees it is that foundations end up 'compartmentalizing' themselves (some focus on literacy and numeracy, whereas others focus on '21st-century skills' like confidence) to try to reduce a wicked, complex issue into what can feel like 'manageable' parts, in order to secure funding for their ideas.

While focus and depth do have benefits, the problem with compartmentalizing like this is that education is inherently a complicated and wicked process: each 'compartment' is inextricably linked and only when you get all the compartments working in concert does a child get the full benefit of education. For example, my time in Indonesia visiting East Java schools was eye-opening. In much of Indonesia (unlike India) most kids could read, write and count (Bahasa is a relatively easy language to learn, after all). However, they couldn't understand or think critically about what they had read, and there was no habit of reading. There was good literacy – which would have checked the philanthropists' box – but the lack of critical thinking rendered it much less powerful than it should have been. I basically saw first-hand the dangers of 'compartmentalization' at play.

Until 2015, the international community was focused on the Millennium Development Goals as its North Star – the goals the international community wanted to hold itself accountable for. There was an explicit agreement – between the governments concerned and the international donors that funded education – to focus on *access* to education, because it felt tangible. The other drivers of education quality involved working with messy groups like teachers and local politics, which donors felt less confident about influencing.

What happened? Yes, most countries 'succeeded' in achieving the goals on access to education. But it was a largely hollow victory. Hundreds of millions of children now have access to school, and enrolment rates are as high as 98 per cent in many countries – both remarkable achievements. But it also led to schools where no meaningful learning took place for the majority of the children, according to the World Bank's 2018 World Development Report.[24]

Because of the pressure countries felt to meet the Millennium Development Goal access and enrolment targets, governments built schools and enrolled children while adopting a mindset of 'we'll figure the learning and quality aspects later'. The problem was, the 'later' never really came.

This is not an obscure, specific problem within developing countries. Education systems face this kind of problem everywhere. Japan is known for its educational rigour and regularly scores highly in international comparisons like the PISA tests. And yet the Japanese government recently announced that student absenteeism had hit an all-time high: over 160,000 children were absent from school for over 30 days or more, according to official statistics. Each year 300 children commit suicide – prompting the government to pass a suicide-prevention act specifically for schools. This time, the suicides are less to do with parents and more to do with 'black school rules', as the Japanese call them – draconian rules that even dictate the colour of children's underwear – and a persistent worry among Japanese children about the behaviour of their peers, from feeling overwhelmed in large classes to outright bullying. Perhaps not surprisingly, there are now over half a million estimated *hikikomori*, children, mostly young men, who refuse to leave their bedrooms and completely withdraw from society, according to a BBC report.[25]

Japanese teachers were encouraged to think of themselves as mere cogs in the education treadmill. Their job was to provide the content for children to pass the notoriously difficult exams. Full stop. There was no sense of responsibility for people who couldn't succeed within the system. So, the entire Japanese education system effectively turned a blind eye to half a million young people: literally out of sight, out of mind.

By now we should understand why. The principal-agent way of thinking about talent is leading to a focus on data and 'objectivity' because of its core belief: that the principal can't really trust the intrinsic motivation of the agent. Therefore agents have to be 'managed' by this data and objectivity. That then leads to a highly reductionist view of success, based purely on extrinsic measures. And that in turn means talent managers – in this case, teachers – never become true talent nurturers.

This need to standardize and control then ends in a loss of Autonomy and diversity in talent owners themselves (in this case Japanese students), and a lack of diversity in how they view success. The image of the Japanese 'salaryman' – who will wear the uniform of conformity all his life, toiling away as an indistinguishable cog in the wheel of some Japanese conglomerate – is still alive and well, despite the pressures of globalization. These systems of organizing talent and work in Japan are the opposite of intrinsic – and they're unlikely to achieve the end Purpose of work we've discussed: to help and serve others.

*

How can talent nurturers harness their Mastery to combat a 'winner takes all' world? The realm of entrepreneurship is a good place to look at this question, because it's so important to the future of our economies. Every country and city in the world – from Lisbon to Lima – aspires to be the new centre for entrepreneurship, because it's one of the few proven ways to create jobs. Even Paris – not normally known for its entrepreneurial credentials – marketed itself to Brexit-fearing European businesses under President Macron, and it seemed initially to work. Smart suburbs like Neuilly-sur-Seine saw booming house prices from jittery French expats returning from London. Then the *veste jaune* protests hit and the devastation they created across the French capital somewhat burst the bubble.

India is no exception to the entrepreneurship fad. When Prime Minister Narendra Modi was elected in his first term, he wanted to make India a country of entrepreneurship, building from his previous success courting business as chief minister of Gujarat. With good reason: the country needs to create 20 million jobs a year just to absorb the number of new young people entering the workforce.

Harshal Shah leads the incubation centre – which supports new start-up companies – within NMIMS's School of Business in Mumbai. He trained as a lawyer and completed his Masters at Harvard Law School, but the entrepreneurial bug truly got to him: he's eschewed his legal career and now both runs the centre and is an early-stage entrepreneur himself.

Harshal's time in helping shape promising start-up companies has taught him three interesting lessons about what's really needed to nurture (as opposed to merely manage) entrepreneurship talent in modern India – lessons that should apply more widely to how we think about Mastery in talent nurturing. No one prepared him for these lessons; to his enormous credit, he picked them up himself.

The first lesson was around sourcing promising companies in the first place. Initially the incubation centre only focused on NMIMS students and graduates, but it found that current students may not be as committed to their ventures as entrepreneurs in the 'real world'. Opening themselves up to anyone in the Mumbai area has massively improved the quality of the talent pool. It has also allowed the centre to work with a much more experienced entrepreneur pool with the average age (and therefore life experience) of the founders going up by several years. There's an interesting parallel between Harshal's learning and what Selena Rezvani told us about transparently opening up applications for 'stretch opportunities' in the previous chapter on work.

The second lesson was in terms of the types of company that would actually prove successful. The companies Harshal initially favoured were what you would find in an incubator in most parts of the world – typically dot-com firms with crazy valuations and no realistic ways of making profit anytime soon. After the Indian stock market saw its bubble burst, following India's 2016 demonetization and much slower economic growth, there was, however, little appetite for this kind of model. The companies the incubation centre started to favour changed to 'real businesses', with positive cash flow and profits. The incubation centre started to focus on finding large family businesses that shared the same values as the entrepreneurs, and could work with them to integrate or grow their services. Again, this kind of 'match-making' with larger businesses wasn't in the centre's initial brief, but Harshal saw the need and adapted.

The third lesson was in the role of the incubator itself. In its early years, Harshal spent most of his and his team's time on spotting and managing talent – for example, screening applicants and their application forms, and spending hours managing and analysing the 'pipeline' of new applicants, to ensure it had the desired depth and profile. But then he realized that nurturing talent was proving much more important. Now the incubation centre provides everything from back-office services like finance to sales and marketing advice and support. And the crown jewels: a network of 70 entrepreneurs who serve as mentors. These entrepreneur-mentors, Harshal tells me, 'are experienced but still hungry for success and have a practical bent to what they can advise on'.

This way of working and this idea – that talent nurturing is more important than talent management – runs counter to India's modern psyche. The IIT exams that Gaurav eschewed are all about this talent pyramid: use selectivity as the ultimate carrot, and amazing things will happen. It's a 'winner takes all' model that is used in many domains in India.

True Mastery in talent nurturing is really demanding. That's a theme that haunts the tales of even Silicon Valley's most prestigious venture-capital funds, such as Kleiner Perkins. 'Kleiner' once was as influential in venture-capitalist circles as 'Oprah' was in Hollywood, argues Polina Marinova in a brilliant piece in *Fortune*.[26] She traces how the firm subsequently went on a path where it lost early-stage deal after deal – including early opportunities to invest in Uber and Snapchat. It then finally got seduced by the much more stable (but less financially rewarding) game of later-stage investments. As a result, the returns it generated for its investors, though strong by any conventional standards, were a fraction of those of competitors like Benchmark. This led to the firm eventually splitting up as the two sides of the business – early-stage and late-stage investing – grew increasingly disparate.

Reading Marinova's analysis, it almost felt like the adrenaline – the sheer rough and tumble – needed for early-stage investing became simply too much to bear, particularly as its legendary founders, including John Doerr, wanted to focus on other areas.

The problem is that truly nurturing talent – of which early-stage investing is an extreme example – is a hair-raising and often soul- (and money-) destroying process. For every ten investments, venture-capital firms are lucky if two become true successes. But those two generate the returns that make up for the whole fund. For example, an investment fund raised by Benchmark in 2010 eventually gave investors back $25 for every dollar invested.

Talent nurturers have an abundance mindset to talent, realize the crooked path talent takes, focus on reigniting intrinsic motivation as much as passing on technical prowess, and fundamentally take their talent owners to places they wouldn't have gone otherwise.

As we saw in Harshal's case, developing Mastery in talent nurturing is hard; he had to eschew many of the traditional shortcuts that other incubators took. But he had the stomach and nerve to learn and then do what was needed – something that even the most pedigreed venture-capital firms in the world find daunting.

What would it take to move to a mindset of talent nurturing? One that reignites the motivation of both the talent nurturer and the talent owner? A mindset that allows us all as individuals to shape our own talent paths?

To achieve that ambitious vision, we'll need to reignite the Purpose of talent nurturing in the first place.

The restaurant world provides an unusual but interesting background to explore how this can be done. JKS is a restaurant group in London that actually makes that model of talent nurturing a reality. It was founded by three British Indian siblings who trained in business, but were obsessed by food. The group's Indian restaurants are all set up directly by JKS, albeit with a diverse mandate: from Gymkhana, which mirrors the old colonial clubs of the British, laced liberally with old-school punches, and Brigadiers with its Indian bar motif, to South Indian and Sri-Lankan-inspired Hoppers, and Michelin-starred, traditional fine-dining Trishna, with which JKS's food empire kicked off.

But it's the non-Indian side of the equation that offers even more distinctiveness and innovation. Bao's signature Taiwanese fried chicken and milky pork parcels made Taiwanese food what it is in London – and all from the humble start of a food stall in Hackney's Netil Market, where my kids still love going. Equally distinctive is Lyle's, where a small but achingly modern British menu is chalked on the board each day.

Talking about the founders of restaurants like Lyle's and the guys at Bao, JKS co-founder Jyotin Sethi was quoted in an interview with *The Caterer*:[27] 'A lot of people talk about how they are passionate and ambitious...But it's a tough industry and to really make it work you really need that obsession and attention to detail – it is all-encompassing. It is a characteristic of everyone we work with, Indian or non-Indian. You need to have talent, but it's obsession that turns that talent into a successful business.'

It's the way that JKS nurtures new restaurant founders that really impressed me. Jyotin Sethi added in the same interview,

'...we advised [the guys at Bao] on how to convert that [street menu] into a restaurant menu. But ultimately they are completely in control of what they want to cook and the way they want the site to look because I think that is key in terms of the partnership. They want the autonomy and the independence, and we put in our experience and expertise on the business side.'

It's an interesting model of nurturing that makes each restaurant feel different. You could go to Berenjak – one of the latest in the group, modelled on a Tehran cafe – and you wouldn't know there was any connection to Hoppers, with its fiery South Indian and Sri Lankan stews and curries.

Most restaurant groups ask themselves a simple question: 'Have I invested my investors' money effectively?' What I love about JKS is how they ask a deeper question – a question built around a deep understanding of talent nurturing: 'Have I helped take the restaurant owners in my group to a place they wouldn't have gone otherwise?'

The second way to reignite a sense of Purpose is for talent nurturers to hold one principle constant, above all else: the love of the activity itself should be paramount – whether that's the restaurant business, teaching or playing a sport.

Kavitha Krishnamurthy was born in Toronto; her mother was a professional, classical Indian *bharatnatyam* dancer. Kavitha and her two siblings played tennis to a high level. Her first memory, she tells me, is of her brother helping her to grip the racket properly at the age of four. And she started to play tournaments from age 11.

She started progressed on the tennis treadmill in Canada and began to make it to the regional and then national levels, and got as high as 40 in the junior world rankings. That led her to play Junior Wimbledon and the US Open – experiences she credits as life changing. Then she got a place to study and compete at Princeton. Combining both must have been brutal. 'I didn't drink or party, that's never been my style,' she explains. (After speaking to Kavitha, my own time at university spent loafing around in college bars and going to random society events felt quite indulgent. I came away with a deep sense of guilt.)

After Princeton, she decided to turn pro. 'I got prestigious places to play like the Rogers Cup,' she tells me, 'but most of the time it was Challengers and satellite tournaments where I ended up grinding in obscurity...sometimes my mother would join me but it was often me, alone.'

Those three years, 2003 to 2006, were perhaps years of innocence on the pro tour. Federer had only just started his dominance of the men's game and things hadn't quite reached the level of ultra-competitiveness that they have now.

At the end of it, did she love tennis?

'I think I did,' Kavitha tells me. 'After deciding to retire as a pro I left and enrolled on a Masters at Oxford. But I certainly didn't hang up my racket. I still played for the university tennis team.'

Looking back, she thinks tennis provided a great deal. 'Some of my best memories and my best times were on the tennis tour,' she tells me. 'There is so much that I wanted to work on and to push myself on. I learned so much.'

Kavitha's one constant was her father. He seemed a symbol of balance and reasonableness. Some days she would win and many other days she wouldn't. It seemed that it was the unconditional acceptance he provided that really mattered – something we'll explore further when we get on to parenting in chapter 5.

What struck me about talking to Kavitha was that her love for the sport seemed intact, and even stronger, all the way through her experience. It felt like the opposite of reading Andre Agassi's autobiography *Open*[28] many years ago, and the love-hate (and more often hate) relationship he had with the sport (and with his father). His book was searing in its honesty even as the candour of the revelations destroyed many of his close friendships in the sport.

What also struck me was how much Kavitha enjoyed the tour, the travel, meeting people from all countries – the ability to create camaraderie in what could have otherwise been an incredibly lonely existence.

She made it to Princeton and Oxford as well as the professional tennis tour, and now works as a senior executive at Diageo. She looks back at her tennis career not with regret but with a love and fondness that is inspiring. There is no one to 'blame' for her not making it to the very top echelons of the sport. There is nothing to feel bad about. She loved the experience of travelling and competing. And through tennis she created a foundation of skills and experiences – and most of all maturity – that would set her up her whole life.

Part of maintaining that sense of Purpose is to avoid feeling jaded. Too often we fall in love with the activity but not the lifestyle around it. But Federer waxes lyrical about the latest sushi restaurant he stumbles across on his travels. Boris Becker, another Wimbledon champion, tells us much the same thing about his life. Speaking recently to the Oxford Union, he talked about how he enjoyed the travel and the lifestyle.[29]

If you are a friend, coach or parent to an aspiring athlete or talent nurturer to anyone, try to help them stay in love with the 'game' and the lifestyle around it. If you help them keep that intact, then you'll largely succeed whatever else happens.

American Mia Hamm was arguably the world's first true international women's football star. Her advice to aspiring players is simple: 'Somewhere behind the athlete you've become and the hours of practice and the coaches who have pushed you is a little girl who fell in love with the game and never looked back...play for her.'[30]

It's good advice for any talent nurturer who wants to maintain Purpose in the person they are nurturing.

*

Here's an important rule for true talent nurturers: give real Autonomy to your talent owners – even if it means relinquishing power yourself.

Federer was lucky to have a series of coaches who took him to a certain level and then, with good grace, allowed him to move to a different coach at the next level. Remember my English teacher pushing me to apply to Cambridge, even after I'd left his school and chosen an entirely different subject. This requires the talent nurturer to really prioritize the motivation and needs of the talent owner, often above their own.

I've always been a distant admirer of venture-capital legend Vinod Khosla. Khosla was a Kleinier Perkins partner for almost 20 years before setting up his own fund, Khosla Ventures. He makes the point that entrepreneurs (the talent owners) think a lot about the choice of their co-founders, but not at all about the investors they take on. The problem with that is that taking on investors inevitably means accepting their influence. His maxim, which he shared in a speech to Bowery Capital, is that 90 per cent of investors add no value to the company and 70 per cent of investors add negative value.

Khosla uses the metaphor of Mount Everest: it's easy to envision it but hard to envision the multiple paths to get to the top. Investors who can help you take the unplanned path to the summit are the real minority. They're like a gold Sherpa, in his eyes.

With Khosla's wealth and experience, you'd think he would have all the answers. In fact, the opposite is true. The core of Khosla's philosophy is trusting the people he invests in – the entrepreneurs. But along with that trust, he also acts as a critical friend. 'Khosla Ventures does its part by favouring brutal honesty over hypocritical politeness in our feedback, while supporting entrepreneurs in their growth objectives,' Khosla once wrote.[31]

'I feel a board shouldn't have to vote on anything except their confidence (or not) in the management. In 25-plus years of being on boards, I have never once voted against a management team except on the question of whether the CEO should be changed... I feel free to argue informally, to have real, sometimes uncomfortable discussions, and to leave the final decision to the team that will execute it. It is hard for a team to execute well...if they believe the board is going to make the final decision on an issue.'

In more than 25 wildly successful years in the business, Khosla has become even more of a fervent believer in the value and judgement of company founders. 'It's always better for a founder to grow into being a CEO. When there's a choice, the founder's vision, culture and approach are usually more important than "good management" alone,' he concludes. The insightful book *The Founder's Mentality*[32] backs up Khosla's philosophy with swathes of business evidence. Companies that remain led or influenced by their founders, the book finds, are more successful in almost every realm – certainly in intrinsic areas like company culture, but even on fully extrinsic criteria such as sales and profits.

Indeed, Khosla Ventures has now created an entire support team designed to nurture talent that is independent of the investment team. This is increasingly needed as Silicon Valley founders seem to get younger and younger with the advent of new web technologies.

The spirit of Autonomy in philanthropy is, as we've seen, rare, so we should celebrate when it does happen – and particularly when it happens at scale. The Ford Foundation – one of the US's most venerable foundations – invested $1 billion in social-justice organizations around the world, in a new programme called BUILD. BUILD is about giving power back to charitable grantees, including long-term (five-year) committed funding. It gives grantees access to the specialized expertise they want, but doesn't direct them on what that expertise should be. Nor what the organizations should do and what their overall strategy should be.

Interim results suggest the approach – and particularly the longer-term funding – has made the non-profit organizations it nurtures more versatile, helping them to focus more on strategy, and develop stronger peer relationships (and, critically, relationships with the Ford Foundation itself).[33] That's the irony: by letting power go, you actually deepen the relationship with those you are nurturing. BUILD is developing what other smaller family foundations – such as the Peery Foundation – have described as a more 'grantee-centric' approach.

Khosla Ventures and the Ford Foundation are two of the heavyweights in their respective sectors. If they can relinquish power, surely others can too.

Another aspect of relinquishing power for wise talent nurturers is to know when you can add value – and when you can't. Robert Dighero is a general partner at Passion Capital, an early-stage investment fund which has invested in many successful early-stage start-ups in the UK, including jobs site Adzuna and online bank Tide (whom I proudly bank with). Passion Capital usually puts one of their partners on the board of the companies to start with, but gradually evolve their role as more mature capital comes in. That partner might move, for example, from being on the board to being a board observer as the company gets bigger and larger venture firms provide more capital. All the way through, however, there's a constant: a huge respect for the time of the founder and their management team. Robert tells me it's a start-up's most precious resource.

I ask Robert how he knows whether a founder is right to invest in. He tells me that the decision has nothing to do with sector (Passion are sector agnostic) or comparing them to other founders through some 'objective' yardstick. It has to do with passion, the passion that comes from finding a problem that they literally can't live without solving. And the second thing is a founder's resilience – no matter how many problems appear, and through the inevitable changes in direction that start-ups have to go through.

At the end of our discussion, Robert concludes: 'Most of the founders would have gotten there anyway. We help them a little.' I'm not so sure about that. But the modesty is as disarming as it is unusual in those who should be nurturing talent.

Finally, talent nurturers also need to deploy and role-model a much broader form of Mastery – one that transcends the actual domain they work in. These broader forms of Mastery can then be harnessed by the talent owner (if they want to) in very different areas and fields.

Whether or not you go all the way to becoming a Wimbledon champion, succeeding at something truly matters and can have knock-on effects for the rest of your life. I remember speaking to Sir Alasdair Macdonald, the inspirational former head teacher of Morpeth School in Tower Hamlets, a highly disadvantaged part of east London. Over the decades of his headship he'd transformed Morpeth from a school where no one wanted to go to one of the most flourishing schools in the country.

When I asked him what his secret was, I was expecting words like curriculum, teaching, OFSTED. Instead came out two words that completely threw me: 'table tennis'. Alasdair explained that the children – and parents – of the school felt they were literally good for nothing so they needed a beacon of hope. Table tennis was the easiest, least expensive and most practical activity to focus the whole school on. London schools are rarely blessed with masses of space, after all. He began a big table-tennis initiative across the school, and brought world-class coaching and training in. Now Morpeth regularly vies for national championships at all age groups. And if you draw a correlation between the school's table-tennis success and its wider success (including in academics), you can see an almost perfect straight line. Succeeding at something can be a huge 'multiplier' for everything else in your life.

Rebecca Feickert and Brian Reynolds are co-founders of Trey Athletes. Trey works to develop US college athletes (with an initial focus on basketball) into well-rounded college graduates – and to protect them from the lucrative but myopic college sports system. College sports, they tell me, is now a $7-billion annual industry in the US, fuelled by TV deals and alumni donations that are highly correlated with college sports-team success.

'Parents feel like their child has won the lottery if their child has won a college scholarship,' Brian tells me. But the objective truth is that, even from that point, the chances of being able to turn professional – and join the National Basketball Association (NBA) – are about 2 per cent. Yet the whole system of college does little to nurture the broader talents of the 98 per cent of college athletes who won't be able to turn pro.

In fact the US college sports system seems hell-bent on achieving the exact opposite – creating an effective educational and social apartheid. Although college athletes are often 'big men' on campus, they're encouraged to live and spend time with their teammates, and not overly socialize with anyone beyond for fear of getting 'distracted'. They're also encouraged to take easier courses that are not academically demanding so they can devote the lion's share of their time to sport.

Trey Athletes is fighting the good fight towards a broader vision of Mastery for athletes, working with the athletes' parents to ensure there is commitment to develop their Mastery in everything from academics to the socio-emotional skills that will be so critical to their wider life and work success.

The importance of creating a broader Mastery is backed up by neuroscience. In his provocative book *The Talent Code*,[34] Daniel Coyle writes about myelin, the neural substance that adds vast amounts of speed and accuracy into our behaviour and thoughts. It's literally an insulating layer that forms around our nerves which allows electrical impulses to move quickly along the nerve cells.

Much of the focus of the study of myelin has been around deep, deliberate practice that allows repeated patterns to form in a very specific discipline. But there's a new frontier in which we badly need evidence around how myelin works – and that's in the process of 'learning to learn'. 'Learning to learn' is what we need most in our education and talent-management systems: the ability of talent owners to look at the external trends and signals around them, and know how to evolve their talent accordingly.

This 'learning to learn' characteristic in talent owners is so important. When I started my early career in strategy consulting, I worked for David Newkirk. He was a brilliant and larger-than-life (in every sense) American. I was always fascinated by how he interviewed candidates for the firm. Or, rather, didn't interview them. He eschewed most of the standard consulting questions and case studies (which usually involved quite inane questions, including asking a candidate to estimate how many golf balls there were in the world) and asked them to talk about something they were already passionate about, which could involve anything from drama to wine to rowing. He would ask them deeper and deeper questions in their chosen area. He was looking to see if they had developed a true Mastery in an area they were passionate about. If so, he told me, he believed that they could develop a similar Mastery in the high-powered world of strategy consulting.

I didn't fully buy his approach then, but I do now. The problem is his approach is becoming increasingly rare. Achieving Mastery for a talent nurturer today is much more complicated than it used to be – but also more rewarding. Being a college coach of the future, for example, might mean being an interlocutor between the sports, academic and pastoral domains of a higher-education institution. It's a lot more complex than the already challenging task of getting athletes to jump through hoops as adeptly as they can. But at least when they jump, it will be through hoops that are truly worth it.

Overall, we've seen in this chapter that we are in a deep and fundamental talent mess – one that is creating success for a few winners, not us all. And in so many aspects of life.

If you're a talent owner – whether in the labour market or the sports field or the concert hall – I hope this chapter has given you some hope and changed some of your mental models. Remember the three core rules of being a talent owner. Know your own unique Purpose – why you love what you do – and keep that paramount.

Express that Purpose in a way that is distinctive – we don't remember Federer just for the grand-slam titles, it's really for the old-school grace and charm of the game he reignited. Don't listen to that claptrap about 'survival of the fittest' – remember Darwin was really talking about diversity. Stand out, be different.

As a talent owner, insist on Autonomy in what you do and how you do it – from practising in the way that keeps you most motivated to how you set up your schedule and your life. Federer turned heads for playing so late in his career, largely because he played fewer tournaments and committed to less travel so he could have more time with his children.

And remember to develop Mastery not just in the narrow domain you are in, but also in the transferable skills that will help define your next talent and success chapter.

Finally, look out for the right talent nurturer – the one who really understands you and believes in you. Sometimes – if you're lucky –

they land in your lives unexpectedly (as teacher Paul Henderson did in mine). But more often than not you'll need to search for them. Don't give up looking, even if it takes time; the right one is out there somewhere. And when you do find them, hold on to them and keep learning and growing with them as far as you can, knowing that your next chapter might need a new nurturer.

If your day job is already about talent – if you're a teacher or coach, work mentor or venture capitalist – see if you can become the best type of talent nurturer you can possibly be.

Don't get seduced by incentives and so-called 'accountability' to the person who pays your bills. Your core Purpose and responsibility are to the people you are nurturing.

Employ an abundance mindset, stay steady even when they take the most crooked paths, and light that lamp of intrinsic motivation in them – the underlying love of the activity itself. That love of the activity will in turn translate to success in whatever else they do in their lives, whether it's related or not.

Resist (where possible) giving too many answers; focus instead on asking the right questions.

And, finally, invest in your own Purpose, Autonomy and Mastery as a talent nurturer – so you can truly fulfil your own potential.

I hope this chapter makes us all think more broadly about what it takes to create a society and world where the talents of many, not just a few, can be nurtured. Let's expose 'meritocracy' for what it truly is.

We all deserve so much better.

The 'winner takes all' mentality pervades so many aspects of our lives, even the most personal – including what we look for in our soulmates, and how we parent.

In the next chapter we'll move from the worlds of work and talent to the more personal. We'll look at how the extrinsic pressures we've seen in both work and talent are putting deep stresses on the Purpose, Autonomy and Mastery in our key relationships – particularly our romantic relationships, which are proving ever more important for achieving our overall happiness in life – and how we can use motivation thinking to improve them.

'I want to feel completely vulnerable, completely naked, completely exposed and absolutely secure.'

Howard Thurman[1]

4

Intrinsic Relationships: From High Stakes to High Safety

'Zayna' is a French national of Arab descent who lives in the smart Paris suburb of Neuilly-sur-Seine. She married her native French husband in her early 20s, while they were both completing their undergraduate studies at a prestigious French business school.

Fifteen years and two children later, their marriage broke up.

When I asked 'Zayna' to explain why, she first told me she didn't really know. And it felt like she and her husband didn't really want to know. 'Both of us were exhausted. We didn't try counselling or anything. We sort of just let it happen...'

French women's magazines and cinema, 'Zayna' says, have traditionally made divorce look easy, perhaps even glamorous – as witnessed by anyone who has watched countless films featuring Gérard Depardieu and Catherine Deneuve. That's being challenged in new French cinema. *L'Economie du couple* (2016), for example, is a gripping psychological take on a French divorce where the husband can't afford to move out of the common house until a settlement is reached. It echoes longstanding HBO series *The Affair* with Dominic West and films like Netflix's *Marriage Story* in the US, which more transparently show some of the side-effects of divorce – both on the couple and on their children.

'Zayna' tells me a story that breaks my heart. Once, to stop a fight between her kids while they were playing, she told them: '*Chacun son tour*.' ('Each his turn.') To which her daughter immediately shot back: 'Why couldn't it be "each his turn" with you and daddy?'

There seems little doubt that 'Zayna' regrets what happened. 'In our working life, we have this attitude that we have to make things work. Even though we care so much less about work than about our kids. Perhaps we need the same attitude to marriage. Because divorce really sucks for the kids.'

'Zayna's' divorce was quick and easy because it was labelled as '*amiable*' (friendly). Like many other countries, France has moved to a 'no blame' divorce law as its primary model. What haunts 'Zayna' still is the sense that she and her husband could have fought harder to keep the marriage, but at the time their emotions were wrought. 'In Paris life is hard. You come home exhausted. And then we would fight constantly about small things – whether or not the kids should watch TV, silly things like that.'

Another source of fighting was over interference from both sets of grandparents. This part of our discussion reminded me of a Russian proverb an old friend, Sasha Berson, attributes to his grandmother: 'Children and their grandparents are united by a common enemy.'

'When you have a child, one person in the couple has to make a sacrifice, to slow down. Many women now don't want to do that,' 'Zayna' adds. And, she tells me, when the tiny minority of men are willing to try, the result is often social scorn. 'When a man in our local parent community decided to take Wednesdays off, which is allowed by law, he was looked on weirdly by everyone – and especially by the mothers in the group.'

'Zayna' grew up in a well-to-do family in her home country. Common to the upper-middle class there, the family had a cook, household help and a driver. She thinks her parents had it much easier than she does now.

She acknowledges that France is a relatively progressive country in terms of family-friendly policies and balance, with paid parental leave and universal and affordable childcare. (This is backed by a 2019 UNICEF study that shows that France does relatively well in the rankings of family-friendly policies, but is behind countries like Sweden, Norway, Iceland, Estonia and Portugal.)[2] But 'Zayna' touches on something that Richard Reeves, Senior Economic

Studies Fellow at the highly respected Brookings Institution also notes about the US – that in matters like these, national policies can only go so far.

The bigger challenge is social norms. When another French couple I know divorced in the upmarket Parisian suburb St Germain-en-Laye, their daughter didn't bat an eyelid. Previously she'd been in the minority in her school for having parents who were still married.

What's emerging from all this is that divorce has many features of a 'social pandemic': once it becomes widespread, it weakens both a couple's and wider society's defence mechanisms. It becomes seen as more and more inevitable and part of the natural state of events.

What is also striking – and to me, shocking – about 'Zayna's' story was that none of her or her then husband's friends tried to counsel them, let alone talk them out of it. When divorce becomes the 'new normal', we really are in societal trouble.

Laura Mucha is a writer who has interviewed hundreds of couples around the world, from Finland to Nigeria. She points to new evidence in her book *We Need to Talk About Love*[3] that suggests that even relatively happy couples now are at a higher risk of divorce. And the killer punch: children of divorced parents are significantly more likely to believe in the acceptability of divorce themselves. She also mentions a 17-year US study of 2,000 couples that shows when low-conflict couples divorce they are less happy afterwards; and their children's wellbeing is unmistakably lower.

The financial implications of divorce are important, too. 'Zayna' was upfront with me about her financial situation: 'We are lucky in that each of us has a good salary. But each of us is now unquestionably poorer. If you like, there are "diseconomies of scale"', she told me, borrowing a phrase from economics. Tight French post-divorce arrangements mean that both parties strictly share time with the child, including on weekends and holidays. And each has to secure accommodation large enough to comfortably house the children while they are with them. Quite literally, 'Zayna' tells me, that means having to buy two of everything.

Global divorce rates provide a more nuanced story. They have risen since the 1950s, and over 40 per cent of married couples today will divorce at some point – over two-thirds in countries like Spain and Luxembourg. But taking a generational perspective provides some more optimism. According to researchers Esteban Ortiz-Ospina and Max Roser,[4] younger couples in countries like the UK and the US seem to be bucking that trend: among that age group, they're likely to stay together longer before breaking up. So much so that overall divorce rates have roughly halved since their peak in the 1990s.

But there's a catch alongside this optimism. Ortiz-Ospina and Roser's analysis suggests that marriage rates have also fallen in the majority of countries across the world. This is especially true for younger people. For example, of men born in 1930, 83 per cent were married by the age of 30. But among those born in 1980, only a quarter were married by the same age. This broader trend holds across all age cohorts, and for men and women. Is the fear of divorce putting people off considering marriage in the first place?

It's worth saying of course that marriage is not the only form of a stable relationship. And each of us has our own views on the institution, as do different societies: Indian attitudes are a night-and-day contrast to Scandinavian ones. In Europe and the US, a majority of people see co-habitation – or living together – as much the same thing as marriage. But even using that yardstick, the proportion of people living together (whether married or not) has *also* declined overall in many parts of the world.[5] For example in the UK, the number of people living alone has increased by a fifth over the last 20 years and totals over eight million, according to a 2019 survey by the Office of National Statistics.[6] A very similar trend holds true for northern America.[7]

This chapter isn't about debating the merits of marriage or co-habitation. Rather, it is about how we can form stable, happy and fulfilling romantic relationships in whatever form we think is most appropriate. This is important because research suggests that we are increasingly dependent on our key romantic relationships – with girlfriends or boyfriends, partners or spouses, heterosexual or same sex – for harnessing our overall happiness in life. Family-studies scientist Christine Proulx has tried to assess this issue robustly. The relative contribution of marriage quality to our overall happiness, she finds, has doubled over 30 years, and now likely explains almost 40 per cent of our overall happiness.[8]

What does all this add up to? In short, a world of 'relationship haves and have-nots'. Those who are lucky enough to enter into a committed relationship are much more likely to stay together, or at least stay together longer, than they would have in the past. But many will forgo the institution of a marriage or stable relationship altogether.

In the US at least, marriage is increasingly becoming the preserve of the upper class, Richard Reeves at Brookings has discovered.[9] Only 59 per cent of middle-class children live in married households, compared to 75 per cent in 1979, 2020 data suggests. And this sharp decline in marriage rates is even sharper among the lower-middle class.

Reeves describes marriage as a 'high commitment' financial strategy. With the stagnation of wages for many Americans, middle-class and working-class men are effectively being priced out of this important societal institution in the first place. They basically don't feel they have the financial security to be a dependable breadwinner for their family, even when most women in the household also work.

The stakes of modern relationships are terrifyingly high. If we find a committed partner we're much more likely to be happier and more motivated in our lives. But the risk of not achieving this is growing – even more so if we are economically disadvantaged. This is an important problem to find some solutions to, and that's what we'll attempt to do in this chapter.

We'll use motivation thinking to diagnose our current relationship malaise. For those of us in relationships, we'll use motivation thinking and the key elements of Purpose, Autonomy and Mastery to ask how we can become better partners. This will boost our collective motivation and happiness in the relationship itself, and in our wider lives. For those of us who aren't in relationships but aspire to be, we'll ask how we can better set up our search to find the right mate – and glean some clues on what to look for.

Let's start with the uber-question: What is the true purpose of a romantic relationship in the first place?

Eli Finkel – a professor at Northwestern University – has studied this in a sweeping and brilliant new historical analysis of US marriage trends.[10] His research suggests that, in the 17th century, marriage was mostly about food, shelter and protection from violence – literal hygiene factors in terms of what we've learned about motivation theory. From the 19th century to the 1970s, however, Finkel finds that the primary function of marriage moved to what we might consider to be higher-order hygiene factors – particularly love, companionship and sexual fulfilment.

From the 1970s onwards, however, 'self-actualization' factors –

'self-discovery, self-esteem and personal growth' – have become core to modern marriage, unleashing what Finkel calls the 'expressive self' and the 'authentic self'. Relationships guru Esther Perel takes a similar perspective on modern marriage in her interview with *The New Yorker*, arguing further that the liberation of rules, order and duty in our relationships has led to the need for a 'freakin' negotiation' in virtually every aspect.[11]

That's not to say that areas like sex don't remain important. Obstetrician Rajiv Sreekumar, who has a booming infertility practice in Chennai, tells me that he has to counsel couples to actually make time for sex. 'So many women now tell me that they don't find enough time in the week,' he tells me. 'I tell them to calendar and diarize.'

Esther Perel argues that sex is increasingly a hygiene factor in modern marriage: if it's good, it doesn't affect the success of marriage that much; but if it's bad or non-existent, it can significantly undermine it.

But overall, the role of marriages and serious relationships is increasingly seen in how they emotionally nurture both partners. And that is creating the trend towards what Finkel calls 'all or nothing' marriages. When they work, they provide the most nurturing environment possible for each individual, and for the couple as a whole, to thrive and provide a sense of emotional safety and attachment.

India is going through a real transition of attitudes in this regard. Dr Nappinnai Seran, who made a mid-career change to become a counsellor in Chennai, is experiencing a booming demand for her services – to such an extent that she now has offices in different parts of town. (Chennai's traffic is as fierce as any Indian metro, so clients are reluctant to travel beyond their local area.) 'Couples are quite emotionally lost,' she told me. 'They have high expectations that aren't grounded in anything. They are not sure what they should hope for. Amid all this there are lots of external pressures and stress.'

Research by Stanford sociologist Michael Rosenfeld suggests that online dating has become the most common way American heterosexual couples meet.[12] It's overtaken such old-fashioned 'niceties' such as being introduced by a friend or flirting in a bar.

'AJ' is a veteran of these dating apps, including Tinder. He's a successful London-based entrepreneur, in his mid-40s and single, and has experienced more than his share of the London and New York dating scenes. He has been on one or two dates per week for over two decades, which gives us a large data set to glean insights from.

I am expecting to feel more than a small pang of jealousy, particularly as he shows me the successful 'swipes' from upcoming dates on his Tinder account. I do have a little pang, of course (AJ is a good-looking guy, and seems to attract equivalent matches).

But more than anything I feel a sense of liberation – for getting married before the dating world ratcheted up in its intensity.

Perhaps unsurprisingly, AJ is withering about what motivates the multi-billion-dollar companies behind the biggest dating apps. 'Their purpose is to sustain their revenue, so the last thing they want to do is help people actually find their match,' he believes emphatically.

From his dating forays, he's learned a lot about what really motivates people on dates. It's worth stressing upfront that this is one person (and particularly one man's) lived experience, but nevertheless it provides some interesting insights:

'People think they know what they want. I think women subconsciously look for "will this person provide me with offspring and a better life?" They look for power and position – success and long-term security. They want, essentially, "winners". They're fine if the success is self-generated or inherited, and also if the man is on an upward trajectory in his career and on his way to success.

'Looks are only one of several factors women look at,' he adds. 'That's very different for men.' He's not claiming that either sex is more noble than the other. In his view, it's extrinsic for both sexes – just a different type of extrinsic in each case.

AJ's views are based on his own lived experience, and they may not be the most comfortable for those of us who want to believe in the best of human nature. But, for better or worse, they seem to be backed up by a reasonable degree of recent evidence.

Psychologists Norman Li from Singapore Management University, Oliver Sng from University of California Irvine and their colleagues have conducted various experiments using online-dating and speed dating methods. Unlike past studies into dating, these have included a wide socio-economic mix of candidates at all stages of the spectrum. And for the first time they have included people who aren't classically good-looking in the design of their studies.

Men and women, Professor Li concluded, 'prioritize different qualities when screening each other in online chats and speed-dates – women want men who are at least average in social status while men want women who are at least moderately physically attractive.'[13]

Previous studies, which were not as carefully designed, had suggested that both men and women were much less clear about what they wanted, and that there was a much smaller gender difference. But Li and Sng's findings do reinforce previous 'mate preference' research that Li conducted with Douglas Kenrick.[14] According to Li, 'The new study helps to dispel politically correct – but factually misguided – notions of a gender-neutral world where men and women want the exact same kind of mates.'

Li's findings further build on a study by Shackelford, Schmitt and Buss almost a decade earlier, which had taken a more global perspective, surveying 10,000 adults across six continents.[15] This study found that men tended to prioritize physical attractiveness and health, whereas women prioritized status, resources, dependability and intelligence. These were 'basic criteria to keep in mind before choosing more specific attractive qualities'.

It's really important to stress the point about 'basic criteria'. Social status and looks (for women and men respectively) appear to be hygiene factors for those looking for love, in a similar way to how sex appears to be a hygiene factor to sustain relationships. Beyond these hygiene factors, the research suggests, we're much more individual and subjective. 'Mystery', chemistry and romance still play an important role in how we select our mates. But the basic criteria matter too.

Here's the challenge: the rise of online dating and match-making may be actually increasing the importance of these hygiene factors, to the point they are becoming 'wannabe' motivators. They're the dating equivalent of the employers trying to make fancy office perks (such as the coffee machines) motivators that we saw in our chapter on work.

That's certainly AJ's view. Dating apps are a social disaster, he believes, not just because of the online behaviour they directly create, but how they bleed into normal life and change our wider everyday expectations. He points to the way that apps deliberately stimulate us visually and provide immediate external validation, and the highs from dopamine – the neurotransmitter that sends messages through our nerve cells – that each match ignites in our brain.

Social psychologist Jeanette Purvis has written a dissertation on Tinder.[16] She likens online dating to drug addiction. For drug addicts, the expectation of the drug causes a greater release of dopamine than the drug itself. 'Similarly, for those who may be expecting the next swipe on Tinder to lead to reward, serial swiping can start to look and feel a lot like an addiction,' she concludes.

Recent data seems to back this up, even in studies conducted by large dating sites themselves. One in six singles admitted in a 2017 Match.com survey that they felt addicted to the process of finding a date. Researchers from Ohio State University have further found that when social anxiety was compounded by loneliness, online dating 'led to compulsive use and then negative outcomes'.[17]

We've talked before about the dangers of contingent rewards – and online dating appears to be the ultimate example. A study by The Manifest found that 93 per cent of dating-app users had deleted a dating app at least once in the last nine months, and only a small minority of these because they had found a committed partner.[18] Jessica, a dating-app user in Toronto, said, 'They feel like a waste of time...Most of the time, it's really discouraging to use dating apps, and it feels like you'll never meet someone you actually like [or] want to be with.'

Despite these concerns, an independent study by the Pew Research Center found that 30 per cent of American adults said they had used online dating sites, and 12 per cent of them had got married or found a committed relationship through them – a 39 per cent effective 'success rate' in their view.[19]

Here's a killer fact, however, from the Pew's research: two-thirds of users had never even been on a date with someone they'd met through the app. When the dopamine triggered comes from the expectation rather than reality of a date, that's perhaps not surprising.

AJ also points to deteriorating standards of online dating behaviour. An example is the now fairly common practice of 'ghosting' dates, where one other party literally just doesn't show up, or sends a cancellation message minutes before the agreed time. He cites a key reason: there is no reliable way for both parties on a date to leave mutual feedback. Unlike an Uber or Airbnb, online dating site users aren't able to 'rate' each other's behaviour. 'And with millennials, the idea of negative feedback can sometimes be alien anyway.' He points to Greg Lukianoff and Jonathan Haidt's biting *The Coddling of the American Mind*[20] as a vindication of the fragility of young egos – but also acknowledges that he is generalizing across a very diverse group. Pew's US survey more scientifically documents the extent to which these 'bad dating behaviours' have become ubiquitous, as well as the phenomenon of women becoming hounded and harassed on sites.

Online dating is 'leading to a really consumeristic mindset where it's all about creating maximum convenience for yourself as the user. Whereas modern love should be like fish love,' AJ adds, borrowing a quote from former chief rabbi, the late Jonathan Sacks,[21] 'where you are really focused on the happiness and fulfilment of the other.'

AJ's story reveals something about the paradox of (almost) infinite choice that dating apps have unleashed. Like me, AJ trained as an economist and starts chattering excitedly about optimal stopping theory. 'Studies show that after about 35 dates you should have found your match. Beyond that there is no real point to go further,' he proclaims.

Dating apps and websites were set up to liberate us from limited options. But all this choice creates a similar feeling to 'buyers' remorse', even on dates where there is some connection and chemistry. No matter how well it goes, there's always a lingering feeling that someone out there could be just that little bit better. It's almost as if online apps are designed to create a 'dating lifestyle' that's as extrinsic as it gets.

What's the best advice to survive the crazy modern dating world based on the couples I've spoken to who have found a genuine and authentic relationship? Find something you intrinsically love – a hobby or activity – and find your flow, and in the process try to find love naturally.

*

It's not just Purpose that's being compromised in our current approach to romantic relationships – Autonomy is, too. Our Autonomy to live lives as genuine individuals, over and above the romantic relationship we are in. It's a real risk to our personal inner drive and motivation.

An important reason for marriages or committed relationships becoming 'all or nothing' – borrowing Finkel's phrase again – is that our other human relationships are factoring less in our day-to-day life. Finkel presents compelling data that shows the time spent by married people with wider friends and acquaintances has been on a consistent downward trend over the years. So, too, is time spent with parents, siblings or other close family.[22] Meanwhile the time people spend engaging in their local community – such as the local cricket club or Scouts group – has been showing even more precipitous declines, something Robert Putnam alerted us to some years ago in his powerful book *Bowling Alone*.[23] For example, Finkel cites data showing that, in 1975, Americans averaged two hours a day with friends and relatives and away from their partner, irrespective of whether they had kids. By 2003, a generation later, it had fallen to just over an hour per day.

The most startling finding from the University of Minnesota is that couples are spending considerably more time together *en famille*,[24] as the French say. Family life is increasingly monopolizing all our discretionary time, in the 'real world' at least – at the expense of friends, extended family and the wider community, and, most critically, as couples alone. You may be asking yourself, but isn't quality time as a family a good thing? Yes, but not if it's making us increasingly isolated as individuals from our wider networks and communities.

Finkel cites a study by Elaine Cheung, also at Northwestern University, that shows that the more 'diversified' our social portfolios are – the more people we can go to for help with different emotional states – the higher our quality of life.[25] Wharton professor of psychology Adam Grant finds that even relationships that involve weaker ties – where we only check-in with each other occasionally – can still be emotionally rewarding,[26] even if they are activated only once in a while. Reaching out very occasionally can actually be really fulfilling, he argues. Richard Ryan agrees, arguing that there is little correlation between the 'dosage' of a human relationship and its quality – what matters more is *how* people relate to each other in the human interaction itself. In other words, while spending more together as a family has many benefits, it's important we keep our eyes and ears (and most of all, our minds) open to a much wider range of people and don't shut ourselves off from the world.

There's a further pressure that comes from work. Our social lives are increasingly dictated by our social class – and our social class is ever more dictated by our work and working identities. We've managed to create two 'binds' in this regard – one for women and one for men – and this puts further pressure on our relationships.

We know from chapter 2 that the true Purpose of work is to help and serve others. But we also saw that achieving this Purpose involves significant investment of our time in gaining the smart essentials of Mastery at work.

The problem for women is that most of these essential activities such as information gathering, networking and increasing visibility and trust among the most senior leaders of the organization, tend to take place outside office hours: at dinners, networking drinks, speaker talks and often just in the bar or pub – at times when women take the main responsibility for childcare. We might have hoped that the recent trend towards home working might alleviate these pressures, but in fact it seems to have accentuated them. According to a large-scale British Ipsos survey conducted in the peak of the Covid-19 lockdown, even though most men were also working from home, the lion's share of childcare and household chores still fell to women.[27] That's why it's so important that time devoted to the 'smart essentials' of Mastery – such as training or networking – happens as much as possible during the working day, because placing these activities outside working hours sadly makes it harder for many women to access them.

Where does that leave women? They know their talents are as deserving of nurturing as their partner's. But equally they know these talents are much less likely to be nurtured in practice, due to the heavier demands on their time.

Needless to say, this is a deeply unfair state of affairs and one that prevents half of our world's talents from being truly nurtured. If there's one single contributor to a 'winner takes all' world that we've discussed, this must surely be it. But it's the pressure it creates on modern relationships that is particularly noteworthy for this chapter.

Anne-Marie Lucey is a leading divorce barrister based at Trinity Chambers, and her clients mostly come from London and Essex. Since starting at the bar in 2005 she has handled over 3,000 divorce cases. About 60 per cent of her clients are married or in civil partnerships and the others are living together.

She confirms that this 'work bind' is a major contributor to the divorce cases she sees in heterosexual marriages: women often have to make continual career sacrifices for the sake of the family. 'Having children is like throwing a bomb into the marriage,' Anne-Marie tells me. 'It can be a good bomb but more often than not it's a nuclear bomb.' She gives as an example 'a female GP who works a couple of days a week, while the husband becomes a surgeon. This creates a sense of creeping resentment all through the marriage.'

Although women definitely get the shorter end of the straw, it's not that much better for men either. Meredith Bodgas, based in Baltimore, is the editor of the leading US magazine *Working Mother*. Ironically, given the magazine's title, she's recently focused the magazine on campaigning with employers about changing the demands on men in the workplace. There is still an expectation among American men, for example, that they should be available for meetings after 5pm – even if those meetings have no clear end time agreed, and consequently drag on into the early hours of the morning.

If a woman's career and salary plateau after having a family – which is what many studies across developed countries show – then the male partner has to bring in a continually higher relative share of the household earnings, particularly as children grow up and are more expensive to raise. This bind often leads to further tension and to men being pressured to devote even less time to the wider network of relationships that are so important to their lives.

What's created is a vicious cycle that amplifies traditional gender expectations, and with it gender stereotypes, and traps both women and men in the process. And lands both in a motivational trap.

As we'll see throughout this book, every aspect of our lives is inextricably interlinked from a motivation perspective. I strongly believe that employers are deeply responsible for some of the broader motivational issues in our lives – particularly in our relationships. They need to respond, and they need to do so thoughtfully but fast.

Modern relationships have incredible potential to liberate intrinsic motivation in our lives, both as individuals and as part of a couple. But it's becoming harder and harder to achieve that potential – and one of the key challenges is around how we spend and prioritize our time.

*

What about achieving Mastery in our relationships? And how can we use that Mastery to motivate the other person and ourselves so we feel more motivated as a couple overall? These feel like critical questions. The key question is Mastery of what?

What may seem like a conflict based on a specific issue, for example a couple's desire to have children, reveals something much deeper at play.

Pradeepa Narayanaswamy is a fertility coach. But she isn't trained in medicine. Instead, her new and fast-growing speciality is helping her clients through the often difficult weeks and months that may or may not lead to conception. Like me, Pradeepa is of South Indian origin, but is now based in the US, outside Dallas. She has a global client base that she connects to mostly by video call. 'A husband and wife can come with a ton of information,' she says. 'So much information that they are simply overwhelmed. Couples are not taught how to go through a difficult situation together.'

In the case of Pradeepa's clients, friends and family are often at a loss to know how to support them. Pradeepa tells me, 'They often end up doing things that are not supportive. For example, the first thing *not* to say is "Relax, it will just happen".' Because, as the data clearly shows, it simply may not.

Researchers Ashok Agarwal, Aditi Mulgund and Michelle Renee Chyatte have produced pioneering new estimates of the incidence of infertility around the world.[28] Previous data had suggested 15 per cent of all couples globally – or almost 50 million couples – were infertile. But, the researchers showed, this massively underestimated the global rate of male infertility, particularly in Africa and in Central and Eastern Europe. Previously about half of all infertility cases were thought to be caused by the woman, and only 20 to 30 per cent by the man (with the rest due to joint factors). The new research suggests that the man's role could actually account for as much as 70 per cent of all cases in some geographies.

Despite this, it's still women who usually start the coaching relationship with Pradeepa. Even after the husbands get involved, she finds they can often be very controlling of what they want their wives to do and say in front of her. Men can be fearful of losing face, especially if the cause is 'theirs'.

Therefore rapid improvements in infertility technology – the most prominent being the growth of IVF – have not led to the dramatic falls in infertility that many scientists would have predicted, according to the World Health Organization.[29]

But while talk of physical ducts and tubes – and other associated anatomy – occupies much of the airtime in Pradeepa's coaching sessions, there's an underlying emotional issue: 'We are not paying enough attention to our partners in the first place.'

What masquerades as an issue about infertility begins to unravel much deeper issues the couple is facing in terms of a shared identity and values. 'What united the couple before was social status, particularly if they are of Indian origin,' Pradeepa explains. 'Now they are struggling to find common values...And you have to go deeper to explain what you *really* mean by common values. For example, it could be the same attitude that both members of the couple have to raising children, or how they see their relationship with money.'

Pradeepa's craft is as much about couples counselling as it is about the journey of having children. And while infertility coaching as a field may be new, in other ways it continues a longstanding tradition. The problem is that formal couples counselling may not be as effective as it could be, mainly because by the time couples begin counselling it's already too late, and they aren't really committed.

This is apparent when I speak to divorce lawyer Anne-Marie about her experience in the UK. Although half of her clients have seen counsellors, it's rare that counselling changes much – mostly because couples generally attend only a few sessions. 'People think, it's not working, so that's it.' There's a reluctance, she thinks, to work on a marriage and try to find a way through.

Couples who are on the route to divorce have to undergo a further 'mediation' process, but I learn from Anne-Marie how ineffective that process usually is too. 'Mediation is often seen as a tick-box exercise,' she says – a step that's simply required by law. 'It's more of a predivorce preparation of arrangements rather than a serious attempt to turn things around.' Tellingly, out of roughly 3,000 cases she has seen, she can think of no more than a handful where mediation has changed the outcome.

What we need to master as couples is the ability to have deeper conversations, either as a couple or with professional help. We need to learn how to enter into these more challenging discussions which are fundamentally about our emotional safety. Too often we don't enter into them in the first place – mostly because of our fear – or when we do, it's far too late.

Using motivation thinking, how can we redefine the Purpose of our key romantic relationships? We have misunderstood modern relationships as providing all the emotional nourishment and motivation we'll need in our lives, but that isn't realistic. Our lives are incredibly complex, and asking one person to provide all this nourishment is too much.

While it is unrealistic to expect our partner to be able to fulfil all of our wants and needs, the core Purpose of a relationship is to provide us with a sense of emotional safety, a sense of attachment.

According to attachment theory developed by psychologist and psychiatrist John Bowlby and subsequently Mary Ainsworth, there are three dominant attachment styles for a relationship: secure, anxious and avoidant.[30]

Each style pretty much means what it says on the tin. Avoidance styles tend to value emotional independence greatly, anxious styles tend to want a lot of closeness and express insecurities, and secure styles tend to be reliable and consistent in relationships.

In their revealing book *Attached*, Amir Levine and Rachel Heller[31] explain that understanding your attachment style can help couples better understand each other. You can learn how to adapt to each other's styles and help foster that sense of emotional safety.

Cristina Escallón – a Colombian organization-behaviour consultant and business school guest lecturer, based in London – explained to me the neuroscience around this. What makes us humans so different as a species, Cristina argues, is the way our brains have developed. Because our brains are not fully developed when we are born, we are unique in that we are completely dependent on others for survival in our early years. This creates a strong social instinct early on, which is compounded by the fact that our earliest years have the greatest influence on how our neural pathways develop, creating all sorts of beliefs about ourselves and the world around us.

As a result, Cristina explains, our reptilian brains – ever alert since we are young – have a fundamental 'social survival' instinct. Just as we instinctively waited for our mothers or carers to respond to what we did, we may seek the same social response and approval through much of our lives. Our brains remain on edge, always fearful and trying to protect us from potential danger. And when danger – or even negative feedback – is perceived, we can react as if we are in physical danger: cortisol pumps rapidly, over-stressing our brains and bodies.

How we experience fear is critical. Cristina believes there are three fundamental human fears: the fear of safety (emotional, physical and financial), the fear of not being good enough and the fear of not being loved enough.

Unconditional positive regard, a concept developed by psychologist Carl Rogers,[32] may be helpful to apply here. It's the idea that we love someone without judging them – and don't see them differently according to their social status or other extrinsic factors.

Being able to talk about the pressures we face and our insecurities is so important. When the kids were very young, Aida and I would often argue over what time to put them to bed. I would be back later in the evening and would want to keep them up so I could spend time with them. But Aida was right when she said that we needed quality time alone and she needed time – after a day that was much more gruelling than my work day – with another adult. But just an increase in couples' time alone will not be enough. We need to use that time to have these more vulnerable conversations.

There's a further complication along with our ever-growing expectations. And that's around the pace of external change in our lives. Since Aida and I were married over 15 years ago, I've changed my job no fewer than four times – and each episode of change has had its own emotional damage and turmoil with sharp alterations in working, and with it, personal identity. And Aida has changed as often. Add two children, three different places to live, and health scares with both sets of parents, and that adds up to a lot of change.

How we support each other through change – that we individually experience, and that we experience together as a couple – will become an ever more critical factor of relationships, given the rapid changes in modern life.

When I spoke to now renowned chef and restaurateur Asma Khan, I thought I had rarely met a more self-confident woman – and one driven by an incredible sense of Autonomy and Purpose. But even with such a supremely self-confident chef and founder, it's clear the supportive role marriage has played. Her husband Mushtaq was initially nonplussed when she started running supper clubs from their Earl's Court apartment. He has never interfered in the business, just as she doesn't with his work. But his was the art of quiet encouragement, and it was clear the seismic difference that made to Asma.

When Asma was featured – to huge acclaim – on Netflix's *Chef's Table,* she thought Mushtaq had left her to her own devices. It was only later that she realized he had switched on the family TV in their ancestral home in Bangladesh, played the show to the entire extended family and – with quiet but immense pride – made everyone stay in their seats and watch it all the way through. Even for such a brave, confident woman – one of the most inspiring I've ever met – it was the quiet encouragement and non-judgement of her husband and ex-teacher Mushtaq that was critical to her feeling safe.

Similarly, when I moved from a fancy high-paying job as a consultant to set up an NGO, I was extremely lucky to have a partner who didn't have her view of me wrapped in the extrinsic aspects of my working identify. Safety and unconditional positive regard are incredibly important to a relationship today.

The idea of a no-fault divorce can actually be a double-edged sword. When both parties are sure they want to get divorced, it can certainly make the process of divorce much less adversarial. But equally, as we've seen in 'Zayna's' case, it can eliminate some of the 'brakes' towards a divorce taking place, leading to marriages dissolving rapidly and undermining the sense of safety.

If anything, safety appears to be even more important for same-sex couples. Charles Q Lau, in a 2012 study, found that co-habiting same-sex romantic couples break up more readily than heterosexual couples.[33] 'Minority stress' suggests that external pressures put more strain on both members of the couple. However, as our legal systems become more inclusive – through introducing institutions like civil partnerships and same-sex marriage – and our societal attitudes change, we would hope that this difference between heterosexual and same-sex couples would reduce over time.

What about if you're living together but aren't married or in a formal civil partnership? It might mean that you have to put even more effort into ensuring there is deep emotional safety, simply because the legal barrier to separation is much lower.

There are no quick fixes for the scary, unpredictable world we live in. But the Purpose of a strong relationship is to help us feel safe in that world, so we can feel loved and valued regardless.

What about Autonomy as a couple? How do we do things our own way and enjoy happy, healthy relationships without feeling like we need to 'keep up with the Joneses'?

I think there are three key ways.

As we've seen in this chapter, the pressures of modern life are giving us less and less time to spend together in our relationship. That's something that can be addressed by prioritizing time and interests together. I've found that sharing similar experiences can help strengthen that sense of Autonomy. Aida and I try to watch a play together at least once a month, and are greedy with my parents' offer to keep the kids on Friday. Where possible – and especially now that Aida is training to be a psychotherapist – we try to read similar books. Aida has helped suggest some interesting research articles for this book, for example.

The second way we achieve Autonomy is by developing a sense of identity from being a couple, apart from our kids – something that's becoming increasingly hard in the age of 'helicopter parenting' (more on this in the next chapter). Aida and I actively try to meet other couples who either don't have kids, or who don't just want to talk about their kids! Wherever possible, Friday evenings become 'kid free' zones – both physically and emotionally.

The third thing we should do is develop a greater sense of Autonomy for each individual within the relationship. Richard Ryan concludes on the basis of dozens of studies: 'Individuals report feeling more securely attached to, and more emotionally reliant on, partners who are more supportive of their autonomy, and when the autonomy support is mutual, the results are most positive for most relationships.'[34] Perhaps a way to maintain Autonomy for a couple is to maintain deep friendships and some separate interests or passions on each side. I have a group of guy friends I've known since our university days, and they've supported me through all the many iterations of my life.

What can we do to develop Mastery in our relationships?

John Gottman is one of the world's leading authorities on how we can help our relationships thrive. Through his eponymous Gottman Institute he's developed a keen sense of what can make a couple's relationship flourish or flounder.[35] It all comes down to a surprisingly simple thing.

Gottman found that relationships flounder under the cumulative effect of hundreds – perhaps thousands – of 'failed bids' for emotional engagement and attention, which can be devastating over time. Each incremental failed bid creates a small but permanent incision in the heart, and they all add up and contribute to the ultimate relational heart attack.

It made me wonder whether 'Zayna' and her then husband had stopped being able to hear each other's emotional bids amongst the stress of Parisian city life and the screeching of young kids.

'We had a lot of time together,' 'Zayna' told me. 'But it was never meaningful time.' 'Zayna' is right to use the world 'meaningful'. And that's not the same as 'quality time'. The myth of 'quality time' was particularly prevalent in the 1980s and 1990s, when successful career parents assumed they could outsource everything to a nanny or teacher then turn up at the end of a full day and have an engaging hour with their kids where they could impart all their wisdom. The myth still lingers in many parents that I talk to today.

What Gottman's work tells us is there is really no substitute for time as a couple. And that means time when you are able to genuinely engage with each other and listen. The challenge is that these moments are not earmarked or ring-fenced. Unlike a company or country, there are no quarterly earnings reports or annual state of the nations to call attention to them. The important stuff – the bids for emotional engagement and connection – are interspersed, and often masked, in the world of the mundane.

Listening, sensing, therefore becomes critical. We need to master both the listening skills to be attentive to when these moments come along and what psychologists call 'meta-cognition' – the ability to step back from a situation and understand and reflect on our own thoughts and emotional processes once away from the immediate heat of an argument.

We also need to confront the impact of social media on our relationships. Every relationship expert I talked to agreed that 'air-brushed' social media was not a true substitute for 'real world' relationships. Meanwhile, senior executives of tech companies ban nannies and babysitters from using smartphones when they're looking after their own children, according to *The New York Times*.[36] I now put my phone upstairs and try to ensure that it stays there for much of the evening. The boys tell me they're a lot happier about this.

To have strong relationships we have to be physically and emotionally present. It's something I've been terrible at as a parent and a husband, but I'm trying to get a lot better at it. Aida has gone on mindfulness training, and after being interviewed by Michael James Wong on his gentle *Just Breathe* podcast, I've been thinking more about the critical link between mindfulness and intrinsic motivation. Too much of our time is focused on extrinsic distractions. Just being there for each other is so important.

Whatever decisions we make in our life, we need to master – first and foremost – being truly present for each other. If we are fully immersed in these moments together, it's more likely that we'll be fully engaged.

In this chapter we've seen how motivation thinking can help us reset and reframe our relationships. We know that our relationships are some of the most important drivers of motivation and happiness in our lives, but they are becoming increasingly 'all or nothing'. It's critical for us all to get them right.

We need to reorientate the Purpose of our relationships to a much more modest but focused intrinsic goal: providing emotional safety and unconditional regard.

There's a paradox: the modern dating world, in particular online dating, does not encourage emotional safety. Dating companies could respond to this, but their current business models – which provide them with more money the more time we spend on their apps – discourage them; so we also need to shift our individual behaviour in how we use them. Right now, extrinsic factors are prevailing.

Our relationship Autonomy is being jeopardized – particularly our time spent outside our key romantic relationship and (where applicable) immediate family. We can, however, find the confidence and Autonomy to set our relationships up thoughtfully and intentionally, through developing a broader set of interests and friendships, both as a couple and as individuals.

Finally, we need to develop a better Mastery in listening to each other – for which mindfulness might be a helpful tool, as might regulating our use of social media. This would help us to manage those critical but unannounced emotional bids for engagement as they come.

Overall, I hope you're emerging from this chapter with a strong sense of optimism. It's important to remember that we are as much blessed as cursed by choice. It's incredible, in my case for example, that a South Indian could marry a Moroccan through a chance encounter at party in a hipster *arrondissement* in Paris, and then live peacefully and safely in London. It's equally a miracle of modern life that AJ can meet Russians, Germans and Italians on his dating apps as easily as he can English roses. And that couples are increasingly freed from the tyranny of overbearing families and in-laws.

But in unleashing rivulets of freedom and Autonomy, we have also unleashed rivers of complexity and complication that as couples we need to develop new forms of Mastery over.

The fact that the demand for Pradeepa's fertility-counselling services is booming is a great harbinger of change. The South Indian backgrounds that she and I both hail from can be incredibly comfortable and supportive, but simultaneously parochial and stifling. Just before I got married in Chennai, a distant relative told my mother: 'If you had raised Sharath properly, he would have never done something like this.'

Chennai is now a different city. It's more vibrant, cosmopolitan and, most importantly, open in how people think. More than ever, there is freedom for couples to live the way they truly want – and to raise their children in the way they see most fit. And to seek professional help and counselling if and when they need to.

Alongside this opening of possibilities comes a ray of hope, even some sunshine. It shows up in how our understanding of relationships has deepened. It shows up in Pradeepa's success in building deep trust and understanding among the couples she works with, even in the most difficult and uncertain times of their lives.

We have become guilty of thinking in too binary a way about our relationships, just as Indian astrologers have always thought that there is a good match and a bad match. Only a few years ago, we used to think about intelligence in a similar way – we thought some kids were just smart and some not so much.

It was only when Carol Dweck developed her theory of growth mindset that our perspective on intelligence shifted – she showed us that intelligence was malleable, like a muscle in the body.[37] We have come to an equivalent point where we need to rethink our approach to relationships.

The line between whether we can have a successful intrinsic relationship or not is a lot finer than we think. Ultimately, it's up to us to reignite the motivation in our relationships – and reignite it we can.

'Not so long ago, we raised our children to work for us.
They toiled in the fields or helped us mind our shops...
But now it seems, all we do is work for them!'

Overheard in a conversation between a couple
on the London Underground (2019)

5

Intrinsic Parenting:
From Straight Lines
to Zig-zags

'This generation is well and truly screwed.'

The mother and father who tell me this are both successful professionals. Their two younger children attend one of London's top schools, and their eldest daughter is in her second year at Cambridge. Aida and I are sipping wine and chatting in their expansive garden, both of us experiencing a profound sense of 'house envy' as we do so.

'I mean, there's really no way for this generation to be unique or different,' the father adds. 'They look at social media and realize that someone, somewhere out there is just exactly what they are – only bigger and better.'

It turns out that one of their daughters is seeing a counsellor.

She seems to be in as stable and loving a family environment as I can imagine – and seems incredibly focused when we briefly meet her. Seeing counsellors is now quickly emerging as a new social norm in London's more affluent suburbs.

'My daughter insists on me joining her in the counselling sessions,' the mother tells us. 'Perhaps she thinks it's the only place where I'm actively listening to her, and to her feelings.'

Our children are growing up in a world that has never been wealthier, nor more open and connected. But the pressures of our current thinking and helicopter approaches to modern parenting are weighing heavily on our children, and on us as parents too.

It's the second time in just a couple of weeks, after London's first Covid-19 lockdown, that my parenting head has been reeling from what I'm seeing around me. A couple of weeks ago, I'd been waiting outside the courts for my son's group tennis lesson to finish, relieved he could finally play again. The other 'tennis parents' around me, however, were looking decidedly glum.

'To be honest I preferred lockdown,' one father told me. 'I didn't have to do *this*.' By 'this' he meant spending entire afternoons chauffeuring his kids from activity to activity. 'Lockdown life was so much less "programmed",' he added. 'I got to spend a lot more time with my kids and really see what's going on in their lives.'

The 'new normal' was feeling a lot more 'normal' than 'new' for him, and for many of the other dads and mums there.

Aida and I – and our two young boys – are lucky to live in a leafy suburb of north-east London that's both relatively quiet and accessible. In my heart I am a Londoner: I love its diverse, rambling sprawl and the fact that I can still get lost for hours in a new neighbourhood. I love the range of restaurants, the galleries and theatres.

But from time to time, Aida and I fleetingly discuss the attractions of a smaller, quieter life, usually near the coast (both of us grew up on the coast – Aida in Rabat and I in Jeddah). These discussions are usually triggered by the competitive London 'parenting bubble' that surrounds us and the pressure this creates on our children and on us as parents. Like so many parents today, we obsess about getting our boys into the 'right' school.

London isn't even the worst city for this kind of competitive environment. I've talked to third- or fourth-generation members of the richest families in places like Palo Alto, the beating heart of California's Silicon Valley. The ultra-competitive culture of Silicon Valley, and the societal problems that causes are prompting many of these prominent families to uproot their lives. One person I know has moved with his wife and five kids to a small island off Seattle, where he told me his children can live a more much normal, unpressured life.

Whether it's London or Palo Alto, there seems to be a common malaise in our world today: children are suffering from greater anxiety. And it stems ultimately from a deep fear they seem to have of not being good enough, at least by the standards that people around them – including us as parents – have set.

Ultimately, we, as parents rather than schools, have to take part of the responsibility for this malaise. Schools nowadays have to function in a world of 'parental choice', and as a result schools have to operate and 'compete' in a system of OFSTED inspections and academic league tables.

But it doesn't have to be this way.

In this chapter we'll assess these trends – and ask what it would take to reignite our inner drive as parents and, in turn, in our children. As the father of two young boys myself, I can testify to how hard being a parent is today. The message behind this chapter is that we can have a more hopeful future – for our children and for ourselves as parents.

Dozens of rigorous research studies now make one point crystal clear: helicopter parenting, also termed 'overparenting', has taken root among our most affluent parents and is actually deeply harmful to our kids, both in the short and in the long term. However, we know that 'absentee' parenting styles – often the only choice for billions of less fortunate parents today – can be equally, if not more, problematic. We'll delve deeper into this in the chapter.

Perhaps there has also been an element of parental narcissism: in doing the best for our children, we are really doing the best for ourselves – and fulfilling our egos. 'Your children are not your children,' poet Kahlil Gibran once wrote,[1] but that seems to have fallen on largely deaf parental ears today.

In this chapter I want to ask how we can be better parents to our next generation. I think we owe it to them to find a better way, for their sakes, as well as our own. We'll use Purpose, Autonomy and Mastery for the diagnosis of our parental quandaries and to develop some solutions.

How do parents see the Purpose of parenting today? And how does it relate to how they see the Purpose of childhood? It's worth really stepping back to answer this core question to ground our discussion of modern parenting.

Helicopter parenting essentially sees the Purpose of parenting as removing obstacles for our kids, which only delays them dealing with the inevitable future. The term 'helicopter parenting' was coined by Haim Ginott in 1969.[2] The teens he talked to told him their parents would hover over them like a helicopter. An overprotective, helicopter parent discourages a child's independence by being too involved in the child's life. The mother or father basically swoops in at any sign of challenge or discomfort.

There's an interesting parallel trend of outsourcing – to the ballet coach, the tutor and of course (as we've seen) the counsellor. And while emotional distance is not an inevitable consequence of helicopter parenting, the practical pressures it creates reduce the sheer time and intensity of emotional connection between parent and child. That can lead to the example we saw at the start of the chapter – parents needing to hire counsellors just to have honest conversations with their children.

Palo Alto, the epicentre of Silicon Valley, provides an extreme example of where helicopter parenting can lead us. Over the past decade there has been such a significant spate of suicides at the train station in Palo Alto that the community and district government felt a permanent presence – in the form of manned guards – was needed. Virtually all of these suicides have been from teenagers. Mostly, they are the sons and daughters of the well-educated and well-compensated executives of the tech world, or the children of bankers, lawyers and doctors. Many of them are in the top 1 per cent of the country in terms of income and wealth. Young men and women who you would think have it all.

The track guards are disproportionately Hispanic or African-American. They come literally from the other side of the tracks – the much more troubled East Palo Alto or from further away. They do what they can to make ends meet in what is now perhaps the most expensive region in the country. In most countries, the poor have always been entrusted to rear the children of the rich. Now they're being asked to prevent their premature death.

According to surveys of local public schools – generously funded by local property taxes, and among America's finest – over 12 per cent of high-school students have seriously contemplated committing suicide. Teenage stress and anxiety are the new buzzwords in Silicon Valley – as vociferously debated on the cocktail circuit as premoney valuations and artificial intelligence. All of this has happened at a speed that would put the nimblest of Silicon Valley start-ups to shame.

What is happening to modern child-rearing and parenting? Christine Gross-Loh, who has studied the difference between American parents and those in other parts of the world, concludes: 'That which is most American about us – our belief that the future is unwritten – is what is driving us mad as parents.'[3]

Parents who have the money and means, such as these in Palo Alto, are now 'graduating' from helicopter parenting to a new style of 'snowplough parenting' – where parents proactively remove all possible obstacles and impediments upfront out of a child's way. The best recent example of this was the admissions scandal with the University of Southern California, where dozens of wealthy American and Chinese parents – including a star of TV show *Desperate Housewives* – were found to be paying indirectly bribes of hundreds of thousands of dollars through highly paid 'admissions tutors'.

'Go figure this,' Amee Parikh tells me over lunch in Singapore. 'Since the scandal, admissions to USC *have actually gone up significantly*. Asian parents in particular thought, "There must be something really good in this place if everyone wants to get their children in there."'

Amee and her husband Akash run Amansa Capital, a successful asset-management fund based out of Singapore and Mumbai. 'The real problem is that "good enough" is no longer "good enough",' she says. 'A child who wants to learn yoga gets a personal tutor sent to their home. What's wrong with a group class at a studio? And children as young as 15 are being put on internships with banks and finance funds – all through parental connections, of course. What is the point of all this? At 15 in a finance firm you're most likely just going to be a nuisance and get in the way.'

Sara Harkness, a professor at the University of Connecticut, has tried to make sense of these trends:[4] 'Our sense of needing to push children to their full potential is partly driven by fear of the child failing in an increasingly competitive world where you can't count on things that our previous parents could count on,' she writes.

Other researchers have suggested that having immigrant parents in a community or city – such as from China and India – has created even more angst and confusion among American parents in places like Palo Alto. There is this underlying feeling that their kids will now need to 'compete' against new, 'hungrier' immigrant families.

There is no question that this concern over competition is sapping our motivation as parents. Matthias Doepke is a professor of economics at Northwestern University, and is pioneering the new field of 'parental economics'.[5] He finds that in countries with greater inequality, parenting styles (particularly for more affluent parents) are more pronounced – literally more aggressive and helicopter-like.

It's not that different in Indonesia, either. 'Parents really feel they have struggled so much to get to this point. They want to do everything possible to ensure that their children don't have to go through the same struggle,' says Rosita Tehusijarana, a parenting counsellor based in Indonesia's capital, Jakarta.

Rosita talks about an example in her own parenting life. 'My daughter got into a foreign university...that was never the plan... so we had never saved up for it. Most people in my position would have begged richer relatives, or taken out a massive loan. Or taken on a double or triple work shift. We did the opposite. We told my daughter, if it's meant to happen it will happen. It happened a year later and then she eventually got her funding, and in the meantime she volunteered and did an internship in the gap year she ended up having.'

Part of me is inherently sceptical about this. Shouldn't our role as parents in this situation be to make all of the sacrifices we can? Rosita tells me that this just leads to a vicious cycle. 'What happens then is that the parents work all hours of the night to make an income, and then they don't see their children except for weekends. And then the kids start acting up – because what they really want is love and attention from their parents. And that leads to the proliferation of gadgets, too, which are causing so much havoc with our children.'

Julie Lythcott-Haims – previously Dean of freshmen at Stanford University and now an accomplished parenting author – shares lots of examples where parents removing obstacles for their children can work for a while until a breaking point.[6] One story of hers involves a fresh new graduate who gets a prestigious job on Wall Street, and who tells his mother in passing that he's working most days till past midnight. His boss receives a call from the mother, complaining about why he is working her son so hard. The next day the son is fired. Another story involves a Stanford PhD candidate who attends the admissions interview with her mother and yet another story involves a Stanford undergraduate who is woken up each morning and reminded of his class schedule by his mom and dad.

Removing obstacles can feel laudable, until the parent becomes the obstacle to the child's progress. This straight-line parenting approach has undermined the true Purpose of parenting for everyone – particularly for the rich, but it is increasingly the norm for all income groups. And that includes how parents of virtually all socio-economic groups view academic success.

Sneha Sheth is an Indian-American who founded Dost, an NGO that tries to engage parents more holistically in their children's education. Dost works in the slums of Delhi and other Indian urban areas – similar environments to what we saw in the opening chapter.

'There is so much influence on TV and social media,' Sneha says. 'And so much peer pressure. And whereas before, in a village, there used to be multiple caregiving influences on the child, now the parent feels much more alone and isolated.'

Sneha's colleague Krishna Sharma works directly with low-income parents and says that they are most concerned about '*padhai*' – academic instruction. 'Children as young as three are being sent to tuition classes. And children three to seven years old go to school *and* tuition – and then are expected to study at home as well,' she tells me.

To some extent it's understandable. These emerging middle-class parents are making huge financial sacrifices. I've personally entered poor households in Delhi where there are two jars at the front of the house, each containing the household's monthly savings. One for food, housing and essentials; the other jar just for school fees. (Even though – as we saw – India has built a million free government schools across the country, many lower-middle-class parents who have the choice prefer to send their children to low-fee private schools, usually costing a few pounds per month.)

Parents here feel that time spent playing is a huge waste of time. Most parents that Dost surveys say they focus their own parenting time towards helping their children with their homework.

But a strong body of research shows that play is in fact essential for holistic child development, in everything from well-being to academic success. A systemic review of evidence from Golinkoff and Hirsch-Pasek shows that what makes play so unique is how it integrates physical, social, emotional and creative spheres.[7] This is key for lifelong learning. For example, they point to a 2011 study by Mischel and colleagues who show that executive function (or control over impulses) in the early years – typically the years before a child starts formal school – predicts a whole range of things, from SAT scores to health and prevention against substance abuse.[8]

Rosita Tehusijarana, the parental counsellor from Jakarta whom we met earlier, tells me: 'Middle-class parents here are very concerned about academics. *Very concerned*. And they offer all kinds of extrinsic rewards – what I would even call bribes – to achieve that. Trips to Disneyland. That new PlayStation. All in return for coming top of your class.' Julie Lythcott-Haims slams this whole trend as essentially a 'mortgaged childhood', in other words, parents are forcing their children to take a loan out on their childhood – which should be one of the happiest and most formative stages of their lives – for a false 'guarantee' of a successful future.

Is academic success even a ticket to better job prospects and, in turn, a better standard of living? In fast-growing emerging countries like India, we used to think so. Dozens of studies had previously shown a strong link between successive years of school completion and lifetime earnings. But those studies were almost all based on following whole cohorts of kids, rather than following individual children over long periods of time. Jishnu Das is a professor at Georgetown University, and for the first time he's been able to gather data sets based on the latter approach. This research method allows us to see the intricacies of an individual life unfold, rather than just looking at 'average' patterns in cohorts of children, so it's much more individualized and nuanced. What this research is revealing – as he shared in a seminar I attended – is that educational attainment and completion do not seem to explain as much as we thought about how children, many years later, perform in the labour market. In other words, academic success is only one of many factors that appear to predict job success. Social connections and status also seem to persist – socially advantaged kids tend to have a lot of other advantages, including connections and perhaps confidence. This may not be a good thing in terms of equity between young people from different backgrounds, but it does mean that seeing academic success as a be-all and end-all – particularly for children from families of average or above average income – is unlikely to be a wise move. And it does suggest that parents *and* schools need to think about nurturing a much broader set of behaviours in children, including confidence. I hope this chapter will provide some ideas on how.

What if we took a step back from this academic perspective and took an intrinsic view? What about the basic goal of keeping kids happy in school as a starting point? Increasingly research studies back up what British philosopher Bertrand Russell wrote decades ago: 'The good life, as I conceive it, is a happy life…I do not mean that if you are good you will be happy; I mean that if you are happy you will be good.'⁹ Russell was predating ideas of living in the present –

the basis of modern mindfulness – and the now very popular idea of 'flow', a term coined by Mihaly Csikszentmihalyi to describe when someone is fully immersed and engaged in an activity in a way that engenders peak performance.[10]

One of the questions that has baffled us so far, however, is which way the relationship between happiness and academic performance flows. Researchers Walsh, Boehm and Lyubomirsky looked at more than 170 experimental, longitudinal and cross-sectional studies that focused on this link.[11] They concluded that 'the weight of experimental evidence suggests that happy people outperform less happy people, and that their positive demeanour is probably the cause.'

In short, happiness in school is actually a much more important determinant of academic success than we might have initially thought. And what seems to drive happiness in school? Increasingly, the answer appears to be student engagement.

Researchers at Menzies Institute for Medical Research in Australia created an innovative 'school engagement index'.[12] The index was calculated by surveying children in order to understand their motivation to learn, sense of belonging, and participation in wider school and physical activities. The researchers found that each unit of school engagement was independently associated with a 10 per cent higher chance of achieving a post-compulsory school education at some point in the next 20 years. And those who were engaged at school were likely to go on to a professional or managerial career.

In a compelling letter in *The New York Times*,[13] renowned psychologist Adam Grant also argues for the benefits of engaged and active learning, based on hundreds of studies – from school all the way to college.

If children are more engaged in school, they are more likely to be happy – and therefore academically successful. Engagement also enables what the late Ken Robinson, renowned international adviser on education, describes as 'finding your element';[14] the ability to find a much broader definition of intelligence and aptitude that goes beyond specific subjects or extra-curricular domains. This 'element' in turn further boosts engagement and makes you happier – creating a virtuous cycle. And that, in turn, is likely to lead to success along the way.

The problem with the snowplough approach to parenting is that it usually focuses on the academic goal as the end outcome in itself, and then tries to get there in the shortest way possible. We might well achieve the academic outcome (using techniques like rote memorization, and outside resources like tutors), but we don't develop the intermediate skills that are at least as, if not more, important. Skills like being able to think critically or developing deep curiosity. Or the sense of engagement and flow that are so important to develop in the process. Our exam systems aren't great at measuring these things, at least at any scale, so it's easy to bypass them entirely for the obsessive focus on the academic outcomes.

I can imagine many parents – including myself – facing a simple quandary: don't our kids still need to pass, and be successful in, exams?

The sad truth is yes. Covid-19 has forced the education systems of many countries to look again at the value of exams in the first place, given that so many had to be cancelled due to the pandemic. Researchers Jack Rossiter and Might Kojo Abreh looked at exam patterns in many developing countries, and found that many broader factors affected exam results beyond just student ability and motivation, and beyond the quality of teaching they received. In other words, exams may not be anywhere near as 'objective' as we often think.[15]

What does that mean practically for us as parents? Basically, we need to see exams as hygiene factors – as necessary hoops that our children will, for better or worse, need to jump through. But focusing on *how* children pass exams matters so much more – it will determine whether they develop a lifelong motivation to learn, and love of learning, that will really help them succeed and thrive in the world beyond the school gates.

Alfie Kohn has some wonderful examples in his books about how children can become (in his words) 'hooked on learning', and gives many practical strategies for parents, teachers and children.[16] He is scathing of the many 'carrots and sticks' – from praise to punishment

– being used in American classrooms today, which he sees as easy but inferior substitutes to really engaging students. His take on grades is that they are useful periodically as a source of information and feedback for teachers, children and parents; but can become toxic if they are used as an extrinsic incentive or reward for academic performance.

We've seen some of the effects of accountability and performance measures – such as OFSTED inspections and school league tables – on the motivation of teachers in chapter 2. Be equally wary as parents of academic 'league tables' that only show absolute levels or grades – the percentage of children who pass a public exam or who achieved top grades. Much of the results are simply gained through selection of children in the first place. It's a dirty and relatively unknown secret discovered in the OECD's PISA tests – the common tests that a sample of children in many countries sit, to provide cross-country comparisons – that many 'top' schools around the world actually produce very little in what educationalists call 'value-added' for children over and above the effects of selection. Selection of their incoming cohorts of children and (implicitly) of the background of their parents. On similar lines, child expert Paul Tough has described how many renowned US private schools are remarkable for how successful they have been at maintaining their kids in the upper echelons of social class. And at the same time, how remarkably few alumni from those schools have broken new ground in a field or discipline, or made a truly meaningful difference to the world, given the privileges and advantages most of these children have had.[17] We need to ask so much more of our so-called 'top schools' – and of our schools everywhere.

At STiR we thought hard about how to develop an intrinsic motivation to learn among children. And we built tools that explicitly measure attributes like whether a child wants to be in school, trusts their teacher and feels emotionally safe; this is done by measuring simple behaviours such as whether children are actively asking questions of their teacher and are engaged meaningfully in the classroom tasks at hand. These are obvious attributes but ones that very few rigorous studies actually measure, as Dave Evans of the Center for Global Development tells me when we meet in his Washington office.

This is my biggest worry about well-meaning initiatives like No Child Left Behind in the US, and OFSTED's outsized power in the UK. They probably have reduced academic variability between schools, but mostly through narrowing and reducing the curriculum (as well as some quite flagrant teaching to the test).

And all the while we continue to overload our kids with content in a few areas, while reducing the breadth of their curriculums, so much so that we distract the teacher from her core role of building a deep, genuine and human relationship with the child – as Steve Hilton argues in *More Human*.[18] Indonesia, for example, has 16 official subjects that children must study at primary school – and that more or less continues to secondary school too. Education experts there feel that teachers have little time to do more than superficially 'dip in and out' of all these subject areas, using rote memorization. As a result, any chance for deep or meaningful learning is lost. I went to visit a school in Yogyakarta, Indonesia's former capital, which had achieved some of the best examination results in the country. But the kids were overwhelmingly sitting at their desks, heads down, just copying into their books what the teacher was saying.

Even the Dalai Lama has been quoted as saying there is a crisis of Purpose among our children and ourselves. He thinks children (and their parents) have become too self-centred and even downright selfish. He elaborates on this in *The Book of Joy*:[19] 'The problem is that our world and our education remain focused exclusively on external, materialistic values.'

I want to make it clear that I'm not suggesting that academic proficiency is not important. We all need to be able to read and write and count effectively, and be conversant in important subjects from history to science. But a good childhood should be so much more.

We've all heard the scare stories of the 'tiger parent' – and we all feel as parents the pressure to compete. In her provocative article 'Why Chinese Mothers Are Superior',[20] Amy Chua explains that the typical Asian mother eschews fun stuff like playdates and sleepovers and focuses on academic and musical accomplishments.

Esther Wojcicki – a parenting writer and mother of three pretty accomplished women, one of whom is the current CEO of YouTube – tells the story of being on a panel standoff against Amy Chua. Esther ended up being labelled and derided as a 'panda parent' for her much softer approach.[21] But don't be fooled by the hype.

The problem with tiger parenting, studies suggest, is that few children of tiger parents end up happy or successful. Once the tiger parenting is removed, most children end up distant. Su Yeong Kim, an associate professor at the University of Texas, completed an exhaustive ten-year study of 300 Asian-American families.[22] She found that the kids of tiger parents had lower grades, were more troubled emotionally and more likely to be estranged from their parents compared to parents who employed more traditional parenting styles.

If we see the Purpose of childhood just within the narrow confines of academic success, we risk prioritizing an important 'hygiene factor' (important as it is) over what will truly motivate and help our kids live a fulfilling life.

Earlier I mentioned the growing trend in outsourcing some key aspects of parenting. This is leading to a loss of Autonomy for parents, and makes it harder for us to help children develop true Autonomy.

If you think a city like London is particularly bad for parental 'outsourcing', this trend is even more pronounced in the middle classes of Africa, which is our world's most rapidly growing population.

Brenda Akite Otika is a member of Uganda's fast-growing professional class. She was born in the capital, Kampala, but finding a head-office role in the international development sector, where she passionately wanted to work, proved tough. This led Brenda to work in more remote villages, engaging directly with communities 'upcountry', as Ugandans tend to call it. Then she became pregnant. One of her colleagues had died in childbirth upcountry a couple of years before, so Brenda persuaded her then employer to allow her to work most of her pregnancy months from Kampala. After the (thankfully safe) delivery, Brenda went back to working in the field and dragged her nanny and young baby upcountry with her. That was until repeated bouts of illness for the baby ensued – problems ranged from hygiene (water bottles were often contaminated) to bumpy dirt roads that took their toll on the baby's body and stomach. Brenda started to leave her (now two) little ones with her parents in Kampala at the beginning of each week and would pick them up at the weekend when she returned to the city.

The drawback was her kids no longer wanted to see her. Accustomed to a new home environment, they now wanted to spend all their time with their grandparents. Brenda worried that she didn't have enough day-to-day contact with her children. This seems to have inspired a profound sense of guilt, so then she hired a permanent maid to look after the kids, particularly when her new job allowed her to spend more time in Kampala.

One evening, she told me she got a call from a man she didn't know. He was doing the electrical wiring on her street. He could see her two girls through the upstairs window of her house. They were alone and there wasn't an adult in sight. It was 9.30pm and Brenda was travelling back from a meeting. The maid had packed her bags and left the girls to themselves.

Now her two little girls – aged eight and six – are enrolled in boarding school, because Brenda felt that was a more reliable way of ensuring a good education given the stresses of her job. It's a mid-range option among Uganda's vast array of schools, and Brenda is taking out a savings plan so she can afford more expensive options in the future. Brenda speaks to the girls on the phone every week and tries to visit them every two weeks.

Brenda dreams of her girls having a happy, rounded childhood and equally – if not more – of them winning a prestigious scholarship so they can attend either a government university or have reduced fees at a private one. But she knows there are huge risks. There are a large number of kids in Ugandan boarding schools who start hanging out in bad groups, then drop out and get expelled, she tells me. Some parents then end up spending further money – which they can ill afford – on 'rehabilitating' them. But others abandon their children altogether. And even if the child does well academically, they can often be pushed out of getting selected into their next school or university by parents who can afford to pay bribes.

I spoke to another parent of young children at a Ugandan boarding school – Brenda Namulinda – who told me that she has learned to 'pick her battles'. She saw many cases of bad bullying or bad hygiene in the boarding halls. If she complains once, she told me, the warden will usually listen. If she shouts too often or too much, there is a high risk of retribution on her kids – either from other kids, or potentially from the staff themselves.

But the options for day school aren't much better. Going to one of Kampala's better academic schools usually means being picked up in the school bus at four in the morning and returning home past nine at night. The stress among parents is particularly strong among mothers, as Ugandan fathers typically see parenting as the role of the women, even though most women work full time as well. That's something both women tell me.

In other parts of the emerging world, the 'fully outsourced' approach can be more prevalent in lower-income parents. Sneha Sheth argues that low-income parents behave like consumers in modern India: you pay the school fees, you expect the school to 'take care of it'. And 'it' means everything from academic performance to values, character and personality development. Low-cost private schools – of which there are more than 300,000 across India – are effectively positioning themselves like the Indian IT outsourcing companies such as Infosys or Wipro.

Although this 'fully outsourced' trend is more common in

emerging countries, there are interesting parallels among poorer parents in richer countries. The charter school movement in the US is a useful example. KIPP (Knowledge is Power Program) was one of the earliest of these, and I learned a lot from their co-founder Mike Feinberg when he visited India many years ago. They've achieved a great deal – an overwhelming number of KIPP students reach college, for example. But KIPP's model worked initially by trying to compensate for the lack of structure in a child's home life by providing it in school. That meant, for instance, a school day that was often hours longer than at a traditional school. It worked wonders while children were in KIPP schools, but often proved to be challenging when the KIPP kids went to college. Without the structure and support, many KIPP alumni sadly became college dropouts.

Clayton Christensen, the late Harvard Business School professor we met in chapter 2, likened this trend of outsourcing to the business outsourcing craze of the 1990s, when companies felt pressured to reduce their assets and focus on their 'core competencies' (according to the management lingo).

Christensen told the cautionary tale of computer company Dell. Dell outsourced more and more to its Asia-based suppliers, to the point where it lost the ability to put together a whole computer. Its Asian supplier then started to create its own line of computers to sell directly to consumers. It took years for Dell to fully recover.

It's a cautionary tale that applies to parents, but in slightly different ways. For some parents everything (by necessity) needs to be outsourced, with boarding schools for the youngest of kids being the most extreme example. Helicopter parents would probably argue that while they outsource all of the individual components (to the teacher, the tutor and the tennis coach), they maintain a high degree of oversight. After all, that's the definition of helicopter parenting – the constant hovering over so that the parent can step in at any sign of trouble.

Christensen however warned that this sense of control by helicopter parents is illusory. Helicopter parents rarely know their child with the emotional depth they would like, simply because they haven't had the time to do so: think of the story of the mother, daughter and counsellor. They can end up emotionally detached and removed, stepping in only in times of need or crisies to solve their children's problems for them. Nevertheless, despite its flaws, helicopter parenting is what many less affluent parents all over the world aspire to. Shows like *Modern Family* have a large following among middle-class Africans with satellite TV, despite the somewhat haphazard helicopter-parenting attempts of many of the characters on the show.

The impact this all has on our Autonomy as parents and that of our children is becoming increasingly clear. Kristin Moilanen, associate professor of child development and family studies at West

Virginia University in the US, argues that more often than not the child might be capable of solving a problem themselves, but the parent interferes before they have a chance to prove it. This leads to a belief that their outcomes are determined by external forces and that they are not capable of living independently and alone.[23]

Overall, there is strong evidence that the Autonomy costs of helicopter parenting can be harmful. Florida State psychologists found that kids who had helicopter parents were more likely to have burnout from work in university, and also had a harder subsequent time transitioning from university to the real world.[24] The key point: over time, kids feel that everything they do is for their parents, so they lose their intrinsic motivation to succeed. Previous studies by Kayla Reed-Fitzke, James Duncan, Anthony Ferraro et al found that helicopter parenting tended to lead to lower self-efficacy – the belief that kids could actually change key events in their lives.[25]

Our current focus on a very narrow definition of Mastery – almost entirely centred on academics – is unlikely to provide our children with the foundations they'll need to be 'life-ready' and 'job-ready', let alone 'world-ready'.

In short, we've seen that we're spending too much time helping kids develop the right fight plan (the perfect grades, the right extra-curricular activities) and nowhere near as much time teaching them how to fight when the plan unwinds, as it so often does in life.

When I talked to many Singaporean parents, they presented an unusual paradox. Singapore's students regularly top the PISA international rankings of student performance. And yet employers in the city-state complain they can't find staff who are self-driven and motivated. The government is trying to take steps to remedy this, but it can't seem to let go of a key pillar, largely due to parental pressure – the examination sorting system. At 11, based on how they do in a national exam, local kids are sorted into different levels of school, which will basically define their chances for the rest of their lives. With such a high-stakes barrier still intact, it's no wonder that the shift to a more progressive system can feel slow. Singapore is hardly alone; England continues to have an equally pernicious system of the eleven-plus that also 'sorts' children into admission, no less brutally, for its more selective secondary schools.

Julie Lythcott-Haims similarly recalls talking to a Silicon Valley entrepreneur who told her that everything he'd achieved in life had been due to his willingness to take risks. And yet, on probing, she found that he'd done everything possible to eliminate any potential for risk among his children.

What do we need to do as parents to support our children to develop Mastery in these broader areas?

It all comes down to how we as parents partner effectively and productively with the schools our children are in. It has to be a genuine partnership. It can rarely be achieved by teachers or parents working alone.

Being completely hands-off and 'outsourcing' everything to teachers and schools is unlikely to be effective, as we've seen. But equally creating competing pressures on our children – from extra-tuition classes to myriad extra-curricular activities – creates the impression among our children that the 'real action' takes place outside of school. And bombarding our children's teachers with emails with little gripes or complaints is only likely to distract teachers from their core job – which is to engage our children in life and learning. A number of London schools have even had to articulate a clear 'communications expectations' policy to parents, reminding them they can't expect teachers to be 'on' 24/7, as we've come to expect in our large corporates.

Indonesia is one of the countries that is getting this mutual partnership between parents and schools right. When I visit the school founded by Pastor Jimmy Peter Kalauserang, on the outskirts of Yogyakarta, the first thing he stresses to me is: 'We as the school cannot do it alone. Ultimately a child spends so much more time with his or her family than with us. It has to be a partnership between us and the parents.'

The school started with Jimmy home-schooling his own children. Now it's grown to several classrooms and (despite having a Christian ethos in a predominantly Muslim country) receives official funding from Indonesia's Ministry of Religious Affairs. That's impressive. What struck me most about the school was how parents integrated through the day – they are free to come into lessons or stay for lunch. It's true that this kind of involvement is difficult for full-time working parents, but the school has made it feel open and accessible, with parents able to visit the school based around their work schedules. But – almost in return for this level of openness and access – parents are expected not to 'over-step'; the roles of Jimmy and the teachers are understood and respected – parents don't 'second-guess' teachers in the way that's perhaps become a norm. The paradox is that by opening up the school in this way, Jimmy has built trust among the parents and perhaps reduced the need for helicopter parenting in the first place.

A day at HighScope Indonesia, a bilingual school in Jakarta, gives me even more insight into how this collaboration between teachers and parents can further boost our children's Mastery. On the first day of the new academic year, I observe a 'joint goal-setting' session – where learning goals are discussed and the child, parent and teacher sign a mutual agreement to focus on these goals during the year, and share regular progress. The session I observe is with an autistic child so the school psychologist and special education needs teacher join in too. This extent of collaboration between parents, teachers and children is as truly inspiring as it is rare to see.

*

Given all these (somewhat alarming) trends, we need to learn how to fight back. Let's start with how we can reframe our core Purpose.

This starts with how we think about our children's time at school. Do they enjoy being there? Do they love learning and are they intrinsically motivated to learn?

If you focus on a child's engagement in class and school, on their intrinsic motivation to learn, it's much more likely that they will become a lifelong learner. That's what you can stress when you talk to them about their experience at school and whether they are enjoying it.

Carol Dweck's work on growth mindset has shown that many children have a fixed view of their abilities, which can be fatal for their life chances. However, focusing on effort and enjoying the experience of learning for its own sake can unlock this fatalism. I'm a big believer in this. My sons' school, for example, provides both attainment and effort grades for each child. But ideally the effort should be because of a child's intrinsic motivation to learn, not because they're driven by extrinsic rewards like a PlayStation or trip to Disneyland. The source of effort truly matters: is it intrinsically or extrinsically driven?

Therefore, how we encourage and talk to our kids really matters. This is the source of a near-constant fight with my mother when she tries to praise our boys. She'll congratulate them when one is the 'top of the class' in a particular assignment or test they did. I try to tell her that being top of the class is something they can't directly control. I prefer to praise them when their teacher tells them they were deeply engaged in the exercise at hand, or if they put exceptional effort in. (Sadly, like most fights between sons and mothers, this is one I'm unlikely to win.)

It's also important to remember that the 'perfect kid' – the kid who doesn't struggle – is only storing trouble up for later in life, as we saw with the students at academically gifted KIPP schools.

Ultimately, so much about developing a broader Purpose in our children is also about helping them see things from another person's perspective – and see how they can contribute to helping that other person. How can we ensure our children see their Purpose as helping and serving others – whether family, school, local community or the world at large? It can be as simple as asking children to assist with domestic chores, which studies show is a rarity in middle-class households these days. Or it could follow the lead of a child at my sons' school, who, each time he goes into London, takes food that he can leave with a homeless person he will inevitably meet on the street.

At the core of developing a broader Purpose in our children is nurturing their sense of empathy. As we've seen from the Dalai Lama's comments, our children are too often preoccupied only by themselves and can't imagine the world from another person's eyes. Studies by Ashoka and the Harvard Graduate School of Education show that empathy is one of the strongest predictors of how narrowly or broadly young people will engage in different areas of life, such as in their work and relationships. Greater empathy tends to translate to greater kindness.

It's worth us modelling empathy for our children. Recently, my wife and I took my mother out for her birthday, at a local French restaurant, along with our two boys. That evening Eashan was tired, cranky, grumpy and, frankly, a real pain in the backside. He ended up spoiling the mood for us all. And he wouldn't even talk to the young waitress who was doing her best to cheer him up and make him smile.

My mother explained to the waitress that we had just come from a 12-hour flight. I will never forget how the waitress responded. 'You know, I've been up since 6am myself, working my first job with the council,' she said. It was well past 9pm at this point. 'I don't know why I do this myself sometimes.'

It was a throwaway comment, almost to herself in passing, but it reminded me of how lacking in empathy our current generation of children will end up if we don't turn things around.

Normally I would have let it go and, like my mother, excused Eashan's behaviour on the basis of the long flight. But writing this chapter perhaps changed my perspective. When we got home, I asked Eashan to reflect on his behaviour, and about how he would feel if someone else spoiled his own birthday in the same way he had spoiled my mother's. And I told him that we would cancel his forthcoming birthday party as a way of remembering the importance of thinking about others – both his grandmother and the waitress who had been trying so hard to cheer him up.

He was clearly upset but, interestingly, didn't protest or resist. And he didn't even seem to mind when the party actually didn't take place a few months later (despite lots of anxiety from both Aida and me).

The next morning, I asked him to write a page on what he had learned from the night before. This is what he wrote:

My Behaviour

Yesterday my behaviour was bad even though it was my grandmother's birthday. I was even grumpy when the waiter tried to make me happy before dinner was served. And I really was rude to the waiter last night and I didn't say please or thank you at all. And I have learned that you can't always think about yourself, you have to think about family and friends. You have to think about people who are kind and you have to be respectful or kind to everyone. And yesterday all I cared about was myself and you should help people. And in the future I want to help people and care about everyone. And not to be grumpy or miserable at anyone in special occasions.

Eashan

I think children know when they cross lines – much more than we often give them credit for.

Schemes like Teach For India and Teach For America have given many graduates a much greater connection to the world, and a sense of moral responsibility for making a difference to it, through the experience of teaching for two years in a challenging school. This tends to stay with them for the rest of their lives.

There is a legendary story that goes around Teach For All circles, about an Internal Revenue Service (IRS) form that was causing huge problems for disadvantaged teenagers applying for college. A leader within the IRS heard about this issue, conducted internal discussions and moved mountains to make the form a relic of history. And did this within days.

How on earth did that happen? The IRS is rarely known for such entrepreneurialism. That's easy. The director in question was a former employee of Teach for America in its early days.

Purpose is something that we can cultivate in our children. We just need to consciously make sure it's a broad sense of Purpose, not a narrow one – and then deeply encourage it.

The more supportive of our children's Autonomy we are, the more our kids will generally flourish – and the more motivated and satisfied we are likely to be as parents too.

Richard Ryan writes that when parents support their children's

Autonomy, 'their children are more autonomously motivated, engage more positively in school and have higher well-being.' He cites an analysis by Ariana Vasquez across 36 separate parenting studies as the basis for this.[26]

I talked earlier about parental narcissism and the risk of not being able to separate one's own identity with that of one's children. Since the 1940s, John Bowlby's pioneering research at London's Tavistock Clinic, which we touched on previously in chapter 4, has spawned over 20,000 studies on the notion of 'attachment theory'. Bowlby's core tenet was that a child has to develop a secure attachment to their caregiver, particularly their mother. Parents need to respond carefully to children's signals and create a reciprocal pattern of interaction. If secure attachment is not in place early in childhood, Bowlby's research found, it can lead to all kinds of emotional insecurities for children later in life.

Attachment theory has become the bedrock of modern parenting, and it also influenced the move to a more child-centred approach in teaching. Of course, secure attachment (compared to the avoidant or ambivalent styles we saw in the previous chapter) is a good thing in itself, but it has been taken to such an extreme that we now see no separation between us and our children. And that means pushing children as an extension of ourselves and projecting their success as our success.

There's an obvious insight coming from all this – for parental attachment to be successful, you also need separation. Anyone who has watched a neck-and-neck sporting final knows what it's like when your favourite team or player loses at the very end. But we know at the end of the day that the player or team is not us. That's the sense of 'attachment with separation' we need to have as parents. Kahlil Gibran was so right when, as we saw earlier in this chapter, he penned the line: 'Your children are not your children.'

This ability to separate your identity and success from your child's is what I call 'big Autonomy'. For example, it might have been your unfulfilled dream to be a pro tennis player or county-level cricketer. But that doesn't mean your child has to fulfil it.

Once big Autonomy has been addressed, there is plenty we can do to foster what I call 'small Autonomy'. Small Autonomy has a few key dimensions: space, time, people and decisions.

We rarely give our kids much Autonomy over space. US media outlets created a stir when they reported children as young as seven in Tokyo were able to travel on the subway by themselves.[27] This has helped create the momentum for a broader "free-range kids" movement around the world.[28] Data suggests that in most countries our public places have become safer over time, but that unfortunate incidents get reported more, which is why the world can feel more dangerous, as leading thinkers such as Steven Pinker have argued. And that is why risks can feel distorted to us as parents.[29]

That's not saying that giving our children their own space won't sometimes be stressful. When I met Esther Wojcicki at her book launch in London for *How to Raise Happy and Successful Children*, she told a hilarious story about when she left her young grandkids in a Target store and asked them to roam around by themselves and complete their shopping until she came to pick them up. The grandkids were fine; their mother Susan, however, was much less happy about the whole escapade.

Giving our children their own space means allowing them to enjoy an activity without our constant presence. Former US Vice-President Al Gore became famous for attending every one of his son's games. I used to do the same with my son Eashan's cricket matches – until I started to write this book and needed the spare time. I find Eashan does just as well, if not better, when I'm not there. And now I just attend the most important matches he plays.

Autonomy of time is another rare thing for children today. Shuffled from activity to activity, the only way they play with others now is through structured playdates. When I was young, I used to spend long summers with my grandparents in Chennai. These were the days when there was half an hour of English TV daily on Doordarshan, then the sole permitted government TV channel. I learned quickly to play street cricket, as well as read a book in a day. Being able to manage their own energy and boredom is critical for kids.

Autonomy for our children means exposing them to diverse people. Wojcicki believes that children's time with grandparents in the US is carefully managed because parents are worried about exposing them to a different parenting style, and in particular grandparents relaxing iron-clad routines. From what I've seen there is a similar trend in the UK and other developed countries too. But one of the best things about parenting in earlier times was that kids were exposed to multiple caregivers, friends and family. The same applies to friendship. A parent in my sons' school actively tries to control who her son's 'best friend' is based on whom she personally approves of. That stops kids from learning to interact and deal with a range of people.

Finally, we should try to empower children to have Autonomy over even small decisions. For example: give them a shopping list of what the family needs to buy and ask them to find the best (and best value) choice of products within that. This is something my wife and I have started trying when we're in the supermarket. It seems to work wonders, particularly in helping the boys figure out how to make decisions based on real budgets and understanding they can't have everything they want to buy.

Anything you can do to increase Autonomy for your children, big or small, can help. For example, Aida and I have tried to spend a good part of our summers living in one of the countries where STiR works. This has meant bringing our kids with us, and where possible putting them in a local school for a month – we've done this in Uganda, Indonesia and India. It's not for academic benefit, but because it helps them learn to settle in quickly, and meet new people and cultures, and gives them the confidence and empathy these things can bring. We feel incredibly lucky to have been able give them this exposure. I hope it's one of the things they'll truly remember about their childhoods.

One of the things that really struck us from our trips was how little time children in London have just to play with, and entertain, children of the same age without being chaperoned or structured. In Singapore, staying with a close friend, our boys immediately became part of a broader group of 20 children who played together along East Coast Park. Their parents largely left them in peace and didn't interfere. This approach worked through supervision by the older kids in the group, and the children always stayed within eye and earshot of the parents. We noticed how much more the boys developed and learned to be independent, including learning how to manage issues and conflicts directly with other kids, rather than relying on adults to intervene. This approach is one we've been trying to bring back to our lives in London.

Finally, let's talk about adopting a Mastery mindset as a parent – and the kind of Mastery we want to nurture in our children.

A common theme of the extreme parenting approaches we've seen so far – from helicopter to snowplough – is the assumption that life for our children can be, and will be (if we are a good enough parent), a 'straight line'. They will have a clear path they can safely follow to a happy and successful life.

As we've seen in this chapter, however, the link between school attainment and success in life is only partial, and doesn't form the entire picture. That also mirrors my own personal experience. Once they graduated into real life, the most 'successful' classmates of mine from Cambridge or INSEAD were not by a long way the most academically successful – at least according to extrinsic definitions, such as wealth or conventional status. Nor were the academically most successful necessarily happier (either personally or professionally) or more fulfilled.

One of my classmates from my Cambridge college committed suicide. A year after graduating I found myself weeping at his funeral. He was of East Asian origin and gay, and he had been going through deep issues around identity that the 'bubble' of university life hadn't prepared him to confront – and that he hadn't felt confident confiding in others about.

By trying to draw a straight line that just isn't there, we are fundamentally deceiving our kids about the nature of the real world they are about to enter.

A new Mastery mindset as parents should not be focused on creating (or, rather, praying for) the straight line. We should embrace our children's life as an inevitable zig-zag – and, indeed, embrace the uncertainty that brings. Because it will be one of the key things that keeps our children truly alive and motivated.

There are two important ways we can do this. The first is through role-modelling as parents. Vineet Bewtra, who used to work for Omidyar Network, is one of the voices I really respected during my time in philanthropy. Vineet once told me about the 'success narrative' that entrepreneurs display time and time again on big podiums at conferences. In these contexts, entrepreneurs tell their stories in a straight line – where one event leads logically to the next – guided of course by wisdom and brilliant decision-making on their part. But entrepreneurship, Vineet noted – and my own entrepreneurial experience would certainly reinforce his point – is almost never a straight line. Vineet quoted the Mike Tyson adage both for entrepreneurship and for life as a whole: 'Everybody has a plan until they get punched in the mouth.'

Success in entrepreneurship is about knowing that the dark side will inevitably come. Times when you'll have to make decisions that will upset people you deeply respect and care about. Times when you are on the ropes and struggling to stay in the proverbial ring. In nine years of leading STiR, which was relatively well funded, we hit the financial ropes – the risk of going out of business – no fewer than three times.

All too often, we project the same 'success narrative' onto our children. I could not have asked for more committed and loving parents, but that was also the narrative they projected onto me. My mother often told me and my brother, 'I was top of my class at school and at medical school.' I'm sharing that with no spirit of blame – that's what parents then were taught they should do to inspire their children to aspire and work hard.

Rosita Tehusijarana says the single most powerful thing I've heard in all my discussions with parents and parenting experts. 'At the end of the day, children don't follow what we as parents say. They follow what we do.' She's alluding to the power of role-modelling.

If we want our kids to master the zig-zag of life, we need to show them our vulnerability through the same struggles. That's something that most Indian parents – and parents from many other places – find very difficult to do. I'll forever be grateful for the sacrifice my parents made when we left Saudi Arabia abruptly, all really to protect our education. The English medical system did not value experience from elsewhere all that much, so both my parents had to take initial career side-steps before they found a way back to doing what they truly loved. The savings that they'd painstakingly accumulated from their time in Saudi Arabia – their original motivation for going there – were quickly burned on our return, due to adjusting to a new cost of living, including housing. It must have been a very challenging time for them, but they didn't feel comfortable sharing it.

If we don't open up about our own struggles and vulnerabilities, we perpetuate that myth of the straight line, and that does our kids a disservice much later in life. I try now to talk to my children about what's happening in my life, including at work – whether there's been a difficult situation with a donor or team member, or a challenge in writing this book (of which there have been many).

The second thing we can provide is a spoonful – à la Mary Poppins – of what I call 'own-label parenting'. I started my career as a management consultant to the food industry in the days when supermarkets were first creating their own-label products in everything from ketchup to toilet paper. In many areas, supermarkets' own products are just as good. The same goes for parenting.

After a heart-to-heart with Eashan, we decided he wasn't that interested in competitive tennis. I must admit that I had mixed feelings about this as I love the sport so much, but I knew I had to respect his instincts. So we've decided to give up on the tournaments, at least for a while, and play a lot more together. I'm never going to be as good as his former tennis coach – so, yes, there are definitely some drawbacks from reducing the level of 'outsourcing' – but now we have an activity where we can experience the zig-zag together.

In 2018, the Palo Alto city government announced that its Cal Train station would soon no longer be manned by guards, but rather by cameras with a hundred-foot visibility ahead of them. Of course, this being Silicon Valley, artificial intelligence and predictive analytics would 'alert human agents to intervene' in the case of suicide attempts, according to the government notice.

I found myself so depressed when I read that announcement. Yes, the city government had superficially tackled the symptoms of the problem, but it had done nothing to address the root causes.

Our children and we as parents deserve so much better.

Where does this leave us as parents? Just as we should be wary of comparing our children to others, we should be careful not to compare ourselves too much with other parents. Facebook groups and websites like Mumsnet – a boon in providing useful information – can also stoke a great deal of peer pressure. Let's also be careful not to jump too quickly to assumptions about how others parent, particularly people with different backgrounds. When academics surveyed Chinese-American and Asian-American parents, they found that only a small minority were employing anything like what you could call tiger-parenting strategies – completely contrary to exaggerated American parental imagination.

We need to develop our own sense of Mastery, too. Sneha Sheth is currently using texts and WhatsApp messages to nudge Delhi parents into good behaviours, but long term she sees potential for creating parent self-help groups that are led by more experienced parents in communities. Rosita Tehusijarana has already set up a couple of such groups in Jakarta and, using a mix of case studies and discussions, she's helping parents find ways out of common pitfalls, including the over-focus on academics, the unbalanced relationship between parents and teachers and the desire to remove all our children's obstacles out of the way.

Our children's lives will not be straight lines. The world – in terms of technology, social and political change – will be a hard one to predict, if you believe anyone from McKinsey to Yuval Noah Harari.

The things we currently obsess about as parents – the grades, the trophies, the schools they get into – should be seen as hygiene factors and not the be all-and end-all. While we are at it, let's drop the parenting buzzwords and remember our key Purpose as parents is to help our kids embrace, master – even revel in – the zig-zag of life.

'If you want to go fast, go alone;
but if you want to go far, go together.'

African proverb[1]

6

Intrinsic Citizenship:
From Divided to
United

'It's time to put away the harsh rhetoric,' Joe Biden declared in his 2020 presidential acceptance speech. 'To lower the temperature. To see each other again. To listen to each other again. To make progress, we must stop treating our opponents as our enemy. We are not enemies. We are Americans.'[2]

The irony was the American electorate didn't seem that motivated about being united. Only 19 per cent of US voters in the 2020 election said they wanted a president 'who can unite the country', according to CNN exit polls.[3]

In this chapter we are going to move our focus from individual aspects of our lives to our role as citizens in the countries and world we live in. As we've seen throughout this book, the broader forces that affect our individual lives – including the pervasive trend towards 'winner takes all' – create an enormous number of pressures and stresses on us as individuals. These pressures are affecting our individual motivation and behaviour in everything from how we show up to work to how we parent.

Through the course of the book we've explored the ways we can offset these pressures as individuals and how we can reignite our personal inner drive. But it would be misleading to pretend that acting alone, as rugged 'lone rangers', will be enough to solve the gaping problems that we and our world face.

Political analyst Tom Bentley is the author of a provocative Demos report 'Everyday Democracy: Why we get the politicians we deserve'. 'Our political culture perpetuates the myth that strong leaders bring about change single-handedly,' he writes, and then points out: 'Rather than relying on the authority of office, real leadership means motivating people to solve problems for which there are no easy answers.'[4]

But there is hope from applying motivation thinking to this critical problem, and that hope comes in how we reignite our intrinsic motivation as citizens – and, in doing so, create the right motivation for our leaders and politicians.

I'm not going to pretend this will be easy. Our trust in the motivation and intent of our politicians and elected leaders is at an all-time low. An Ipsos MORI Veracity Index created just before the 2019 British general election suggested that only 14 per cent of Brits trusted politicians to meet the most basic leadership requirement of telling the truth – and that only rose marginally to 17 per cent for government ministers.[5] The survey put our politicians on similar levels of trust as advertising executives. Although these are British figures, it's a phenomenon that we see replicated in almost every country in the world.

We are going to explore what it would it really take for us to align our motivation as citizens with the motivation of our politicians. Some of the insights might surprise us, but they're essential if we want to have any hope of addressing the scale of the problems in front of us – problems that, as we've defined before, are inherently 'wicked', with no easy technical solutions.

Before we jump in, I want to clarify an answer to one question, which often haunts our thinking as citizens. Are politicians even motivated by Purpose, by the desire to help and serve us as citizens, in the first place?

A surprisingly robust body of evidence suggests that, on average, they are. Timothy Besley and Maitreesh Ghatak, both professors at the London School of Economics, have developed an extensive 'mission' theory of politician motivation – where politicians view public life and office as their mission (or Purpose), which is more important than personal benefit.[6] That theory has now been tested and validated in many parts of the world. Other studies have shown how ownership (Autonomy) and sense of community (Purpose) are highly correlated with the personal drive of politicians. The research also suggests that politicians demonstrate these traits far more than people in other, profit-driven professions. Besley and Ghatak have a further interesting finding from their surveys: when politicians are successful, they develop a 'warm glow' which closely ties to our definition of Purpose.

I spoke to two members of the British House of Lords and they broadly concurred with this view. Lord (Jim) Knight, a former education minister under Gordon Brown, told me: 'You can't be a modern politician without some form of intrinsic motivation.' Baroness (Sally) Morgan, who played a key role under Tony Blair, also agrees. 'I remain on many MP WhatsApp groups, and I see from everyday conversation how much they all care. There are many much easier ways to make money or gain power, after all.'

Baroness Morgan's point about money is an interesting one. Of course political corruption still remains a major problem in many countries (though it has been falling steadily in most countries, according to studies by the World Bank).[7] But evidence suggests that for most politicians – similar to what we've seen in other professions – money is a hygiene factor, not a true motivator.

Studies in the US, Finland and Mexico have shown that increasing pay can attract different pools of candidates with varying educational backgrounds to enter politics.[8, 9, 10] But equally in contexts where politicians are already well paid compared to alternative professions, increasing pay has little effect. A study of an increase in pay of Members of the European Parliament actually led to some negative effects, including increasing absenteeism.

When politicians are less worried about covering their own and their staff's costs, they also appear to be less beholden to special interests and more inclined to create policies that improve welfare for all. Researchers Renee Bowen and Cecilia Mo, for example, show that in American states where governors earn more money, the minimum wage tends to be higher and corporations contribute a higher share of tax revenue – policies that favour ordinary citizens over the interests of particular groups.[11]

But what about that other temptation, power? Trained in a heady cocktail of management theory and psychoanalysis, INSEAD's Professor Manfred Kets de Vries has found that the most common leadership style at the top of many organizations is that of a narcissist. He concludes that 'derailment at the top is often due to the excesses that come with this behaviour. In these instances, position and disposition seem to interact in mysterious ways. Ultimately the rot sets in.'[12] Kets de Vries is writing about power in all types of organizations, but our lived experience should give us plenty of examples of where we have seen such behaviour in our top politicians.

David Laws, a former minister for schools in the British Conservative/Lib Dem 2010 coalition government, talked to me about the different roles of intrinsic and extrinsic motivation as you progress through a political career. 'At the beginning, as you get into politics, you are driven more by intrinsic motivators. Once you get into office you have to deal with the government and it feels like survival…Only a small number of people really control what is happening in government – and often you hear news from a newspaper headline, just as everyone else does.' That can be very demotivating. David believes that it's critical to maintain a sense of Purpose and Autonomy, even if you aren't in the 'inner circle'.

What does this tell us? First, that narcissistic tendencies and the quest for power can indeed derail our leaders away from their core Purpose of helping and serving us. At the same time, however – just as we saw in almost every profession, including teaching – there is already a strong degree of intrinsic motivation in most of our political leaders. It's how the systems and surrounding culture affect them, eroding their intrinsic motivation, that seems to be causing many of the problems in our politics and countries today. It's not that different from other professions, but of course the consequences are so much more severe for us all.

In this chapter we'll ask how, as citizens, we can fight back. We'll use our familiar Purpose, Autonomy and Mastery framework in two ways. The first step will be to diagnose the key challenges in the motivation of our politicians today. The second step is to look at how we need to change our own motivation and behaviour as citizens, so we can collaborate better with our politicians and our fellow citizens, and realize the countries and world we truly want. And to find new solutions to these truly 'wicked' problems.

What's the core of the Purpose problem facing our politicians today? At the core is how difficult it is to truly unify a country, particularly when, as we saw in the views of the US electorate, few of us as citizens may want to be 'unified' in the first place.

When Ethiopian Prime Minister Abiy Ahmed was awarded the 2019 Nobel Peace Prize, it was formally for solving a 20-year long border tension and war with neighbouring Eritrea. 'Abiy' (as his supporters call him) had also been active – the Nobel Committee noted – in supporting the peace processes of other African nations, notably Sudan. But it was his early attempts to unify Ethiopia that gained more attention on the global stage. Within his first year of being elected, Abiy had freed political prisoners, liberalized the press, relaxed the country's draconian NGO laws and elected women to half of the cabinet and – for the first time – to the role of the country's president. Most fundamentally, for the first time he'd tried to bring the country's many ethnic groups into a common national identity – of being, first and foremost, Ethiopians.

It's that last part that's recently been the most challenging – and the most dangerous. And it seems mostly because of the suspicions it's unleashed from each ethnic group that others are getting more 'special' treatment. The ethnic tensions it's generated – with each of the country's nine ethnic groups jockeying for position – has led to 2.5 million people being displaced, and ethnic skirmishes that have led to thousands of lost lives. Whether Abiy eventually succeeds in unifying the country will matter hugely for the future of Africa (in which Ethiopia is the second largest country). Recent indications have not been so positive – with signs of more authoritarian actions, military strikes and election delays. There's a real risk that, if it's not turned around, Ethiopia will go the way of other countries ruled by 'old men' of Africa.

But it's not as if richer countries don't have their challenges with their own 'tribes', too. As I walked into Addis airport that first time in late 2018, bleary eyed with the early-morning arrival, even I could sense the hope and excitement that year. I felt a deep envy for the sense of national hope I was seeing, because for the past three years, my own adopted country – the United Kingdom – had exploded into its own version of tribal warfare, all centred around two warring 'tribes' – 'remainers' and 'leavers'. The debate Britain has had about Brexit – which has consumed so much of the country's emotional energy – seemed to take little heed of the views of our 'experts', who were warning of all kinds of risks to our economy and national security.

The havoc this was creating for the UK's global reputation was staggering. Scenes of former House of Commons Speaker John Bercow trying to maintain order in parliament played across global televisions. Votes of no confidence – of nothing less than outright mutiny against Prime Minister Theresa May by members of her own party. And then (similar to many African countries) an entire suspension of parliament – or 'proroguing', as Brits learned the process was called – was put into motion by her successor Boris Johnson. The fact that the UK had no formal written constitution only added to the sense of Westminster's suspense and intrigue.

It was in the midst of this chaos that I visited Singapore with my family. As we wandered around former colonial buildings, one of my old friends, Pradeep, told my kids: 'See how the British used to rule the world. Now they can't even rule themselves.'

At the heart of Brexit – whatever your views, whether you believed in leave or remain – was a huge vacuum of Purpose. A majority of Brits wanted to escape the EU, it seemed fair to say, because they couldn't see a deeper sense of Purpose in why being an EU 'citizen' mattered to them. It was striking how every politician's speech in favour of remain – across the political spectrum, from David Cameron to Jeremy Corbyn – invoked the logic of economics and convenience, and not that of a deeper Purpose in being part of the European project's vision of a unified people and continent.

Here was the irony: the case for leave – or 'sovereignty', to invoke

Brexiteer language – was equally obscure. What was the sovereignty we were going to have to bear so much pain to achieve actually for? Besides the opportunity to negotiate bespoke trade deals, there was almost nothing provided in terms of a broader national Purpose around what Brexit was actually for. And as our leaders – and all of us as citizens – got sucked into the negotiation drama, there was even less energy to clarify and articulate this Purpose.

It reminded me of the wiry lawyer in the Netflix film *Marriage Story*, played by Alan Alda, who reminds a divorcing couple of how much emotional energy husbands and wives usually spend arguing about custody. Only to find that by the time the divorce takes place, they're so exhausted that they almost have no emotional energy left to spend with their children.

As President Kennedy opined several decades ago, the job of any politician – and, by extension, political party – must be to define a clear national Purpose. Why has this erosion of national Purpose been so marked in so many of our countries today?

A large reason is that we have been focusing on the extrinsic – and particularly the idea of 'zero-sum' politics: one faction gaining at the expense of another. Instead of fostering a common national Purpose, we see an increase in political factions.

In *The Federalist Papers*,[13] three of America's founding fathers – Alexander Hamilton, James Madison and John Jay – foresaw this danger hundreds of years ago. Madison in particular defined a 'faction' as a number of citizens, whether a majority or minority, who were united and activated by 'some common impulse of passion, or of interest, adverse to the rights of other citizens, or to the permanent and aggregate interests of the community'.

Factions, Madison believed, arise because public opinion forms and spreads quickly. But they can be reduced if the public is given time to explore these issues properly. To prevent factions, Madison strongly argued for a representative rather than direct democracy. In this way enlightened members of the public – serving as elected politicians – would serve the public good.

So, hundreds of years after these exact risks were identified, why do we seem to have the most tribal, dysfunctional politics in so many parts of the world?

'Populism' – a term which has been thrown around to describe recent trends – tends to define two groups, according to political theorists Mudde and Kaltwasser:[14] the 'pure people' versus the 'corrupt elite'. It's been a narrative exploited both by the left and by the right.

It's in the US that these developments become even more interesting. Here Amy Chua – the Chinese-American advocate of the 'tiger mom' we met in the previous chapter – makes a compelling argument. Writing in the *Guardian*, she notes that 'political tribalism' has become the dominant feature of US politics because every group feels persecuted.[15] Fifty years ago, she argues – the time of John F Kennedy – people like Martin Luther King were pushing the idea of a Great Society. As King put it: 'a promise that all men, yes, black men as well as white men, would be guaranteed the unalienable rights of life, liberty and the pursuit of happiness'. Chua argues that although the left was always concerned with minority oppression and disadvantaged group rights, they tended to be 'group blind'.

Chua notes that even as recently as the 2004 Democratic National Convention – in a speech that propelled his career – a then relatively unknown Senator Barack Obama declared: 'There's not a black America and white America and Latino America and Asian America; there's the United States of America.'[16] It was a great – and well-orated – defence of national Purpose. But seeing so little progress against this idea has, Chua argues, moved the country away from universalism, viewing it – in her words – as 'an attempt to erase the specificity of the experience and oppression of specific marginalized groups'. She cites as a vivid example a Black Lives Matter rally where an organizer told white protestors taking part to take their 'rightful' place at the back.

This has led to – in her view – white identity politics. When every other group was told to take pride and solidarity in their racial or ethnic identity, 'white Americans have for the last several decades been told they must never, ever do so'. And that's what has led white voters to feel like a persecuted minority, Chua argues – and in doing so, helped propel the success of Donald Trump. 'People want to see their own tribe as exceptional, as something to be deeply proud of; that's what the tribal instinct is all about,' she concludes. It's not so different to what Abiy Ahmed has been facing in Ethiopia. And it's taking us further and further from our core national Purpose.

It's this lack of national Purpose, and the pattern of tribal politics, that increasingly make us see the world in 'zero-sum' game terms – that one group or faction's gain has to be at the expense of another's. That, in turn, is deterring potentially strong new MPs from now running for office in the UK and other countries. It's also demotivating those already in parliament. Sally Morgan and Jim Knight both confirmed this trend. And in Lord Knight's case, it led him to bemoan the vanishing of the 'One Nation' tradition of politics in Britain, where politicians see their role as serving the whole country, not just the factions that gave them their vote. *The Economist* has also noted how requiring strong 'Brexiteers' in the current UK cabinet – rather than simply the best people suited for cabinet jobs – has led to a weak pool of talent.[17]

To mark how severe these trends in British politics are, Labour MP David Lammy has written a book focused on the question of tribes, arguing that it's the make-or-break issue for us all today.[18]

If all of us as citizens are being increasingly tribal in our views and beliefs, how can we expect the politicians who are meant to serve us to be able to champion a true national Purpose? The onus is on us as much as on the politicians we elect, to change our collective mindset.

There is another issue that deters our politicians from creating true national Purpose – and that relates to the wider trends around inequality that we've touched on elsewhere in the book: by dividing our societies into 'haves' and 'have-nots' – or, as we've seen, 'winners' and 'the rest' – it's making it almost impossible to create a Purpose that straddles the needs and priorities of both groups.

Let's delve into why that's the case. Remember our discussion of hygiene factors – necessary requirements that don't truly motivate us. The Cold War at its height led to a deep fear over our own survival. Anyone who can't remember how far this was ingrained, even in the psyche of young schoolchildren, should visit some of the secret nuclear bunkers in the English countryside. A 1984 survey of 1,100 Toronto schoolchildren found that many of them reported feeling helpless and powerless at the prospect of a nuclear war.[19] A citizen's sense of peace and security are what you might call 'macro' hygiene factors.

When the Iron Curtain came down and the Cold War ended, the world breathed a huge, collective sigh of relief. Leading thinker Francis Fukuyama even declared 'the end of history' in his bestselling book.[20] Democracy, he pointed out with no small level of triumphalism, has repeatedly been a fundamentally better system than any other. Now the battle of that question was over – he argued – everything else following it would just be 'events', not real history.

But there proved to be a fundamental flaw in Fukuyama's logic. And that was around his belief in the other engine of Western values: capitalism and the belief that its spoils would 'trickle down' to everyone.

Capitalism has certainly led to soaring incomes and wealth in many countries, both in the West and elsewhere. In India, where I spent the first part of my life in the 1970s and many childhood summers in the 1980s, I learned quickly at first hand the symptoms of socialism: the back-breaking efforts of my grandfather to get a landline installed in his house, to take just one example. The state monopoly would only deign to provide its service in its own sweet time (which often meant years) without the strong incentive of a bribe. I remember 'socialist' India as a rather grey, joyless place – so different from the noisy, vibrant energy that you see unleashed in any Indian city you visit today. Throughout this huge socialist experiment, India's human development indicators from poverty to health to women's welfare to education also remained abysmal, as economists Amartya Sen and Jean Drèze found in their ground-breaking research.[21]

But the prescribed dose of capitalism – which was administered like a medicine to many poor countries, such as India, by the likes of the World Bank and the IMF when they made their loans – came with a nasty, undeclared side-effect. And that side-effect was inequality.

We would all hopefully agree that one of the most important things a society should achieve for its citizens is happiness. The

US Declaration of Independence, of course, famously calls for the 'pursuit of happiness' to be the nation's main goal. It's ironic that it's taken us until very recently – decades after national income was being measured – to even try to measure national happiness robustly. The UN, for example, only started compiling its annual World Happiness Report in 2012.

Nobel prize-winning economist Sir Angus Deaton and Nobel prize-winning psychologist Daniel Kahneman made world headlines from a joint-research paper[22] that found that $75,000 was the average personal income level above which happiness more or less plateaued. Even before that threshold was hit, however, there were what economists call 'diminishing returns to happiness' – every extra dollar brought a lower and lower amount of happiness.

Yes, you heard me right. There were almost *no* increases in happiness above the $75,000 threshold. Which would seem to be an extreme validation of what motivation theory predicts. Money is important, but almost entirely as a hygiene factor. There is therefore a 'ceiling' effect. Deaton and Kahneman's findings seem to resonate with other cross-country studies of these trends. According to the *Berkeley Economic Review*, a 100 per cent change in GDP per capita leads to only a 30 per cent change in happiness (measured through their happiness index).[23]

What does that mean practically? Finnish citizens appear to be substantially happier than US citizens, despite being a quarter poorer than the US in per capita income. Countries 'use' per capita income gains more or less to generate happiness gains, the Berkeley economists concluded. But it's how the additional income is used – whether to make lasting changes to citizens' welfare, for example through improving public health or education, or whether it's distributed mostly to the 'winners' we met in our success chapter – that seems to matter the most.

Here's the most important takeaway: while average (or mean) income in the US for example is $58,000, the median – a much more representative average because it doesn't get 'pulled up' by the extremely wealthy – is actually just above $30,000. Average incomes for most people on median incomes in the West – after adjusting for inflation – haven't increased much at all over the last 20 years. And this has led many to characterize those who voted for Brexit as citizens who have 'nothing to lose'. Remainers, on the other hand – who are typically more urban, have a higher income and usually a higher level of education – felt on that path to affluence. They, by contrast, had a huge amount to lose.

It's therefore no surprise that the countries with the most 'populist' movements – the UK, US, India, Hong Kong, Brazil, Philippines – have some of the highest inequality in the world, and the lowest rates of intergenerational mobility.

In other words, the economic costs of an event like Brexit feel much less important for citizens who don't think they have a chance to get on the rungs of the happiness-GDP ladder in the first place. It's almost the opposite of the 'fuck-you money' attitude that exists in places like Silicon Valley, where an employee may have enough money to leave an unreasonable employer – it's 'fuck you, I have nothing to lose'.

So, where do these trends leave our modern politicians? Basically, in a very tough position.

Now politicians have two audiences, two 'tribes' to contend with – those on the happiness-GDP ladder and those not. The second tribe is of course much more populous. It's going to be the braver politicians – the Abiys of this world, echoing the Kennedys of the past – who are going to be confident enough to even try to create a common sense of national Purpose. Then find out how challenging that really proves to be.

This is going to make any kind of political direction and decisions increasingly hard to justify. One of the things that was so notable about the Brexit discussion in the UK was which 'goalposts' were being used to judge success – something that had a whiff of ambiguity throughout. Is it an economic goalpost or is it a purely intrinsic (sovereignty or Autonomy) goalpost? We seemed to constantly be moving between these in any argument – and the criteria the country's leaders were using throughout the debate were never very explicit.

For politicians, it's increasingly tempting to manipulate the drivers of intrinsic motivation – and at times falsely represent them.

Brexit might mean more Autonomy for Britain, or it might mean being sandwiched between the US, China and Europe and squeezed in every possible way. No one really knows. But 'take back control' has no subtlety; it's much easier for politicians to not get into these nuances at all.

Equally, in the US, a story of Purpose that panders to whites left behind in the economic race and makes them yearn for a nostalgic yesteryear makes many people profoundly uncomfortable. The econonic disparities and inequalities that cause the concerns are significant and real, but this kind of nostalgia tends to divide an increasingly racially diverse country.

All of these trends seem to move us further away from a true national Purpose that unites us all. And of course trends in traditional and social media only accelerate this problem. Most of the people in Westminster I talked to bemoaned how social media made it impossible for politicians to have a genuine conversation with the whole nation. I heard Tony Blair give an intimate talk in Cochin, India, about how his conversation with the nation was always a three-fold narrative: a lot done, a lot to do and a lot to lose.

That's completely different from the political micro-segmentation – the slicing and dicing – that social media and the internet have created today. The Conservatives received much criticism, for example, in their 2019 electoral campaign for including 28 different social media ads based on voter 'micro-targeting'.

Social media is the ultimate example of the famous Burger King slogan 'Have it your way'. Whatever your political views already are, they'll be reinforced and amplified by the online messages and conversations around you.

Basically, we've created a vicious cycle where politicians can't create a national Purpose in the first place because their countries are so divided. And that in turn creates even more distrust among citizens.

Just as it's becoming increasingly difficult for our political leaders to create a true sense of national Purpose, they're also finding it hard to exercise true Autonomy in what they do – and that impinges directly on their intrinsic motivation.

One of the biggest problems is that the climate of distrust between us and our political leaders has encouraged us to put our politicians under incredible scrutiny both in our social media and with every word being monitored on national television.

Remember the idea of representative democracy – we trust our elected leaders to make overall good decisions. But that's not how it feels, and the distrust we feel ends up polarizing us.

Dan Honig, an expert on public-service reform, shared with me an interesting study[24] conducted in the US around the time when C-SPAN – the US channel that broadcasts live political debate in both houses – launched. Following the example of 'grandstanders' like Newt Gingrich, politicians became much more polarized and unwilling to make compromises when they were on live TV.

So now, many commentators argue, the US House of Representatives and Senate are more like chambers of self-starting 'entrepreneurs' who follow their own instincts and their own bank of voters rather than the broader party direction. Jonathan Rauch is a US political commentator who has been examining these trends. He observes that 'there is no such thing as the party leader'. Each politician, he argues, now pursues their own interests 'like excited gas molecules in an overheated balloon'. Rauch goes as far as to describe it as 'chaos syndrome'. He argues that a 'rogue politician' in the US nowadays can't even be fired by his party leader.[25]

Let's think back to the work chapter and the importance of 'guided Autonomy'. Remember our challenges at STiR when the meetings of teachers were a 'free for all' in terms of what they focused on. There's a powerful parallel here. We need to balance the Autonomy of individual politicians with the Autonomy of their party, and the Autonomy of the overall leader. Just like in work, Autonomy for politicians needs to be channelled and 'guided'.

In this context, Rauch echoes what Dan Honig told me: middlemen – civil servants and a whole army of political 'fixers' – were essential people to make the chaos more organized and to create the 'sausage machine' of compromise that's often required in politics. In other words, they help to be guides for channelling the Autonomy of individual politicians and parties on both sides of the political aisle.

But the advent of new political 'sunshine' (or transparency) laws that were introduced in the 1970s makes everything accountable and open; now everything – down to who a politician meets each day – has to be disclosed. This has impeded rather than helped compromise.

To compound these Autonomy challenges, this excessive scrutiny – as well as perhaps the temptations of narcissism we've discussed – encourages our political leaders to over-centralize power. Part of the problem with modern politics, according to the UK's former Liberal Democrat education minister David Laws, is that the forces of accountability – targets and social media – lead to 'personality politicians' where only between five and ten people really lead the country. The intense media spotlight, he argues, means that there is pressure to 'personalize and own everything'.

'The UK has a hundred or so ministers – and the truth is most aren't being used,' David adds. 'It's only a few people who really run the country.'

This reached almost farcical proportions when the arrangements for the second English Covid-19 lockdown were leaked to the press before most MPs had any information, prompting furious demands by MPs to treat the institution of parliament and its elected members seriously.[26]

What we are seeing in places like Westminster and Washington is a simultaneous crisis of both leadership and followership. Politicians need to better accept the direction of their party – something that is much easier to do if it is linked to a clear, shared national Purpose. But equally a president or prime minister needs to devolve power to a much wider group of ministers and members of parliament.

As citizens and voters, we need to hold our political leaders to account for creating a truly national Purpose and vision that genuinely is one nation – one that applies to the whole country. But once they do that convincingly, we need to be willing to follow, provide trust and – counterintuitively – avoid second-guessing them and hemming them in with excessive scrutiny on how they achieve that national Purpose. That gives them room to collaborate with each other and find compromise.

The more we insist on a blame and cancel culture as citizens, the more it will tempt our leaders and politicians to centralize power.

Purpose and Autonomy on their own won't be enough if our politicians don't have true Mastery over their roles. Here the evidence is growing that our current parliamentary systems simply aren't up to the task of developing the Mastery that's needed for such critical responsibilities.

Nelson Mandela, justifiably loved by virtually everyone, was nevertheless accused of being more interested in the grand symbolic gesture than the details of government. South Africa's promise, most would agree, irrespective of their political stripes, has not been fully realized. To take just one disturbing example: white South Africans now earn six times as much as black South Africans in average incomes – this is worse than during apartheid.

Mandela, while scrupulously honest himself, was also criticized for not ostracizing the corrupting faction of his party. The jury is still out on new South African President Cyril Ramaphosa, but at least he's admitted some of the ANC's recent shortcomings, something his predecessor Jacob Zuma seemed reluctant to do.

A similar criticism was lobbed at John F Kennedy – that his soaring rhetoric was not always matched by actions that carried the same level of courage and freedom. So Mastery matters as much as Purpose for our leaders and politicians.

On the one hand, politicians need to be expert legislators, knowing exactly how to enact great legislation that achieves the policy objective at hand. And at the same time they need to be adept at going beyond the legislation, and know how to work with their civil service to ensure that laws actually create the intended change on the ground.

As Isabel Hardman points out in her thoughtful book *Why We Get the Wrong Politicians*,[27] British MPs have to collaborate with a much wider range of society members than almost any of the rest of us do these days. Most people tend to socialize, work with and even marry members of the same socio-economic class – one of the factors that's perpetuated the inequality that we've talked about.

This requires two very different skill sets of politicians in countries like the UK – one is the MP's own ability to create the right coterie of advisers around them. The other is knowing how to engage the civil service, and drive and oversee change, while also engaging the energy of a much wider body of people in government. It's a difficult balancing act, but right now there is little in the way of any formal mechanisms for developing Mastery in parliament.

A key framework that leadership expert Ram Charan has created is a leadership pipeline for different levels of managers – and particularly for how 'managers of managers of managers' (which is what prime ministers or presidents usually are) can lead effectively.[28] That has helped large businesses like General Electric be successful. But there is no equivalent for politicians – even though managing a country is as complicated as management gets. We need to invest much more in the management training our politicians get, because it's a critical part of their Mastery. We saw good health policy in many aspects of England's response to Covid-19, for example, but poor management – an abysmal track-and-trace system that, because of the uncertainty it caused, contributed to huge economic damage, and shortages in PPE that put many frontline workers at unnecessary risk. All of these issues could have been a lot less painful if our leaders knew how to manage the sprawling civil services they were in charge of.

We often complain as citizens or voters about the 'Westminster bubble' or the 'Washington bubble' and how our politicians stay on for too long, but the evidence shows that there simply isn't enough time for our politicians to develop a Mastery of their role. Rather than yearn for the days of the 'amateur politician', perhaps as citizens we can help accelerate the move towards politicians who see themselves as true professionals, rather than just professional politicians. That's a key distinction.

Every other profession – from medicine to law – has clear standards, accreditation, membership oaths and values, preservice training and ongoing professional development: all the things that we've seen in our discussion of work that create the smart essentials of Mastery.

But there's almost nothing in place for our politicians, even in our oldest Western democracies such as Britain. Lord Knight confirmed that while there was a 'buddying' system for new members of the House of Lords, it was almost entirely focused on procedural matters – how to find your desk and how to get to the dispatch box.

We need far deeper and more systematic mechanisms in place if we are to resolve this Mastery challenge for our leaders.

We've seen the challenges and tensions that stop us aligning our motivation as citizens with the motivation of our politicians. How as citizens can we respond and fight back?

First and foremost, we need to tie our politicians to a clear goal of defining and articulating a national Purpose – not just one that keeps the faction that elected them happy, but one that unifies us all as citizens.

As we've seen, one of the biggest challenges to this is the division between haves and have-nots.

Fortunately there's a tool which is based on the principles of intrinsic motivation that could help us here, which is gaining support on the left and right of the political spectrum in most countries. And that's the idea of a guaranteed basic income.

Guaranteed basic income refers to the idea of paying every citizen a fixed amount of money each month. Unlike most 'benefits' which are income or 'means' tested, everyone from Bill Gates to a resident of a housing estate would get the same amount. In the US, $1,000 per month per adult – and $500 per child – have been touted as a first potential step, including in Democratic presidential candidate Andrew Yang's 2020 manifesto.

One of the most powerful arguments for a guaranteed income, as Jim Stone argues in *Psychology Today*,[29] is that it avoids the shame and stigma of traditional benefit schemes. In an earlier life I spent almost two years of my life as a management consultant at Booz & Company working for the British Department for Work and Pensions. It was a fascinating 18 months, but what struck me most of all was the huge apparatus needed to deliver all of it – including massive government advertising and outreach campaigns to let people know they were eligible for benefits in the first place. Stigma and shame were incredibly strong barriers to people taking up benefits that they were genuinely entitled to.

Similarly, during my work in education, I found that many children who were eligible for free school meals in the UK never took up the benefit because their parents felt ashamed of it. (I'm so pleased that all English children in their early school years are now entitled to free school lunches automatically, irrespective of their families' income.)

Much of what we have to do in the social sector – for example, my work at STiR on education – is about mopping up the effects of income inequality. Education can be an equalizer but we are asking it to equalize against widening inequality and even outright poverty. Academics like Sendhil Mullainathan at Harvard have shown the devastating psychology of poverty: people living on the margins of poverty often suffer from so much trauma and stress that it makes it close to impossible to make good decisions for the long term, and that includes their choices as parents.

Dan Heath's book *Upstream*[30] talks about how we need to solve problems at their source – the root cause rather than the symptoms. Education would be so much more powerful an equalizer if we could solve some of these upstream issues through income.

Nick Hanauer, a financier and education-reform philanthropist, jolted quite a few heads in the education-reform establishment when he wrote that 'Better Schools Won't Fix America' in *The Atlantic*.[31] His strong conclusion: 'In short, great public schools are the product of a thriving middle class, not the other way around. Pay people enough to afford dignified middle-class lives, and high-quality public schools will follow. But allow economic inequality to grow, and education inequality will inevitably grow with it.' A guaranteed basic income could be an important first step towards combatting this.

The most powerful argument of all for the guaranteed basic income, according to commentators, is that it could literally help millions of us as citizens do what we want to do and potentially enter more risky but ultimately more fulfilling careers – including, for some of us, entering politics.

Would it discourage people from working? In fact, quite the opposite if you believe the intrinsic motivation thinking we've explored throughout this book. A meta-study by Richard Gilbert, Nora A Murphy, Allison Stepka, Mark Barrett and Dianne Worku of 16 guaranteed-income programmes all around the world showed that, in over 90 per cent of cases, people did not work any less after the guaranteed income was introduced.[32]

Not only is the idea being hotly debated in rich countries, it's heating up in emerging countries too. India's former chief economic adviser, Arvind Subramanian, made the case for doing this as early as 2008, as an alternative to the expensive subsidies programme that plagued national budgets for years.[33] While subsidies on basics like wheat and gas have contributed to poverty rates halving over the coming years, he found that widespread corruption and fraud were endemic at the same time.

No country has yet implemented a guaranteed basic income – not even a rich country. Yet the Indian state of Sikkim has committed to introducing one by 2022. (It's important to note that Sikkim has a population of just over half a million people – a drop in the proverbial ocean by Indian standards.) In the throes of the Covid-19 crisis many countries have come much closer, at least as a temporary measure. Spain launched a monthly basic-income scheme for the most vulnerable and has indicated that it wants to make it a permanent feature once the post-Covid recovery is over.[34] During the first and second Covid-19 lockdowns the British government paid up to 80 per cent of the salaries of many workers through its furlough scheme; payments were also made to many self-employed workers. And even in a Trumpist free-market America, a short-term bill to give every American $1,000 monthly during Covid inched (painfully and far too slowly) across both Houses and was finally passed.

Should receiving a guaranteed income be 'conditional' on good societal behaviour? There is always the fear that people could spend the windfall on alcohol or tobacco – but this is largely unfounded, according to a World Bank analysis.[35] However, some reframing of what is expected of citizens – such as parents needing to prioritize the funds to support the health and education of their children – can still prove helpful when launching these programmes, according to a review of evidence conducted by the respected Overseas Development Institute.[36]

But can we afford it? Economists like Karl Widerquist argue that if you allow for the fact that guaranteed income will be taxed in the same way as ordinary income, and if you could use it to consolidate other benefits, the net cost isn't anywhere near as high as we would expect – it's relatively small compared to the costs of furlough and other types of scheme governments have attempted during the response to Covid-19.[37]

The other big effect of this: it helps us steer people towards a world post automation. As futurists like Yuval Noah Harari note, trends in artificial intelligence (AI) will lead to even more inequality because owners of capital will be able to make increasing returns from investment from hiring fewer and fewer people. If many of our citizens feel like they've fallen off the economic ladder now, just wait till trends like AI fully kick in.

The core argument for a guaranteed income must surely be that it allows us to embrace these new trends – and even celebrate and rejoice in them. We all know the stories of companies – think of Kodak or Blockbuster – who tried to hang on to old technologies because they were worried new technologies would 'cannibalize' their existing businesses. Blockbuster could easily have been Netflix, but they were too scared of losing their high-margin DVD business. In the end, both companies were reduced to the proverbial ashes – so much so that there was almost nothing in the end to 'cannibalize'.

The Economist built on this point by arguing that while the massive furlough payments made by the British government were needed and justified, they risked keeping old jobs alive beyond their proverbial sell-by date – leading to distortions like too many sandwich shops remaining in the City of London, when more of us will be working from home. Protecting individual workers themselves instead, they argued, would allow these people to be flexible and respond to what an economy needed.[38]

We have much less to lose from change than we do from trying (ultimately futilely) to prevent it. And if we ensured the hygiene factor of a basic income for all, it could free us all up to do what we love. My wife Aida stopped full-time work when our kids were young so she could spend more time with them. It proved to be a godsend, and helped us at least come closer to being the parents we wanted to be, particularly given my crazy travel schedule at STiR. But she almost didn't go through with it because of concerns over our income. An element of guaranteed income would help people make some of these important life decisions and trade-offs in a better and more balanced way. It would also ensure we all have a stake in economic growth – in turn making it easier for our politicians to develop a national Purpose that unites us all.

But, of course, a guaranteed income alone is not enough. We still need to persuade our politicians to articulate a unifying Purpose for all of us as citizens.

What could such unifying ideas be? An obvious one would be to continue to make progress on reducing inequality, and to ensure that growth in a country is shared. A second might be to create a goal focused on common opportunities and threats, from AI and its associated automation to climate change or global pandemics.

Leadership guru Simon Sinek distinguishes between a finite game and infinite game when defining a 'just cause'[39] (or vision for the future) for an individual or organization. Finite games have a defined end point, but infinite games (which are a far more realistic way of looking at how countries develop) don't.

What can we do as citizens to enable our politicians to balance the competing pressures around Autonomy, stemming from the lack of trust from citizens, that's leading to the excessive levels of scrutiny?

As we've seen, we need to give them leeway and trust. But in return we need to ask our politicians for transparent and reliable information. Timely and reliable information hasn't always been forthcoming during the Covid-19 crisis. For example, the decision to enter England into a full second lockdown might well have been the right one, but given the stakes involved – billions of pounds of economic damage to livelihoods and the mental and physical health of citizens – the quality of forecasting of cases that was used to justify the decision hardly inspired confidence. These forecasts were weeks out of date in their assumptions, not even taking into account the most recent regional tier restrictions, and yet were shared on national television. It was only after a Select Committee grilling that the chief scientific adviser to the government admitted the flaws in the analysis and that he regretted the way they had been shared with the public, particularly when a model with updated assumptions was available.[40] The UK Statistics Authority intervened to point out how trust in official figures could be undermined if they were not 'supported by transparent information being provided in a timely manner'.[41] In return for giving our politicians more trust and leeway, we should ask that they make transparent the often hidden assumptions used by our governments to make decisions.

Often seemingly trivial 'technical' details really matter, particularly for some of our most 'wicked issues', such as climate change. For years we heard forecasts from our leaders about what the costs of climate change would be. They were almost always given using what economists call a 'discount rate', which converts future money into today's money. The problem – which very few citizens and perhaps even very few politicians realized – was that the discount rate being used in most economic models was extremely high. So, the huge costs of climate change for forthcoming generations was being 'discounted' to such an extent that they didn't feel significant to us as citizens today. We had been getting the maths wrong for years.

It was only until Lord Stern conducted the Stern Review in 2006 on behalf of the government[42] that the issues around this discount rate truly surfaced. And by then it was far too late, because almost every British bank and financial institution was using this high-discount rate in their economic models, influencing – in the wrong way – how hundreds of billions of pounds were being spent.

This discount-rate issue also applies to important societal investments we make – or, more often than not, don't make. Economist and Nobel Prize winner James Heckman has shown that investments in early childhood care and education – before a child enters formal schooling – are one of the best society can possibly make.[43] There are strong effects on children in everything from lifetime earnings to what educationalists call 'self-regulation' and even mental health. Yet despite the strength of the evidence, few rich countries have made universal or compulsory early childhood education the norm. Again, it relates to the discount rate: although the benefits are so strong, they are many years out into the future and are therefore reduced heavily in magnitude by the use of the high discount rate. These benefits (not coincidentially) often go well beyond traditional election cycles. They literally end up heavily discounted – and indeed, abandoned. And this is something we simply aren't made aware of as citizens by our politicians.

A third example of how we aren't given transparent information as citizens is in how our national income (or GDP) is calculated. GDP is used by our politicians to justify almost any major decision, from Brexit to climate change. Yet the whole way that GDP is calculated is increasingly meaningless and has little correlation with our wider well-being. To take one example, Aida decided to look after our son Sayan herself in his early years; that contributed nothing to GDP because no one was paid for the service. We sent Eashan, however, to a crèche; that counted towards GDP. Moreover, as we've seen, given that almost all of the GDP growth of the last 20 years has gone to the top 20 per cent in terms of income distribution – and within that, the top 5 per cent, 1 per cent and even 0.2 per cent – it's questionable why we should care about GDP growth at all. It stops being a marker for anything really representative and meaningful for most of us in society.

In addition to giving trust to politicians while asking for transparency, another way to enable our politicians to balance the competing pressures around Autonomy is for us all to become 'active citizens'. Tom Bentley of Demos, whom we met earlier in the chapter, makes a compelling case for allowing us all to engage in many more aspects of how our country operates.[44] For example, as its ultimate beneficiaries, we could all be involved in decisions about which local services, which community initiatives and projects, to prioritize investing in. Bentley calls for much more open 'space' for us to engage as citizens in these different areas. Improvements in technology mean this could even be done from the comfort and convenience of our own homes.

Singapore is normally known for a somewhat paternalistic form of government, where the state is generally assumed to be responsible for everything. They have created the Yellow Ribbon Project which encourages previous prison offenders to reintegrate into society, but in an interesting twist, the reintegration is left to the ingenuity and innovation of local communities, with the most innovative approaches highlighted and celebrated.[45]

Citizen Assemblies are another powerful platform where citizens can work together to solve real problems. They have been tried with particular fervour in France and Scotland, but have been less enthusiastically received elsewhere in the UK, according to *The Economist*.[46]

Jeff Edmondson founded Strive Together based in the US, which brings together leaders and citizens from different backgrounds – employers, school districts, parents – to look at the current education reality in their cities and jointly develop improvement plans. The model has spread to cities and districts all over the US and is seeing promising improvements in many key education measures.

We've seen how politics is one of the few professions where there are almost no formal or explicit systems for developing Mastery, from induction and training to ongoing professional development.

When these systems of Mastery are tacit and untransparent, we create a system of insiders, closed connections and patronage. 'Acceptable faces' are encouraged on party lists – people who don't pose serious danger of rocking the proverbial boat. This limits the range and diversity of people who feel comfortable entering politics. The brash and confrontational culture of politics that persists even today in countries like the UK favours what was learned 'on the playing fields of Eton', as more than one politician has jibed in the debating chamber.

Baroness Morgan talked to me about how proactive efforts were made in the past around the selection of MPs, particularly to target women and minorities, but little of this support continues after selection is completed. Assistant editor of *The Spectator* Isabel Hardman argues that, even in selection, rules that require candidates to take six weeks unpaid leave from their current job to run a campaign – with no certainty of a parliamentary seat at the end – still discourage women and candidates from less advantaged backgrounds from putting their hat in the ring.[47] When it's compounded by the complete absence of formal mechanisms to develop Mastery, this reduces diversity of our political leaders even further.

Relatively small changes can make huge differences in how our leaders can develop Mastery. One of the ideas Hardman poses is that it's hard to learn about how effective your policies are when there is almost no feedback provided afterwards. You never see what happened later. What about 'public payback' where politicians are asked to look at what happened to the country years after a bill was introduced (even if a policy was introduced by their predecessor)? It's a bit like lesson study for teachers or an annual review for a business. Additional measures to ensure that committee time is more productive, and to give MPs more direct oversight over bills, could help dramatically, she argues.

Harvard Kennedy School in the US and the Lal Bahadur Shastri National Academy of Administration in Mussoorie, India, promote Mastery in government. And in recent years new schools like the Blavatnik School of Government in Oxford and the Lee Kuan Yew School of Public Policy in Singapore have also emerged. Almost all focus on civil servants, rather than on politicians themselves.

Jamie Cooper, founder of Big Win Philanthropy, provides an interesting exception. She invites promising new African ministers across countries and domains to the Harvard Ministerial Leadership Programme at the Kennedy School. This provides a platform and peer learning across countries. The programme targets ministers early in their careers, when their motivation and ideas are most formative. Irrespective of how long ministers stay in their roles, it's a worthwhile investment relative to its cost both for the minister and for his or her country.

We also need to invest in Mastery as citizens ourselves. The pressures on our school systems to narrow curriculums and 'teach to the test' have decimated the opportunities to provide proper civics education in our schools. iCivics is a pioneering US-based organization founded by celebrated former justice Sandra Day O'Connor. It makes civics education engaging, relevant and fun for schoolchildren across the US – and has even been shown to boost literacy. Citizenship education, when done well like this, can help forge national Purpose in an authentic and thoughtful way.

We also need to be comfortable dealing with uncomfortable topics as citizens, if we are going to learn how to discuss what a national Purpose really means for us all – and that needs to begin in our schools. Writer and broadcaster Afua Hirsch, one of the most insightful commentators on race in modern Britain, points out the irony of our history curriculum leaving a yawning gap between the Tudors and the First World War. All of the inconvenient developments in between – the hotly contested role of the British Empire and the global slave trade – are largely absent from what we discuss in our schools.

This doesn't create the 'muscle' we need as citizens to learn how to discuss and explore the 'wicked' problems that are in front of us today. We need to be open to difficult and sometimes uncomfortable discussions with our fellow citizens, as well as with our leaders. It requires learning to make our own views clear while also being open to listen (with curiosity and respect) to others with very different views. It requires trust in our fellow citizens (as in our politicians) that we all want the best for our country. Most of all it requires the end of the cancerous 'cancel' culture that stops us all feeling able to enter into genuine dialogue. Echoing what we found in the relationships chapter, if we don't feel safe in our relationships with our fellow citizens, how can we play an active role in shaping our countries, and in encouraging our politicians to create that unifying national Purpose for us all?

It's challenging but not impossible. We need to insist on deep and genuine Mastery among our politicians and we need to role-model that by developing genuine Mastery as citizens.

Politics is one of the hardest professions. We need to hold our politicians to account for ensuring a sense of national Purpose but give them more leeway to find compromise on how they achieve it. We need to respect their Autonomy – on the condition that our Autonomy as citizens is respected back. We should insist on them developing true Mastery in their roles: a few hundred elected officials, one leader and a few cabinet ministers have such a disproportionate influence on our lives. And it will be a growing influence given the scale of the 'wicked' problems in front of us, as current events around the pandemic, climate change, inequality and sovereignty and identity have all shown.

There's an interesting parallel with the relationship between our teachers and our schools. As we saw, trying as parents to second-guess our teachers and schools is unlikely to be effective. But equally as parents we need to create the right balance between avoiding helicopter parenting while still actively engaging with our children to ensure they are truly motivated in life. There's a similar dynamic in our roles as citizens.

Most of all, this means trying to abandon the climate of distrust. The more we distrust our leaders and our fellow citizens, the more we tie our leaders in knots or constantly keep second-guessing them, the more they simply stop leading – and start pandering to factions and interest groups, just as Alexander Hamilton predicted.

If we can partner with our political leaders on the path to defining a shared Purpose, we stand a much greater chance of making that dream of unity a concrete reality.

'Inaction breeds doubt and fear. Action breeds confidence and courage. If you want to conquer fear, do not sit home and think about it. Go out and get busy.'

Dale Carnegie[1]

7

An Intrinsic Life: From Resignation to Revolution

Wuhan is the epicentre of the Chinese automotive industry – the source of many of the cars you and I drive every day. But by early 2020 it became the epicentre of something altogether different.

Wuhan Central Hospital is a nondescript, unexceptional hospital – of the type that can be found in many of China's mid-sized cities. ('Mid-sized' is of course relative in China; Wuhan, the largest city in Hubei province, has a population of over 11 million people). But in 2020 the hospital became the site of an extraordinary drama, and no small amount of bravery.

On 16 December 2019, a patient – who worked at a wildlife market – was admitted with an infection in both lungs that was proving resistant to anti-flu medicines. On 27 December, Wuhan city health officials were informed about a new virus. On 30 December Ai Feng, a hospital director, posted this information on WeChat. As did physician and ophthalmologist Li Wenliang, who sent a message to fellow doctors, warning them to wear protective clothing to defend against an infection that he thought had close similarities to SARS.

Four days later Dr Li was summoned before the Public Security Bureau and told to sign a letter where he was accused of 'making false comments' and of having 'severely disturbed the social order', according to the BBC.[2]

By 10 January Dr Li had started to show telltale symptoms – particularly coughing, which then turned into a fever. He was diagnosed with the coronavirus on 30 January.

On 7 February Dr Li died.

This wasn't the only example where doctors' and experts' honest medical views were suppressed. On 1 January an official at the Hubei Provincial Health Commission ordered nearby labs – which had already determined that the virus had striking similarities to SARS – to stop testing new samples and destroy existing ones. On 2 January, Chinese researchers had been able to exactly map the coronavirus genome – but it took a whole week for it to go public.

Similarly, while the Chinese government had informed the World Health Organization (WHO) on 30 December of an 'unknown virus', as late as 14 January the WHO was still announcing that 'the Chinese authorities had seen no clear evidence of human-to-human transmission of the novel coronavirus'.

On 15 January a passenger with the coronavirus left Wuhan for the US. Between 11 and 17 January, during an important regional health-focused summit of the Chinese Communist Party, Wuhan health authorities insisted there were no new cases of the virus.

With all this in the background, on 18 January tens of thousands of families gathered for potluck at the annual Wuhan New Year banquet. It was only on 21 January that the Chinese Communist Party's *People's Daily* first mentioned the coronavirus to the Chinese public – the same day that the US also announced its first ever domestic case.

By 21 January the Chinese government had undertaken a rapid volte-face in its official policy, announcing that 'anyone who deliberately delays and hides the reporting of cases out of his or her own self-interest will be nailed on the pillar of shame for eternity'.[3]

To give fair credit to the government, since 21 January the response to the crisis has been decisive and rapid – with Wuhan, and along with it virtually all of China, rapidly going into full lockdown. And the late Dr Li received a rare public apology from the Communist Party, as well as death-in-service compensation for his family. Dr Li has become a (deserving) national hero, perhaps even a martyr. But only after a social-media storm that shook China to its core.

Dr Shengjie Lai of Southampton University has been developing some of the world's most sophisticated epidemiological models of how the coronavirus has been spreading. The first thing his modelling tells us is that the strong lockdown measures the Chinese government eventually introduced were extremely effective: compared to the 115,000 actual coronavirus cases that had been recorded by the end of February 2020, the equivalent number without such measures would have been close to 7 million – a difference of almost 70-fold. So there is a lot for the Chinese national government to rightly feel proud of.

But Dr Lai's modelling also projects that if the early professional judgements of Dr Li and his seven other colleagues had not been overridden, and if the coronavirus had been publicly acknowledged three weeks earlier, Chinese coronavirus cases would have been 95 per cent lower than they were by the end of February. You heard me right – that's *95 per cent*. Even if the virus had been admitted to just two weeks earlier, it would have been 86 per cent less. And although Dr Lai's mathematical models focus on China, it's highly likely that the global infection rates would have also followed a sharp reduction.

It's hard not to feel a deep sense of anger at the events that have conspired against the world. An anger, it should be stressed, not at Wuhan or China specifically, but at how the professional Autonomy and judgement of caring, sincere frontline professionals were undermined. As we saw in our discussion around work, this has been such a strong feature of our world's response over these past months. Dr Li is just the tragic tip of the iceberg.

It was remarkable how, at the start of the crisis, the relatively relaxed attitude of UK chief medical adviser Professor Chris Whitty differed from the perceptions of many of the frontline NHS workers I had interviewed for the book, who could already see the upcoming signs of strain on hospital beds. And even more disconcerting to receive furious bursts of WhatsApp messages from my fully locked-down friends in China, who thought still requiring English children to attend school 'crazy' and 'irresponsible'. I remember helping Eashan and Sayan put on their school uniform on those final days before the full UK lockdown with a deep unease and a heavy heart – both for the boys and for the dedicated teachers in their school.

The Covid-19 pandemic awoke in many of us a profound sense of reflection about the world we really want to see – and made many of us reflect more deeply about our lives.

In this final chapter I want to talk about how we can make the transition to a more intrinsic life and world. There are, at the core, four principles that can help us move in that direction. And they apply equally whether in the context of us as individuals, our institutions or our societies at large.

From the events in Wuhan – and then the global response that followed – we can probably infer the **first principle**: we should start by *calculating the costs of inaction*. It may be tempting for the wider world to think of intrinsic motivation, and reigniting our inner drive, as nice, positive but ultimately fluffy things. But it's an incredibly foolish – and dangerous, even fatal – way to think.

The events of Wuhan show us that the cost of inaction in intrinsic motivation can be deeply damaging. For our lives. For our economy. Literally for our way of life and being.

Almost all the untold damage this terrible pandemic has done could have been lessened if the Autonomy of Dr Li and his seven brave colleagues had been respected. A key learning for us all is that, if there is ever doubt, we should respect professional Autonomy and err on the side of caution.

The events of those days in Wuhan – which have been painstakingly gleaned from multiple sources by the innovative news website Axios[4] – should be the ultimate reminder of this first key principle. Namely, that we can often calculate the costs of inaction of intrinsic motivation and they can be staggeringly large in almost every sense.

In other sectors, too, we've been seeing first-hand the costs of inaction much more broadly – of not addressing the enormous issues around intrinsic motivation. In the non-profit sector, heads of foundations have been sharing with me what the difficult economic environment has meant for many non-profit leaders and social entrepreneurs – and how it's destroying their sense of Purpose. Referring to how many foundations were not willing to give the charitable organizations they fund the space and flexibility to adjust to these very challenging times, one foundation CEO told me, 'I spoke to three of my grantees this week, and all have been in tears, including the men, due to how unreasonably the foundations who support them are behaving...Before,' she added, it was easy to 'tolerate this kind of poor behaviour among our peers. Now we need to engage in serious conversations with them.'

I have started engaging with the What Works Centre for Homelessness. In my discussions I've found that the role of the outreach officer – or homeless support officer, as some local authorities call them – has seen its Purpose, Autonomy and Mastery drained out of it. Instead, the tyranny of metrics has forced these deeply important workers to apply 'kind' approaches to deeply 'wicked' problems. The pressures of targets have forced them to focus only on the short-term metric of getting people off the street – even though the short-term approaches they employ mean that many homeless people end up back on the street a few weeks later. Overall, we've seen that ignoring the fundamentals of intrinsic motivation can exert a huge cost on us as individuals, on our institutions and on our societies.

*

The **second principle** is to *see the intrinsic opportunity*. Relatively small ways to address intrinsic issues can make a big difference for us all.

David Lubell is the committed and endearing founder of two sister non-profit organizations, Welcoming America and now Welcoming International. Welcoming America was established because he realized how negatively the issue of immigration could play out in local US communities and the potential tinderbox that could explode. As a (proud) immigrant to the UK myself, I have always admired David's approach and resolve, and have been following his work closely over the years.

'There's a big difference between immigration rising from 100,000 to 110,000 in a region in Europe, say, to it recently rising to well over 300,000 in the same region. This is causing stress,' he tells me. It's these changes that can be most explosive – and literally so in the case of many American cities.

David has developed practical tools and approaches that make towns, cities and communities more welcoming – and more open, resilient and tolerant. These range from 'high-touch' (time-intensive) door-to-door community discussions and engagement, to local communication campaigns that paint an alternative reality to the angry messaging from the growing far-right campaigners in East German cities like Dresden. For example, Welcoming America curates and promotes local events that allow immigrants and local residents to connect and spend time together. It also highlights positive stories of the contribution immigrants are making to their communities.

Perhaps fittingly, David has relocated from Boston to Berlin, as he believes the epicentre of the immigration issue has now decisively moved to Europe. Two hundred communities within and outside the US – and increasingly internationally – are now part of the Welcoming America and Welcoming International networks.

David's work is really about rebuilding social capital in local communities. He backs up what Robert Putnam told us in his book *Bowling Alone*, that communities are being 'balkanized'. He believes the core issue is a global loss of empathy in local communities – people are losing the sense of connection and belonging with and understanding of each other. Towns and cities are losing their intrinsic motivation, and what David is doing is reigniting their sense of Autonomy (the sense of being able to chart their own path), Mastery (giving them the skills to compete in the global stage) and Purpose (through his ideas of open, tolerant, flourishing communities).

Although he can't prove a scientific correlation, David perceives a strong link between the level of intrinsic motivation and the social capital a town or city has, which his approach strongly helps to develop, and that town or city's openness to immigrants.

The wonderful news is that Welcoming America can bring an American city into its network for only tens of thousands of dollars per year, and this includes the costs the city needs to bear, such as that of communicating more effectively to its citizens. What a low cost for such an important addition to the social fabric of towns and cities around the world – and for helping to ensure what are the most important aspects of society today: namely openness, empathy and tolerance.

Cynthia Hansen, whom we met in chapter 2, is taking an equally pioneering approach at the Adecco Foundation. Her belief is that diversity in the future is going to be increasingly manifested in terms of cognitive diversity – diversity of thought. It's the ability to get people of genuinely different thinking and skills to work together that really helps teams and organizations mobilize. It's a major step forward towards the vision we've discussed, where all our talent is recognized and nurtured – and she's seen the intrinsic opportunity by convening a disparate group of thought-leaders (of which I've been part) around reimaging talent and diversity in work.

Adina Kalet is an accomplished American physician who had become disillusioned with the state of medical education. 'Today's graduates are no less committed, but medicine has become so corporatized in its approach,' she told me. So she's now taken up an exciting role at the Wisconsin-based Kern Institute for the Transformation of Medical Education. She's brought two philosophers and a sociologist on board to restart this thinking – which could profoundly change how medical schools across the

US approach igniting the motivation of new doctors. Her first task: re-examining the fundamental Purpose of medicine – and medical education in the process.

In sports, David Slemen of Elite Performance Partners has started to work with many leading sports teams – including several English Football Association teams – to make the case for why a 'win at all costs' attitude can be harmful. A more intrinsic approach, focused on deep Mastery rather than competition, is far stronger in the long term. He's been able to articulate to leading clubs why this extrinsic, 'win at all costs' approach is the reason so many otherwise great players 'choke' at key moments of sport. He's created new 'learning networks' – a bit like STiR teacher networks – where the national performance heads of various sports come together regularly to share notes on what can be changed.

In the UK, the National Tuition Service (NTS) has been launched as a partnership between government and philanthropy. As we've seen, private tuition is now a £2 billion industry in the UK – and it is (for obvious reasons) accessed almost entirely by families that are middle class or above. The NTS uses technology and brings together different providers to open up their offerings and bring costs down, with direct funding for the poorest parents to access, helping to offset the 'winner takes all' trends in education we've seen earlier.

Technology can wreak havoc on relationships, from online dating to social-media usage, in a way that makes us less mindful and far more extrinsic, and which contributes to the growing 'relationship inequalities' in our society. But technology, if used smartly, can equally provide an intrinsic opportunity – a way of fighting back. Venture capital fund Spero Ventures is explicitly trying to address the epidemic in loneliness that Vivek Murthy, the US surgeon general, has compellingly highlighted.[5] Spero has invested in Koko, an online network that uses peer communities and AI to allow users to provide support to each other. Users are taught to help each other think more hopefully about the world – and the interactions are supported (but not replaced) with AI to amplify the network. The aim is that users no longer feel isolated and know that many others face similar challenges. Approaches from Koko and other pioneering companies are being used increasingly successfully in areas as sensitive as suicide prevention.[6]

On a personal front, I've seen the intrinsic opportunity in being a more engaged – and hopefully better – parent. Horrific data I saw while writing this book (from Pew Research) showed that the average father in the US spends just 20 minutes of engaged time with his children each day.[7] I've been talking to UK parenting experts like Dr Kathy Weston about how we can reignite and reimagine fatherhood. But more importantly, I've been trying to walk my own talk. Eashan and I now play cricket together in our backyard most mornings (with an increasing array of balls lost in neighbours' gardens), to match his growing passion for the sport; Sayan and I listen to music together. The Covid-19 lockdown forced me to do something I'd never been able to do previously: stay in one place. Ironically, it took me to a place I wouldn't have reached otherwise – and it was a much-needed place: home.

Intrinsic opportunities do come along – and when you see them, seize them, because they may be a lot more feasible, and less expensive, than you think.

The **third principle** is to *manage against the extrinsic downside*.

A theme we've seen through the book is that taking a more intrinsic direction has potential risks and downsides. Rather than try to bury our heads in the sand about these risks, it's much better to identify them proactively and upfront and then actively manage against them.

Take our discussion around parenting and the need to keep our children focused on the love of an activity itself, rather than obsess about competition.

I could not have been more delighted to see a recent initiative by the Lawn Tennis Association (LTA). The LTA wrote to parents of the orange-level players (who are usually between nine and eleven years old) to announce a loosening of competition requirements. The previous points system had created a relentless talent treadmill, as we saw in chapter 5, and was being fuelled by hyper-anxious parents.

So, when they announced the new rules it was, to me, a surprising but very welcome move.

There was a problem, however. And that was that the LTA had not properly thought through how it could communicate this direction clearly to parents of young tennis players, and what concerns they would need to overcome.

The move caused an uproar among many parents. I kid you not, within minutes of the announcement being shared with our regional tennis centre, my tennis parents' WhatsApp group was flooded with dozens of messages from anxious users.

'"Bobby" was really chasing that one,' one message said. 'How is he going to deal with this?'

'How will my child be motivated to keep playing?' another asked.

The problem was that the LTA hadn't explained how their new rules fitted in the bigger picture. When I went on to the LTA website, the picture that emerged was of a sports association that was genuinely trying to prioritize kids playing as much as possible and *enjoying it*. The LTA recognized rightly that the previous competition regime had been undermining this. They had made the small step of change, but hadn't signalled the broader intrinsic direction they wanted to go in – and this only fuelled further the already keen anxieties of parents.

How does this principle apply to another area of life we've discussed, our key relationships?

We've talked a lot in this book about the benefits of keeping a relationship together, but what if a relationship – and particularly a marriage – isn't working? We need to help couples manage these contexts, too. Lucy Williamson is a divorce coach, based in Cambridge, who helps her clients manage the difficult process – an interesting parallel to Pradeepa's fertility coaching. A key principle, Lucy tells me, is around reducing 'divorce hangover' and really ensuring that both parties take genuine ownership for their actions, which involves helping them understand the emotional costs of staying together for largely extrinsic reasons. She provides coaching support to them while going through the difficult divorce process, once a relationship is destined for break-up.

When risks and downsides are managed upfront, it can clear the path for change. In education, another area we've explored deeply in the book, England has launched a non-government Education Commission of its own, with leadership from the Royal Society. Their thoughtful report[e] had many excellent recommendations for the quandaries that schools across the country are facing everywhere. They've provided a roadmap for how schools can nurture much more broadly the lifelong love of learning among children, while also balancing the need for academic rigour. Andreas Schleicher from the OECD, the inventor of the PISA tests that compare education worldwide, summarized the issue as follows: 'Whatever tasks machines may be taking over from humans at work, the demands on our knowledge and skills to contribute meaningfully to social and civic life will keep rising.'

Well said. If we manage against the extrinsic downside, we can all keep rising.

How do we keep moving forward in an intrinsic direction that is truly sustainable? Our **fourth principle,** *finding and taking small steps towards this direction*, is key. Taken incrementally, small steps can build motivation and momentum and put us on a self-reinforcing path.

The Family Independence Initiative in the US is an exciting model to put struggling lower-income families on precisely such a path. It provides cash transfers in a way that builds the Purpose, Autonomy and Mastery of the whole family – all with a view to helping them get back on the housing and economic ladders. The journeys a family undertakes are all designed in small, incremental steps. The critical act is for the family to come together to set their own goals. They then decide a small step to focus on, whether it's a decision around childcare or savings or education tuition.

When small, positive, self-reinforcing steps do occur, they open up a lot of promise for the future. It's true that some philanthropic foundations have not stepped up to the plate during the Covid-19 pandemic. But many others have made important first steps. Since Covid-19, as founder and president of the Chorus Foundation

Farhad Ebrahimi notes in an article in *Inside Philanthropy*,[9] many have been at pains to tell grantees that they can 'unrestrict' their funding to be able to cope flexibly with the crisis, and they have offered additional support, if needed, to weather the storm. Ebrahimi echoes social activist and philosopher Grace Lee Boggs' point that: 'every crisis, actual or impending, needs to be viewed as an opportunity to bring about profound changes in our society'.[10]

I truly hope that this will be an important first step for foundations to move in a direction that fundamentally sees their role as talent nurturers of the organizations they support, as we saw in chapter 3.

The early days of BUILD initiative within the Ford Foundation, which puts non-profits at the centre of the philanthropic process, provides another lesson on the importance of those small but steady steps.

Speaking to Kathy Reich and Victoria Dunning, who were instrumental in driving BUILD, is a lesson in humility. 'I'm not a particularly visionary person,' Kathy told me, 'but I see my work as helping visionary people to achieve their dreams.' There was no predetermined blueprint they could follow, so they started in small steps, gradually bringing on an initial set of grantees, documenting what they were learning, trying out new approaches in response and quickly learning and experimenting.

This method built trust among grantees and also within the foundation's leadership itself. After positive results from the first round, the board has approved a further billion dollars to flow into its second. And an explicit objective of this upcoming second round of funding is to persuade other foundations to follow suit – which would be a huge snowball in dismantling some of the challenges we've seen around talent-nurturing in philanthropy. But it was the small, reinforcing – and highly experimental – steps at the start of BUILD's journey that led each small early snowflake to build – pun intended – into a $2 billion snowball.

In essence, here are the principles for transitioning to a more intrinsic life:

1. Assess the costs of inaction – the impact of not addressing the intrinsic problem at hand.

2. See the intrinsic opportunity, because it may be more feasible than you think.

3. Manage the extrinsic downside, because otherwise you'll hamper progress. This includes articulating the big intrinsic direction.

4. Make small, self-reinforcing steps towards it.

While we've seen these four principles apply to organizations and societies, they apply equally to us as individuals. Let's take examples from a couple of domains – work and relationships.

We've seen in many of the stories in this book how high the costs of inaction can be in personal terms. Management writer Jo Owen tells me about his time flitting between fancy hotels as an Accenture partner, managing the egos of high-flying but high-maintenance consultants, and feeling a sense of emptiness and futility. Chef Asma Khan told me about the overwhelming sense of loneliness that enveloped her while her husband Mushtaq disappeared into the academic bubble of Cambridge life – and how the move to London, and the ability to connect with people with a similar passion, reignited her life and gave her a new direction in starting Darjeeling Express.

Too often, we know this personal cost and feel it deeply and acutely – but we actually suppress in ourselves the sense of pain it brings. Avery Roth is a New York-based leadership coach who helps her clients manage through difficult personal transitions. She tells me that, for many of her clients, it's about letting the 'inner child' within them speak and feel the right to have a voice again. It's that which enables them to acknowledge the pain that their current way of life imposes.

Seeing the intrinsic opportunity is also critical – simply recognizing it when it hits us in the face. Despairing of his current working identity while travelling around the US, by complete chance Jo Owen heard Wendy Kopp – the founder of Teach For America – speak on national radio. Suddenly he found his Eureka moment. The simple act of picking up the phone and calling her – which he could have told himself was crazy – led him to go on to co-found the British equivalent, Teach First, which has become the largest recruiter of university graduates in the UK. That move also gave him the momentum to write his first leadership book, and then carve a portfolio career spanning his involvement with several non-profits, including STiR. The experience and reputation he's gained from his writing and non-profit work have been mutually reinforcing. The rest, as they say, is history.

Melissa Shusterman is a state representative in Pennsylvania, elected in 2018. She told me that seeing the intrinsic opportunity came from realizing how few existing elected officials in her state put ordinary citizens like her 'top of mind'. 'They just weren't looking out for us,' she told me. And it was particularly true, she believed, if you were a woman. Melissa dug into voting records and expenses and could see the lack of progress; the whole political system in her state reeked of complacency. She could also sense – perhaps even smell – the opportunity, and was nurtured by a group helping female politicians to find their unique voice and develop strong grassroots campaigns. Despite many telling her it was a futile task, she ran for office, got elected – and has even been made the state's deputy chief whip.

Even when you see the opportunity, it can feel scary. Avery Roth talked to me about how she coaches her clients to 'take a deep breath and suspend disbelief'. You can be rational all the way through to the final point of a decision. But at that point, she says, you have to trust yourself and, even if you are scared, jump anyway.

Managing the extrinsic downside is equally important in personal transitions. When I spoke to London-based Samantha Clarke, she told me that she thought carefully about the transition from working in advertising to working as a happiness consultant for companies – and what it would mean for her financially and in terms of her self-identity. It would mean leaving a well-paid and conventionally respected job. She told me honestly about the difficult conversation she had to have with her bemused immigrant parents, and the guilt she felt – because they had sacrificed to give her the education and opportunities to take up that well-paid and well-respected job in the first place. But it's clear that, having had the conversation, Samantha is much more at peace with herself and with her new working identity. And she literally pays her intrinsic dues back by coaching start-up CEOs across London's hottest companies – including at Second Home – on how to build happier, more intrinsic workplaces.

Keeping a balance is important when you make these transitions. Francois Coumau is a former eBay colleague of mine, who – like Samantha – traded in a high-powered corporate career to coach and mentor start-up CEOs, but this time on managing growth. He loves his new job but in order to 'keep his toes' in the world of big business, he's taken board seats on a couple of mid-sized listed companies.

Amy Matthews, a Washington DC-based coach, believes the issue of managing the extrinsic downside when it comes to working identity is even more pronounced for women and minorities. For example, in my years leading STiR, I felt awkward going into a gathering of business-school classmates who all worked for businesses like McKinsey or Goldman Sachs. The tag of 'social entrepreneur' made me feel more like a 'weed' that didn't fit in compared to a 'plant' that stood out. I learned to gain confidence in my own working identity and realized that actually many classmates admired me for taking a different path.

The last principle – of committing to a bigger, broader direction by taking small, self-reinforcing steps – is critically important in personal transitions. It means everything doesn't have to be done in one go, and often one aspect of life – work or parenting, for example – can take the lead.

A good example is in our personal finances when we make a big life or work change. There is no point, Samantha Clarke stresses to me, in embarking on a new direction and not having enough financial firepower to see it all the way through. Her recommendation is to start gradually with part-time assignments that allow you to build confidence and financial stability for when you want to make the big move.

Her point is backed by rigorous research conducted by former INSEAD professor Herminia Ibarra, who has looked at how people have made successful career changes.[11] In almost all cases, she finds, they started with small steps, finding ways to 'try out' new career directions while continuing their old ones until they were sure their proverbial new clothes fitted. And, as Samantha suggests, until they had the financial ability to make the transition. But – and this is the key point – they didn't shy away from taking the small steps in the first place, and they embraced the excitement and discovery in what they saw.

Claire Harbour is a coach also helping clients through major transitions, particularly in the area of work. She believes that when people go too fast and make big jumps too early, it can backfire. She told me a story about a promising young manager who was doing incredibly well at his automotive company. So much so that he was seconded to the company's operations in (of all places) Wuhan, though well before anyone had heard of anything like Covid-19.

It was an incredible stimulus: it opened his mind to new cultures, ways of working and living – you name it. But, like a dish that's so fiery that it destroys your tastebuds for the rest of the meal, the exposure and responsibility he was given so early in his career almost made it hard to adjust back to normal life when he returned to the company's headquarters. Now he's stayed in the same role for years and seems to crave comfort and stability above all. Claire wonders if the root cause was overexposure far too early in his working life, and whether his career progression could have been structured by his employer into smaller, more incremental steps.

Aida's career has also been progressing through a series of small steps. Her original goal was to be an accountant – by implicit pressure rather than choice, because her dad worked in finance – but I don't think it was ever something she was passionate about. Through a chance encounter with a friend's friend (a bit like how we met), she became interested in mindfulness and started training at the London Buddhist Centre. In turn, that developed a passion for yoga. And then she enrolled on the foundation course of humanistic counselling, and completed the first year of an undergraduate degree part time.

Now, she's just been accepted at the Bowlby Centre for a four-year professional training degree to become a psychotherapist. That's the same centre that developed attachment theory, which we looked at in the context of both relationships and parenting.

Aida is happier and more passionate in what she is doing, and I feel happy to have been able to support her to make this transition. (She's been generous in supporting my own transition, too.) It's an immense jump – from accountant to psychotherapist – particularly in the French education system where she did her accountacy training and where the expectation is you'll pursue the same career all your life. But these small steps collectively add up to many miles.

*

I am lucky to wake up each morning with a clear sense of Purpose, and I hope that this book has encouraged you to find Purpose in your work. In some cases that will mean changing what you do, but more often I hope that by reigniting, reframing and recrafting your existing work it will give you true intrinsic motivation: the motivation of knowing your work deeply helps and serves others.

I hope that you will find a talent nurturer (or many nurturers!) in your life who can unlock your unique talents in whatever areas are most important for you. When you find a nurturer, help them get you to a place you wouldn't have reached otherwise – and make sure they keep you deeply in love with the activity itself. If you possibly can, be a nurturer yourself to someone in an area that you really care about. If you do, you'll be part of that broader push towards a world that nurtures all.

In creating a more intrinsic way of living, I hope you'll find – or rediscover – a life partner who can keep you feeling safe as they hold you tight at the end of a challenging day.

If you are a parent, I hope you'll be able to help your children see the wood for the trees, in terms of what's really important in a good childhood – and help bring kind, caring human beings into the world who can master the zig-zag of life.

I hope when someone utters some defunct assumption about what motivates us – something like 'money makes the world go around' – you'll call them out.

And, finally, through your votes and influence, I hope you'll push your country's leaders to find their Purpose again – so that they can create a national Purpose.

I hope, most of all, that you'll remember that we tend to regret what we don't do, much more than what we do. We can manage against the downsides and risks of action.

When Rajesh Krishnamoorthy saw the floods ravage his beautiful home state of Kerala, it made him question his priorities and the fast-paced corporate life he lived in Mumbai. The first thing it made him do was return to Kerala and get directly involved in the flood relief efforts.

But the second thing he did, and which resonated even more with me, was look backwards – and with gratitude. Kerala's state of emergency made him realize the importance of his teachers. And so – on a motorbike journey with six of his former classmates – he went on a teacher-appreciation tour all across the state, tracking down all his former teachers. He literally went from village to village, house to house, and had lunch or breakfast or dinner with each of them. As he showed me the pictures – of paper-crisp *apams*, stews and succulent fish *moilees,* all enjoyed and devoured together with his somewhat disbelieving former teachers – it made my stomach rumble as much as it did my eyes water.

Rajesh now sees his Purpose as building a better India – he's currently playing a mentoring and nurturing role to many of the country's most promising non-profit organizations, including STiR. It's been a winding journey, taken in small steps, and he's had to manage it carefully to balance it with the financial needs of his family. But it all started with this simple act of talking to his teachers. Through listening deeply to them, he could hear directly the cost of inaction – the effect his inaction would have on hundreds of millions of his fellow citizens. That's what motivated him to act.

Making the transition to an intrinsic life is not easy, whether as an individual, an institution or a society. But if we follow the four principles – calculate the cost of inaction, see the opportunity, manage the extrinsic downside and take small but self-reinforcing steps – it is possible. And it's probably the most fulfilling and rewarding thing we will do in our lives.

We are all parents in this world, either literally or metaphorically. And our first priority must surely be to leave this earth, as Gaurav Singh (the inspirational founder behind the 321 Education Foundation) would say, a little better than we found it – by reigniting our inner drive as workers, parents, friends, coaches, spouses and citizens.

What better time to rethink what's truly important to us?

What better time, in other words, to unleash the intrinsic revolution that we all desperately need and deserve?

Acknowledgements

Intrinsic would never have been written without the support and generosity of so many friends and colleagues. I'm only able to mention a small number here, but all of you who have been on this incredible journey with me know who you are.

The idea of even writing a book in the first place was triggered by early encouragement from Sema Sgaier and Daniel Franklin.

I'm eternally grateful for the chance meeting with my wonderful agent Rachel Mills, who helped me to develop the idea from just a half-page concept. And – with the support of Alexandra Cliff and other colleagues at Rachel Mills Literary – guided me through my writing journey and the publishing partnerships that were formed in the UK and elsewhere in the world.

Claudia Connal and the team at Octopus Publishing – including Sybella Stephens, Charlotte Cole, Megan Brown and Charlotte Sanders – believed in the premise of the book from the start, and have been incredible collaborators and nurturers. They've been patient and encouraging through the many writing fits and starts, helping this book become the best version of itself it could be.

I would never have been exposed to the field of intrinsic motivation had it not been for my experience founding STiR Education. To that end, I'm eternally grateful to everyone who came on board with me, including our leadership team, colleagues, board, supporters and partners. Most of all I'm grateful for their collective patience as I navigated the most challenging professional adventure of my life. And I want to pay particular thanks to Jo Owen, James Townsend, Nithya Gurukumar, Rein Terwindt, Anamika Srivastava, John McIntosh, Tomos Davies and Jenny Wilmott – who had to endure especially long periods of their professional lives with me! I hope they enjoyed it as much as I did.

I'm also deeply grateful to the partners and advisory council who have helped me get Intrinsic Labs off the ground. It's been a wonderful way to turn the ideas from the book into a concrete reality and see the momentum that's already been created. I'm also grateful to Michaela Tranfield for her stellar support in the Lab's first year. And to Adi Raj, Mike Jacob and Lesley Lotto for their help in getting it off the ground.

I've been incredibly fortunate to have had generous advice and support from other authors and mentors in the publishing industry, including Malcolm Gladwell, Nir Eyal and Dan Heath, to name just a few. I'm grateful also to Ashley Brady, Sasha Berson, Rein Terwindt and John McIntosh for their (gentle) feedback on the book's early versions.

Balancing time to write a book while – at one point – leading two organizations, was definitely a story of some sacrifice. It manifested in untold weekends, evenings and early mornings buried at my inspiring desk at Second Home or writing furiously at the back of a plane. I'm fortunate that Aida, Eashan and Sayan – as they always have – gave me that time generously throughout, and were excited rather than begrudging with the risk I took. And for the help my parents provided in looking after the boys during the many 'writing spurts' the process required. I'm lucky to have such an amazing family around me and it kept me going through even the darkest writing days.

The insights from *Intrinsic* are built off the research and practice of many experts, practitioners and thought-leaders all over the world. The greatest pleasure was the time spent talking with them and burying myself in their research. I hope that my attempt to cover a lot of ground in the book does adequate justice to their remarkable work; and, more importantly, encourages readers to engage more fully with their original work in all its richness, through the book's references and citations. I owe an especially deep debt of gratitude to Richard Ryan and the academic research movement he has co-catalysed around intrinsic motivation.

I'm also grateful to the many people I interviewed, from all corners of the world, who shared their hopes and fears with me so candidly. It simply wouldn't have been the book it is without the perspectives you shared.

Finally, I'd like to thank every reader who engages with *Intrinsic*. Your time is precious; I hope the book is both a source of inspiration and enjoyment, and a useful companion for your own journey ahead.

References

All of the references in each chapter have been detailed to encourage further reading. You can visit intrinsic-labs.com to stay up to date on the latest motivation thinking through newsletters, podcasts and online courses.

1. An Intrinsic Journey

1. As quoted in Clemmer, Jim. *The Leader's Digest: Timeless Principles for Team and Organization Success* (TCG Press, 2003), p84.

2. 'A Billion Brains', *The Economist*, 29 September 2012, https://www.economist.com/special-report/2012/09/29/a-billion-brains (Accessed 11 March 2021).

3. Many thanks to Tim Klein of Boston College for providing this diesel and electric metaphor.

4. Maslow, A H. 1943. 'A Theory of Human Motivation', *Psychological Review*, 50 (4): 370–96.

5. Harlow, H F. 1958. 'The Nature of Love', *American Psychologist* 13 (12): 673–86.

6. Herzberg, Frederick. 'One More Time: How Do You Motivate Employees?', *Harvard Business Review*, January 2003, https://hbr.org/2003/01/one-more-time-how-do-you-motivate-employees (Accessed 11 March 2021).

7. Ryan, Richard M,. and Deci, Edward, L. *Self-Determination Theory: Basic Psychological Needs in Motivation, Development, and Wellness* (Guilford Press, 2018).

8. Pink, Daniel H. *Drive: The Surprising Truth About What Motivates Us* (Riverhead Books, 2009).

9. Dweck, Carol. *Mindset: Changing the Way You Think to Fulfil Your Potential* (Robinson, 6th edn, 2017).

10. Keynes, John Maynard. *The General Theory of Employment, Interest and Money* (Macmillan, 1936).

11. *Education for All: Towards Quality with Equity, India* (National University of Educational Planning and Administration, 2014), https://unesdoc.unesco.org/ark:/48223/pf0000229873?posI nSet=2&queryId=b60ebaad-a215-4783-bb23-e566586961ce (Accessed 11 March 2021).

12. *National Education Policy 2020* (Ministry of Human Resource Development, Government of India, 2020), https://www. education.gov.in/sites/upload_files/mhrd/files/NEP_Final_ English_0.pdf (Accessed 11 March 2021).

13. Harter, Jim. 'Dismal Employee Engagement Is a Sign of Global Mismanagement', https://www.gallup.com/ workplace/231668/dismal-employee-engagement-sign-global-mismanagement.aspx (Accessed 11 March 2021).

14. Gladwell, Malcolm. *Outliers: The Story of Success* (Little, Brown, 2008).

15. 'The Economic Impact of Closing the Racial Wealth Gap', McKinsey & Company, 13 August 2019, https://www. mckinsey.com/industries/public-and-social-sector/our-insights/the-economic-impact-of-closing-the-racial-wealth-gap# (Accessed 11 March 2021).

16. Topping, Alexandra.'"Fear of Failure" Giving UK Children Lowest Happiness Levels in Europe', *Guardian,* 28 August 2020, https://www.theguardian.com/lifeandstyle/2020/ aug/28/fear-of-failure-giving-uk-children-lowest-happiness-levels-in-europe. (Accessed 11 March 2021).

17. Dalai Lama, Tutu, Desmond, and Abrams, Douglas Carlton, *The Book of Joy: Lasting Happiness in a Changing World* (Hutchinson, 2016).

18. Fukuyama, Francis. *The End of History and the Last Man* (Hamish Hamilton, 1992).

2. Intrinsic Work

1. Grant, Adam. 'What Straight-A Students Get Wrong', *New York Times*, 8 December 2018, https://www.nytimes. com/2018/12/08/opinion/college-gpa-career-success.html (Accessed 11 March 2021).

2. Mandavilli, Apoorva. 'H.I.V. Is Reported Cured in a Second Patient, a Milestone in the Global AIDS Epidemic', *New York Times,* 4 March 2019, https://www.nytimes.com/2019/03/04/ health/aids-cure-london-patient.html (Accessed 11 March 2021).

3. Pryce-Jones, Jessica. *Happiness at Work: Maximizing Your Psychological Capital for Success* (Wiley, 2010).

4. West, Michael, Bailey, Suzie, and Williams, Ethan. *The Courage of Compassion: Supporting nurses and midwives to deliver high-quality care* (Kings Fund, 2020), https://www.kingsfund.org. uk/publications/courage-compassion-supporting-nurses-midwives (Accessed 11 March 2021).

5. Christensen, Clayton M, Allworth, James, and Dillon, Karen. *How Will You Measure Your Life?* (HarperCollins Publishers, 2012).

6. Ryan, *Self-Determination Theory*.

7. Shell, Ellen Ruppel. *The Job: Work and Its Future in a Time of Radical Change* (Currency, 2018).

8. Scott, Dylan. 'Kamala Harris's Plan to Dramatically Increase Teacher Salaries, Explained', *Vox*, 26 March 2019, https://www.vox.com/policy-and-politics/2019/3/26/18280734/kamala-harris-2020-election-policies-teachers-salaries (Accessed 11 March 2021).

9. Béteille, Tara and Evans, David K. *Successful Teachers, Successful Students: Recruiting and Supporting Society's Most Crucial Profession* (World Bank Group, 2019), http://documents1.worldbank.org/curated/en/235831548858735497/Successful-Teachers-Successful-Students-Recruiting-and-Supporting-Society-s-Most-Crucial-Profession.pdf (Accessed 11 March 2021).

10. Ryan, *Self-Determination Theory*.

11. Kohn, Alfie. *Punished by Rewards: The Trouble with Gold Stars, Incentive Plans, A's, Praise, and Other Bribes* (Houghton Mifflin, 1993).

12. Bénabou, Roland, and Tirole, Jean. 2006. 'Incentives and Prosocial Behavior', *American Economic Review* 96 (5): 1652–78.

13. Promberger, Marianne and Marteau, Theresa M. 2013. 'When Do Financial Incentives Reduce Intrinsic Motivation? Comparing Behaviors Studied in Psychological and Economic Literatures', *Health Psychol.* 32 (9): 950–7. Erratum in: 2013. *Health Psychol.* 32 (11): 1148.

14. Ryan, *Self-Determination Theory*.

15. Wronski, Laura, and Cohen, John. 'The Next Silicon Valley Exodus—Over 25% of Tech Sector Wants Permanent Work From Home', *CNBC*, 20 May 2020, https://www.cnbc.com/2020/05/19/how-silicon-valley-work-from-home-forever-will-hit-every-worker.html#:~:text=In%20the%20new%20CNBC%7CSurveyMonkey,often%20than%20they%20used%20to (Accessed 11 March 2021).

16. 'More Than 60 Per Cent of the World's Employed Population Are in the Informal Economy', *International Labour Organization*, 30 April 2018, https://www.ilo.org/global/about-the-ilo/newsroom/news/WCMS_627189/lang--en/index.htm#:~:text=employed%20population%20...-,More%20than%2060%20per%20cent%20of%20the%20world's%20employed%20population,work%20and%20decent%20working-%20conditions (Accessed 11 March 2021).

17. O'Grady, Sarah. 'No Desire to Retire, Say Over-50s', *Express*, 15 November 2018, https://www.express.co.uk/news/uk/1045907/retirement-no-desireto-retiresay-over-50s (Accessed 11 March 2021).

18. Savage, Maddy. 'Burnout Is Rising in the Land of Work-Life Balance', *BBC Worklife*, 26 July 2019, https://www.bbc.com/worklife/article/20190719-why-is-burnout-rising-in-the-land-of-work-life-balance (Accessed 11 March 2021).

19. Gratton, Lynda and Scott, Andrew J. *The 100-Year Life: Living and Working in an Age of Longevity* (Bloomsbury Publishing, 2016).

20. Lin, Blossom Yen-Ju. 2013. 'Job Autonomy, Its Predispositions and Its Relation to Work Outcomes in Community Health Centers in Taiwan', *Health Promotion International*, 28 (2): 166–77.

21. Parsons, Sharon K, et al. 2003. 'Determinants of Satisfaction and Turnover Among Nursing Assistants. The Results of a Statewide Survey', *Journal of Gerontological Nursing*, 29 (3): 51–8.

22. Gladwell, Malcolm. *The Tipping Point: How Little Things Can Make a Big Difference* (Little, Brown, 2000).

23. Levitt, Steven D, and Dubner, Stephen J. *Freakonomics: A Rogue Economist Explores the Hidden Side of Everything* (Allen Lane, 2005).

24. Interview with a west London resident (anonymous), August 2020.

25. Guilfoyle, Simon J. *Intelligent Policing: How Systems Thinking Approaches Eclipse Conventional Management Practice* (Triarchy Press, 2013).

26. Obama, Barack. *Dreams From My Father: A Story of Race and Inheritance* (Canongate Books, 2007).

27. Obama, Barack. *The Audacity of Hope: Thoughts on Reclaiming the American Dream* (Canongate Books, 2008).

28. Martel, Yann. *Life of Pi* (Canongate Books, 2002).

29. Ross, Terence F. 'Is It Ever Okay to Make Teachers Read Scripted Lessons?', *Atlantic,* 10 October 2014, https://www.theatlantic.com/education/archive/2014/10/is-it-okay-to-make-teachers-read-scripted-lessons/381265/ (Accessed 11 March 2021).

30. 'The State of Education: Workload', National Education Union, 16 April 2019, https://neu.org.uk/press-releases/state-education-workload (Accessed 11 March 2021).

31. Prtichett, Lant. *The Rebirth of Education: Schooling Ain't Learning*, Center for Global Development, 2013, https://www.cgdev.org/sites/default/files/rebirth-education-introduction_0.pdf (Accessed 11 March 2021).

32. Stecher, Brian, et al. *Improving Teaching Effectiveness: Final Report: The Intensive Partnerships for Effective Teaching Through 2015–2016* (RAND Corporation, 2018) https://www.rand.org/pubs/research_reports/RR2242.html (Accessed 11 March 2021).

33. Ravitch, Diane, *The Death and Life of the Great American School System: How Testing and Choice Are Undermining Education* (Basic Books, 2010).

34. Stark, Lisa. 'Prison Time Begins for Atlanta Educators Convicted in Cheating Scandal', *Education Week*, 10 October 2018, https://blogs.edweek.org/edweek/District_Dossier/2018/10/prison_time_begins_for_atlanta.html?s_kwcid=AL!6416!3!266402628866!b!!g!!&cmp=cpc-goog-ew-dynamic+ads+recent+articles&ccid=dynamic+ads+recent+articles&ccag=recent+articles+dynamic&cckw=&cccv=dynamic+ad&gclid=EAIaIQobChMI7IHS5_Xl6wIVDOJ3Ch0DDAywEAAYASAAEgJu9PD_BwE (Accessed 11 March 2021).

35. Gladwell, *Outliers*.

36. Epstein, David. *Range: How Generalists Triumph in a Specialized World* (Macmillan, 2019).

37. Ramadan, Al, et al. *Play Bigger: How Rebels and Innovators Create New Categories and Dominate Markets*, (Piatkus, 2016).

38. Nemo, John. 'What a NASA Janitor Can Teach Us About Living a Bigger Life', *Business Journals*, 23 December 2014, https://www.bizjournals.com/bizjournals/how-to/growth-strategies/2014/12/what-a-nasa-janitor-can-teach-us.html (Accessed 11 March 2021).

39. 'Workspace As Creative As You', Second Home, https://secondhome.io/ (Accessed 11 March 2021).

40. Chandra, Vikram. *Sacred Games* (Faber & Faber, 2011).

41. Duranti, Avanti, et al. *Safety Concerns and Reporting of Crime*, IDFC Institute, 2017, https://www.idfcinstitute.org/site/assets/files/12318/satarc_april272017.pdf (Accessed 11 March 2021).

42. Laloux, Frederic. *Reinventing Organizations: A Guide to Creating Organizations Inspired by the Next Stage in Human Consciousness* (Nelson Parker, 2014).

43. Heath, Dan, and Heath, Chip. *Switch: How to Change Things When Change Is Hard*, (Random House Business, 2010).

44. Gillet, Nicolas, et al. 2013. 'The Role of Supervisor Autonomy Support, Organizational Support, and Autonomous and Controlled Motivation in Predicting Employees' Satisfaction and Turnover Intentions', *European Journal of Work and Organizational Psychology* 22 (2): 450–60.

45. 'Transforming the Education Workforce: Learning Teams for a Learning Generation', The Education Commission, 2019, https://educationcommission.org/wp-content/uploads/2019/09/Transforming-the-Education-Workforce-Full-Report.pdf (Accessed 11 March 2021).

46. Nisen, Max. 'Why GE Had to Kill its Annual Performance Reviews After More Than Three Decades', *Quartz*, 13 August 2015, https://qz.com/428813/ge-performance-review-strategy-shift/ (Accessed 11 March 2021).

47. 'InDay Speaker Series with Selena Rezvani', YouTube, 2 May 2012, https://www.youtube.com/watch?v=Q5ttK0XQ5lg&ab_channel=LinkedIn (Accessed 11 March 2021).

48. Crehan, Lucy. *Cleverlands: The Secrets Behind the Success of the World's Education Superpowers* (Unbound, 2017).

49. *Reducing In-School Variation: Making Effective Practice Standard Practice,* Training and Development Agency for Schools, 2009, https://dera.ioe.ac.uk/1276/1/isv_guide.pdf (Accessed 11 March 2021).

50. Keller, Scott, and Meaney, Mary. 'Successfully Transitioning to New Leadership Roles', McKinsey & Company, 23 May 2018, https://www.mckinsey.com/business-functions/organization/our-insights/successfully-transitioning-to-new-leadership-roles (Accessed 22 March 2021).

51. Grant, Adam. *New York Times*.

52. Pryce-Jones, Jessica. *Happiness at Work: Maximizing your Psychological Capital for Success* (Wiley, 2010).

3. Intrinsic Success

1. Ridgers, Bill. *The Economist Book of Business Quotations* (Economist Books, 2021).

2. Badenhausen, Kurt. 'Roger Federer's Uniqlo Deal Pushes His Endorsement Earnings to Highest By An Athlete', *Forbes*, 2 July 2018, https://www.forbes.com/sites/kurtbadenhausen/2018/07/02/roger-federers-uniqlo-deal-pushes-his-endorsement-earnings-to-the-worlds-highest/#3b50d61d42a1 (Accessed 11 March 2021).

3. 'Novak Djokovic: When Crowd Chanted "Roger" I heard "Novak"', YouTube, 14 July 2019, https://www.youtube.com/watch?v=8jf3Z6XfqFM (Accessed 11 March 2021).

4. Lazear, Edward, and Rosen, Sherwin. 'Rank-order Tournaments as Optimum Labor Contracts', Working Paper No. 401, National Bureau of Economic Research 1979, https://www.nber.org/system/files/working_papers/w0401/w0401.pdf (Accessed 11 March 2021).

5. 'Remarks by the President in Back to School Speech in Philadelphia, Pennsylvania', The White House, 14 September 2010, https://obamawhitehouse.archives.gov/the-press-office/2010/09/14/remarks-president-back-school-speech-philadelphia-pennsylvania (Accessed 11 March 2021).

6. 'Some Universities Are About to Be "Walking Dead"', PBS, 25 May 2020, http://www.pbs.org/wnet/amanpour-and-company/video/some-universities-are-about-to-be-walking-dead/ (Accessed 11 March 2021).

7. Deming, David J. 2017, 'The Growing Importance of Social Skills in the Labor Market', *Quarterly Journal of Economics*, 132 (4): 1593–1640. https://scholar.harvard.edu/files/ddeming/files/deming_socialskills_qje.pdf (Accessed 11 March 2021).

8. Markovits, Daniel. *The Meritocracy Trap* (Allen Lane, 2019).

9. Sandel, Michael J. *The Tyranny of Merit: Why the Promise of Moving Up Is Pulling America Apart* (Allen Lane, 2020).

10. Aisch, Gregor, Buchanan, Larry, Cox, Amanda, and
    Quealy, Kevin. 'Some Colleges Have More Students From
    the Top 1 Percent Than the Bottom 60. Find Yours.', *New
    York Times*, 18 January 2017, https://www.nytimes.com/
    interactive/2017/01/18/upshot/some-colleges-have-more-
    students-from-the-top-1-percent-than-the-bottom-60.html
    (Accessed 11 March 2021).

11. Dweck, *Mindset.*

12. Bowers, Chris. *Federer* (John Blake, 2013).

13. Mahesh, Shripiya. 'The Questions That Matter', 1 September
    2020, https://shripriya.com/blog/2020/09/01/the-questions-
    that-matter/ (Accessed 11 March 2021).

14. 'Protégés of Nobel laureates are more likely to thrive',
    The Economist, 11 October 2019, https://www.economist.
    com/graphic-detail/2019/10/11/proteges-of-nobel-laureates-
    are-more-likely-to-thrive (Accessed 11 March 2021).

15. Sandel, *The Tyranny of Merit.*

16. Darwin, Charles. *On the Origin of Species by Means of Natural
    Selection, Or, The Preservation of Favoured Races in the Struggle
    for Life* (John Murray, 1859).

17. Scoville, Heather. 'Survival of the Fittest vs. Natural Selection',
    ThoughtCo, 11 August 2019, https://www.thoughtco.com/
    survival-of-the-fittest-1224578 (Accessed 11 March 2021).

18. Le Page, Michael. 'Evolution: A Guide for the Not-Yet
    Perplexed', *New Scientist*, 16 April 2008, https://www.
    newscientist.com/article/mg19826522-400-evolution-a-guide-
    for-the-not-yet-perplexed/ (Accessed 11 March 2021).

19. Heffernan, Margaret. *A Bigger Prize: How We Can Do Better
    than the Competition* (PublicAffairs, 2014).

20. Jensen, Michael C, and Meckling, William H. 1976. 'Theory of the Firm: Managerial Behavior, Agency Costs and Ownership Structure', *Journal of Financial Economics* 3 (4). https://dx.doi. org/10.2139/ssrn.94043 (Accessed 11 March 2021).

21. Rush, Dominic. 'US Bosses Now Earn 312 Times the Average Worker's Wage, Figures Show', *Guardian*, 16 August 2018, https://www.theguardian.com/business/2018/aug/16/ceo-versus-worker-wage-american-companies-pay-gap-study-2018 (Accessed 11 March 2021).

22. Giridharadas, Anand. *Winners Take All: The Elite Charade of Changing the World* (Penguin, 2019).

23. Dasgupta, Koral. 'Kota Suicides: With Each Child, the Mother Dies the Cruelest Death', *Quint*, 10 May 2016, https://www. thequint.com/voices/blogs/kota-suicides-with-each-child-the-mother-dies-the-cruelest-death (Accessed 11 March 2021).

24. *Learning to Realize Education's Promise: The World Development Report 2018*, World Bank, 2018, https://www. worldbank.org/en/publication/wdr2018 (Accessed 11 March 2021).

25. Kremer, William, and Hammond, Claudia. 'Hikikomori: Why Are So Many Japanese Men Refusing to Leave Their Rooms?', BBC World Service, 5 July 2013, https://www.bbc.co.uk/ news/magazine-23182523 (Accessed 11 March 2021).

26. Marinova, Polina. 'How the Kleiner Perkins Empire Fell', *Fortune*, 23 April 2019 https://fortune.com/longform/kleiner-perkins-vc-fall/ (Accessed 11 March 2021).

27. Gerrard, Neil. 'JKS Restaurants: Sibling Harmony', *The Caterer*, 11 December 2015, https://www.thecaterer.com/news/ restaurant/jks-restaurants-sibling-harmony (Accessed 11 March 2021).

28. Agassi, Andre. *Open: An Autobiography* (HarperCollins, 2009).

29. 'Boris Becker Full Q&A Oxford Union', YouTube,
14 March 2019, https://www.youtube.com/
watch?v=ofhulQPMZio&ab_channel=OxfordUnion
(Accessed 11 March 2021).

30. Hey, Danna. 'Why You Need to Play for Her', *Odyssey*, 17 May
2016, https://www.theodysseyonline.com/playing-for-her
(Accessed 11 March 2021).

31. 'If, When and How to Avoid Hiring a CEO', TechCrunch,
10 November 2012, https://techcrunch.com/2012/11/10/
if-when-and-how-to-avoid-hiring-a-ceo/ (Accessed 11 March
2021).

32. Zook, Chris, and Allen, James. *The Founder's Mentality: How
to Overcome the Predictable Crises of Growth* (Harvard Business
Review Press, 2016).

33. 'Developmental Evaluation of Ford's BUILD Program:
Initial Findings', Ford Foundation, February 2018, https://
www.fordfoundation.org/work/learning/research-reports/
developmental-evaluation-of-fords-build-program-initial-
findings/ (Accessed 11 March 2021).

34. Coyle, Daniel. *The Talent Code: Greatness Isn't Born. It's Grown.
Here's How.* (Bantam Books, 2009).

4. Intrinsic Relationships

1. Quoted in Finkel, Eli J. *The All-or-Nothing Marriage: How the
Best Marriages Work* (Dutton, 2017).

2. 'Sweden, Norway, Iceland, Estonia and Portugal Rank Highest for Family-friendly Policies in OECD and EU Countries', UNICEF, 13 June 2019, https://www.unicef.org.uk/press-releases/sweden-norway-iceland-estonia-and-portugal-rank-highest-for-family-friendly-policies-in-oecd-and-eu-countries/ (Accessed 11 March 2021).

3. Mucha, Laura. *We Need to Talk About Love* (Bloomsbury Publishing, 2020).

4. Ortiz-Ospina, Esteban, and Roser, Max. 2020. 'Marriages and Divorces', Published online at OurWorldInData.org, https://ourworldindata.org/marriages-and-divorces (Accessed 11 March 2021).

5. Ortiz-Ospina and Roser. 'Marriages and divorces'.

6. Hill, Amelia. 'Cohabiting Couples Fastest-growing Family Type, Says ONS', *Guardian*, 7 August 2019, https://www.theguardian.com/uk-news/2019/aug/07/cohabiting-couples-fastest-growing-family-type-ons (Accessed 11 March 2021).

7. Ortiz-Ospina and Roser. 'Marriages and divorces'.

8. Proulx C M, Helms, H M, and Buehler C. 'Marital Quality and Personal Well-being: A Meta-analysis', *Journal of Marriage and Family.* 2007; 69:576–593.

9. Reeves, Richard V, and Pulliam, Christopher. 'Middle Class Marriage is Declining, and Likely Deepening Inequality', *Brookings*, 11 March 2020, https://www.brookings.edu/research/middle-class-marriage-is-declining-and-likely-deepening-inequality/ (Accessed 11 March 2021).

10. Finkel. *The All-or-Nothing Marriage.*

11. Schwartz, Alexandra, 'Love is Not a Permanent State of Enthusiasm: An Interview with Esther Perel', *The New Yorker*, 9 December 2018, https://www.newyorker.com/culture/the-new-yorker-interview/love-is-not-a-permanent-state-of-enthusiasm-an-interview-with-esther-perel (Accessed 11 March 2021).

12. Rosenfeld, Michael, et al. 2019. 'Disintermediating Your Friends: How Online Dating in the United States Displaces Other Ways of Meeting', *PNAS*, 116 (36).

13. 'Do Men and Women Really Look For Different Things In a Romantic Partner?', *Medical Xpress*, 26 August 2013, https://medicalxpress.com/news/2013-08-men-women-romantic-partner.html (Accessed 11 March 2021).

14. Li, Norman P, et al. 2002. 'The Necessities and Luxuries of Mate Preferences: Testing the Tradeoffs', *Journal of Personality and Social Psychology*, 82 (6): 947–55.

15. Shackelford, Todd K., Schmitt, David P., Buss. David M. 'Universal Dimensions of Human Mate Preferences', *Personality and Individual Differences* 39 (2005) 447–458.

16. Purvis, Jeanette Lee. 'Strategic Interference and Tinder Use: A Mixed-method Exploration of Romantic Interactions in Contemporary Contexts', (PhD. diss., University of Hawai'i at Manoa, 2017) https://scholarspace.manoa.hawaii.edu/bitstream/10125/62739/2017-05-phd-purvis.pdf (Accessed 11 March 2021).

17. Coduto, Kathryn D, et al. 2020. 'Swiping for Trouble: Problematic Dating Application Use Among Psychosocially Distraught Individuals and the Paths to Negative Outcomes', *Journal of Social and Personal Relationships*, 37 (1), 212–32.

18. Cox, Toby A. 'Swiping Right in 2020: How People Use Dating Apps', *The Manifest*, 5 February 2020, https://themanifest.com/app-development/swiping-right-how-people-use-dating-apps (Accessed 11 March 2021).

19. Perez, Sarah. 'Pew: 30% of US Adults Have Used Online Dating; 12% Found a Committed Relationship From It', *Tech Crunch*, 6 February 2020, https://techcrunch.com/2020/02/06/pew-30-of-u-s-adults-have-used-online-dating-12-found-a-committed-relationships-from-it/ (Accessed 11 March 2021).

20. Lukianoff, Greg, and Haidt, Jonathan. *The Coddling of the American Mind: How Good Intentions and Bad Ideas Are Setting Up a Generation for Failure* (Penguin, 2018).

21. '"The Love That Brings New Life into the World" – Rabbi Sacks on the Institution of Marriage', Rabbi Sacks, 17 November 2014, https://rabbisacks.org/love-brings-new-life-world-rabbi-sacks-institution-marriage/ (Accessed 11 March 2021).

22. Finkel. *The All-or-Nothing Marriage*.

23. Putnam, Robert D. *Bowling Alone: The Collapse and Revival of American Community* (Simon & Schuster, 2001).

24. Genadek, Katie R, et al. 2016. 'Trends in Spouses' Shared Time in the United States, 1965–2012', *Demography*, 53 (6): 1801–20.

25. Cheung, Elaine, et al. 2016. 'Emotionships: Examining People's Emotion-regulation Relationships and Their Consequences for Well-being', *Social Psychological and Personality Science*, 6 (4): 407.

26. Weverbergh, Raf. 'The Network Always Wins: Scientific Proof That Your PR Strategy Should Focus More on Giving and Less on Taking', Finn, https://www.finn.agency/adam-grant-give-take-reputation-PR-strategy (Accessed 11 March 2021).

27. Azcona, Ginette, Bhatt, Antra, and Love, Kaitlin. 'Ipsos Survey Confirms That COVID-19 Is Intensifying Women's Workload At Home', UN Women, 9 July 2020, https://data.unwomen.org/features/ipsos-survey-confirms-covid-19-intensifying-womens-workload-home (Accessed 11 March 2021).

28. Agarwal, Ashok. 2015. 'A Unique View on Male Infertility Around the Globe', *Reproductive Biology and Endocrinology*, 13 (37).

29. 'Global Prevalence of Infertility, Infecundity and Childlessness', https://www.who.int/reproductivehealth/topics/infertility/burden/en/ (Accessed 11 March 2021).

30. Cherry, Kendra. 'What Is Attachment Theory?', Verywell Mind, 17 July 2019, https://www.verywellmind.com/what-is-attachment-theory-2795337 (Accessed 11 March 2021).

31. Levine, Amir, and Heller, Rachel S F. *Attached: The New Science of Adult Attachment and How It Can Help You Find – and Keep – Love* (Jeremy P. Tarcher, 2012).

32. Rogers, Carl. *Client-Centered Therapy* (Constable and Company, 1951).

33. Lau, C Q. 'The Stability of Same-sex Cohabitation, Different-sex Cohabitation, and Marriage', *Journal of Marriage and Family*. 2012;74:973–988.

34. Ryan, *Self-Determination Theory*.

35. 'What to Do After a Fight' The Gottman Institute, https://www.gottman.com/ (Accessed 11 March 2021).

36. Bowles, Nellie. 'Silicon Valley Nannies Are Phone Police for Kids, *New York Times*, 26 October 2018, https://www.nytimes.com/2018/10/26/style/silicon-valley-nannies.html (Accessed 11 March 2021).

37. Dweck. *Mindset*.

5. Intrinsic Parenting

1. Gibran, Kahlil. *The Prophet* (Knopf, 1995).

2. 'Helicopter Parent', Haim Ginott, https://www.haimginott.com/blog/helicopter-parent (Accessed 11 March 2021).

3. Gross-Loh, Christine. *Parenting Without Borders* (Penguin Random House USA, 2014) https://www.penguin.com/ajax/books/excerpt/9781101609064.

4. Day, Nicholas. 'No Big Deal, But This Researcher's Theory Explains Everything About How Americans Parent', *Slate*, 10 April 2013, http://www.slate.com/blogs/how_babies_work/2013/04/10/parental_ethnotheories_and_how_parents_in_america_differ_from_parents_everywhere.html?via=gdpr-consent (Accessed 11 March 2021).

5. Doepke, Mattias, and Zilibotti, Fabrizio. *Love, Money, and Parenting: How Economics Explains the Way We Raise Our Kids* (Princeton University Press, 2019).

6. Lythcott-Haims, Julie. *How to Raise an Adult: Break Free of the Overparenting Trap and Prepare Your Kid for Success* (Bluebird, 2015).

7. Singer, Dorothy, et al. *Play = Learning: How Play Motivates and Enhances Children's Cognitive and Social-Emotional Growth* (Oxford University Press, 2006).

8. Lythcott-Haims. *How to Raise An Adult*.

9. Russell, Bertrand. *New Hopes for a Changing World* (Allen & Unwin, 1951).

10. Csikszentmihalyi, Mihaly. *Flow: The Psychology of Optimal Experience* (Harper & Row, 1991).

11. Walsh, Lisa C, et al. 2018. 'Does Happiness Promote Career Success? Revisiting the Evidence', *Journal of Career Assessment*, 26 (1). DOI: 10.1177/1069072717751441.

12. 'School Engagement May Be Secret to Success' University of Tasmania, https://www.menzies.utas.edu.au/news-and-events/media-releases/2013/school-engagement-may-be-secret-to-success (Accessed 11 March 2021).

13. Grant, Adam, and Sweet Grant, Allison, 'Kids Can Learn to Love Learning, Even Over Zoom', *New York Times*, 7 September 2020, https://www.nytimes.com/2020/09/07/opinion/remote-school.html.

14. Robinson, Ken. *Finding Your Element* (Allen Lane, 2013).

15. Rossiter, Jack and Kojo Abreh, Might. 'COVID-19 Has Forced Exams to Be Suspended Across West Africa. Should They Be Overhauled Before They Restart?', Center for Global Development, 20 March 2020, https://www.cgdev.org/blog/covid-19-has-forced-exams-be-suspended-across-west-africa-should-they-be-overhauled-they (Accessed 11 March 2021).

16. Kohn. *Punished by Rewards*.

17. Tough, Paul. *How Children Succeed: Grit, Curiosity, and the Hidden Power of Character* (Houghton Mifflin Harcourt, 2012. MLA, 8th ed.), https://scholar.google.com/citations?user=iItny3IAAAAJ&hl=en.

18. Hilton, Steve. *More Human: Designing a World Where People Come First* (W H Allen, 2015).

19. Dalai Lama et al. *The Book of Joy*.

20. Chua, Amy. 'Why Chinese Mothers Are Superior', *Wall Street Journal*, 8 January 2011, https://www.wsj.com/articles/SB100 0142405274870411150457605971352869875 4 (Accessed 11 March 2021).

21. Wojcicki, Esther. *How to Raise Successful People: Simple Lessons for Radical Results* (Houghton Mifflin Harcourt, 2019).

22. Kim, Su Yeong, et al. 2013. 'Does "Tiger Parenting" Exist? Parenting Profiles of Chinese Americans and Adolescent Developmental Outcomes', *Asian American Journal of Psychology* 4 (1): 7–18.

23. Moilanen, Kristin. 'Helicopter Parents and "Hothouse Children"—WVU Researcher Explores the High Stakes of Family Dynamics', *WVU Today*, 18 November 2019, https://wvutoday.wvu.edu/stories/2019/11/18/helicopter-parents-and-hothouse-children-wvu-researcher-explores-the-high-stakes-of-family-dynamics (Accessed 11 March 2021).

24. Wellock, Bill. 'FSU Research: Helicopter Parenting Hinders Children's Self-control Skills', *Florida State University News*, 13 November 2019, https://news.fsu.edu/news/2019/11/13/fsu-research-helicopter-parenting-hinders-childrens-self-control-skills/ (Accessed 11 March 2021).

25. Reed-Fitzke, Kayla, Duncan, James, Lucier-Greer, Mallory, Fixelle, Courtney, Ferraro, Anthony, 'Helicopter Parenting and Emerging Adult Self-Efficacy: Implications for Mental and Physical Health', *Journal of Child and Family Studies*, October 2016.

26 Ryan, Richard. *Self-Determination Theory*.

27. Hoy, Selena. 'Why Are Little Kids in Japan So Independent?', Bloomberg, 28 September 2015, https://www.bloomberg.com/news/articles/2015-09-28/in-japan-small-children-take-the-subway-and-run-errands-alone (Accessed 11 March 2021).

28. https://www.freerangekids.com (Accessed 11 March 2021).

29. Pinker, Steven. *The Better Angels of Our Nature: Why Violence Has Declined* (Viking, 2011).

6. Intrinsic Citizenship

1. Goldberg, Joel. 'It Takes a Village to Determine the Origins of an African Proverb', *NPR*, 30 July 2016, https://www.npr.org/sections/goatsandsoda/2016/07/30/487925796/it-takes-a-village-to-determine-the-origins-of-an-african-proverb (Accessed 12 March 2021) Requoted by Cory Brooker in the 2016 US Democratic National Convention.

2. 'Joe Biden Acceptance Speech', Aljazeera, 8 November 2020, www.aljazeera.com/amp/news/2020/11/8/joe-biden-acceptance-speech-full-transcript (Accessed 12 March 2021).

3. McCloskey, Jimmy. 'First US Election Exit Poll Claims Voters More Worried About Economy Than Covid', *Metro*, 3 November 2020, https://metro.co.uk/2020/11/03/first-us-election-exit-poll-claims-voters-more-worried-about-economy-than-covid-13531203/ (Accessed 12 March 2021).

4. Bentley, Tom. *Everyday Democracy: Why We Get the Politicians We Deserve* (Demos, 2005), http://www.demos.co.uk/files/everydaydemocracy.pdf?1240939425, (Accessed 12 March 2021).

5. Clemence, Michael. 'Trust In Politicians Falls Sending Them Spiralling Back to the Bottom of the Ipsos MORI Veracity Index', Ipsos, 26 November 2019, https://www.ipsos.com/ipsos-mori/en-uk/trust-politicians-falls-sending-them-spiralling-back-bottom-ipsos-mori-veracity-index, (Accessed 12 March 2021).

6. Besley, Timothy J, and Ghathak, Maitreesh. 2005. 'Competition and Incentives with Motivated Agents', *American Economic Review* 95 (3): 616–36.

7. *Doing Business 2020: Comparing Business Regulations in 190 Economies*, World Bank, 2020, http://documents1.worldbank.org/curated/en/688761571934946384/pdf/Doing-Business-2020-Comparing-Business-Regulation-in-190-Economies.pdf, (Accessed 12 March 2021).

8. Ferraz, Claudio, and Finan, Federico. 2009. 'Motivating Politicians: The Impacts of Monetary Incentives on Quality and Performance', National Bureau of Economic Research.

9. Bowen, Renee T, and Mo, Cecelia. 2016. 'The Voter's Blunt Tool', *Journal of Theoretical Politics*, 28 (4).

10. Bó, Ernesto Dal, et al. 2013. 'Strengthening State Capabilities: The Role of Financial Incentives in the Call to Public Service', *The Quarterly Journal of Economics*, 1169–1218.

11. Bowen and Mo. 'The Voter's Blunt Tool'.

12. Kets de Vries, Manfred F R, *You Will Meet a Tall, Dark Stranger* (Palgrave MacMillan, 2016).

13. Hamilton, Alexander, Madison, James, and Jay, John, *The Federalist Papers* (1787).

14. Mudde, Cas ,and Kaltwasser, Cristóbal Rovera. *Populism: A Very Short Introduction* (Oxford University Press, 2nd edn, 2017).

15. Chua, Amy. 'How America's Identity Politics Went from Inclusion to Division', *Guardian*, 1 March 2018, https://www.theguardian.com/society/2018/mar/01/how-americas-identity-politics-went-from-inclusion-to-division (Accessed 12 March 2021).

16. 'Obama's 2004 DNC Keynote Speech' YouTube, 27 July 2016, https://www.youtube.com/watch?v=ueMNqdB1QIE (Accessed 12 March 2021).

17. 'The Talent Dearth in Britain's Government', *The Economist*, 18 July 2020, https://www.economist.com/britain/2020/07/18/the-talent-dearth-in-britains-government (Accessed 12 March 2021).

18. Lammy, David, *Tribes: How Our Need to Belong Can Make or Break Society* (Constable, 2020).

19. Buck, Stephanie. 'Fear of Nuclear Annihilation Scarred Children Growing Up in the Cold War, Studies Later Showed', Timeline, 29 August 2017, https://timeline.com/nuclear-war-child-psychology-d1ff491b5fe0 (Accessed 12 March 2021).

20. Fukuyama. *The End of History and the Last Man*.

21. Drèze, Jean and Sen, Amartya, *An Uncertain Glory, India and Its Contradictions* (Princeton University Press, 2013).

22. Kahneman, Daniel and Deaton, Angus. 2010. 'High Income Improves Evaluation of Life But Not Emotional Well-being' *PNAS*, 107 (38): 16489–93.

23. 'Beyond GDP: Economics and Happiness' *Berkeley Economic Review*, 31 October 2018, https://econreview.berkeley.edu/beyond-gdp-economics-and-happiness/ (Accessed 12 March 2021).

24. Graham, David. 'C-SPAN Isn't All Good', *The Atlantic*, March 2019, https://www.theatlantic.com/politics/archive/2019/03/how-c-span-made-congress-and-washington-worse/585277/ (Accessed 12 March 2021).

25. Rauch, Jonathan. 'How American Politics Went Insane', *The Atlantic*, July/August 2016, https://www.theatlantic.com/magazine/archive/2016/07/how-american-politics-went-insane/485570/ (Accessed 12 March 2021).

26. Johnston, John. 'Tory Minister Nadhim Zahawi Has Condemned the "Corrosive" Leaking of the Government's Latest Lockdown Proposals', *Politics Home*, 9 October 2020, https://www.politicshome.com/news/article/nadhim-zahawi-leaking-condemn-coronavirus (Accessed 12 March 2021)

27. Hardman, Isabel, *Why We Get the Wrong Politicians* (Atlantic Books, 2018).

28. Drotter, Stephen J, et al. 2001. 'Building Leaders at Every Level: A Leadership Pipeline', *Ivey Business Journal* May/June.

29. 'Would a Basic Income Increase National Happiness?', *Psychology Today*, 24 August 2015, https://www.psychologytoday.com/nz/blog/clear-organized-and-motivated/201508/would-basic-income-increase-national-happiness?amp (Accessed 12 March 2021).

30. Heath, Dan. *Upstream: How to Solve Problems Before They Happen* (Bantam Press, 2020).

31. Hanauer, Nick. 'Better Schools Won't Fix America', *The Atlantic*, July 2019, https://www.theatlantic.com/magazine/archive/2019/07/education-isnt-enough/590611/ (Accessed 12 March 2021).

32. Gilbert, Richard L, et al. 'Basic Income and the Motivation to Work: An Analysis of Labor Responses in 16 Trial Programs', https://www.academia.edu/37692463/Basic_Income_and_the_Motivation_to_Work_docx (Accessed 12 March 2021).

33. 'A Universal Basic Income for India?', Center for Global Development, 20 April 2017, https://www.cgdev.org/media/universal-basic-income-india-arvind-subramanian (Accessed 12 March 2021).

34. Ng, Kate. 'Spain Approves National Minimum Income Scheme', *Independent*, 29 May 2020, https://www.independent.co.uk/news/world/europe/spain-national-minimum-income-universal-basic-coronavirus-ubi-economy-a9538606.html (Accessed 12 March 2021).

35. Evans, David, and Popova, Anna. 'Do the Poor Waste Transfers on Booze and Cigarettes? No', World Bank Blogs, 27 May 2014, https://blogs.worldbank.org/impactevaluations/do-poor-waste-transfers-booze-and-cigarettes-no (Accessed 12 March 2021).

36. Bastagli, Francesca, et al., *Cash Transfers, What Does the Evidence Say?* Overseas Development Institute, 2016, https://assets.publishing.service.gov.uk/media/57bafa91ed915d1259000002/Cash_transfers_what_does_the_evidence_say_Full_Report.pdf (Accessed 12 March 2021).

37. Widerquist, Karl. 'The Cost of Basic Income: Back-of-the-Envelope Calculations', IDEAS, https://ideas.repec.org/a/bpj/bistud/v12y2017i2p13n4.html (Accessed 12 March 2021).

38. 'Why Rishi Got It Wrong', *The Economist*, 29 October 2020, https://www.economist.com/leaders/2020/10/29/why-rishi-got-it-wrong (Accessed 12 March 2021).

39. 'Great Leaders & Organizations Advance a Just Cause', Stephen Shedletzky blog https://simonsinek.com/discover/great-leaders-organizations-advance-a-just-cause/ (Accessed 12 March 2021).

40. 'Covid: Regulator Criticises Data Used to Justify Lockdown', BBC, 5 November 2020, https://www.bbc.co.uk/news/health-54831334 (Accessed 12 March 2021).

41. 'Coronavirus: Govt will "Strive to Improve" Data After Watchdog Criticises Downing Street Presentation', Sky News, 6 November 2020, https://news.sky.com/story/coronavirus-watchdog-warns-downing-street-news-briefing-data-could-confuse-the-public-12124762 (Accessed 12 March 2021).

42. Stern, Nicholas, *The Economics of Climate Change: The Stern Review.* HM Treasury, 2006, https://www.lse.ac.uk/granthaminstitute/publication/the-economics-of-climate-change-the-stern-review/ (Accessed 12 March 2021).

43. Heckman, James J. 2011. 'The Economics of Inequality: The Value of Early Childhood Education'. *American Educator*, Spring, https://files.eric.ed.gov/fulltext/EJ920516.pdf.

44. Bentley. *Everyday Democracy*.

45. 'Helping Them Enhance Their Skills Acquisition and Career Growth', Yellow Ribbon, https://www.yellowribbon.gov.sg.

46. 'Citizens' Assemblies Are Increasingly Popular', *The Economist*, 19 September 2020, https://www.economist.com/international/2020/09/19/citizens-assemblies-are-increasingly-popular (Accessed 12 March 2021).

47. Hardman, Isabel, *Why We Get the Wrong Politicians*.

7. An Intrinsic Life

1. Dale Carnegie (@DaleCarnegie) Twitter,
   1 January 2018, https://twitter.com/dalecarnegie/
   status/947829791398547457 (Accessed 22 March).

2. Hegarty, Stephanie. 'The Chinese Doctor Who Tried to Warn
   Others About Coronavirus', BBC News, 6 February 2020,
   https://www.bbc.co.uk/news/world-asia-china-51364382
   (Accessed 12 March 2021).

3. 'Coronavirus: What Did China Do About Early Outbreak?',
   BBC News, 9 June 2020, https://www.bbc.co.uk/news/
   world-52573137 (Accessed 12 March 2021).

4. Allen-Ebrahimian, Bethany. 'Timeline: The Early Days of
   China's Coronavirus Outbreak and Cover-up', Axios, 18 March
   2020, https://www.axios.com/timeline-the-early-days-of-
   chinas-coronavirus-outbreak-and-cover-up-ee65211a-afb6-
   4641-97b8-353718a5faab.html (Accessed 12 March 2021).

5. Murthy, Vivek H, *Together: Loneliness, Health and What
   Happens When We Find Connection* (Wellcome Collection,
   2020).

6. Yakobovitch, David. 'AI Is Helping in Suicide Management',
   Towards Data Science, 6 July 2020, https://towardsdatascience.
   com/ai-suicide-management-c2b483e8c756 (Accessed 12
   March 2021).

7. 'Parents Now Spend Twice As Much Time With Their
   Children As 50 Years Ago', *The Economist*, 27 November 2017,
   https://www.economist.com/graphic-detail/2017/11/27/
   parents-now-spend-twice-as-much-time-with-their-children-as-
   50-years-ago and 'Parenting Children in th Age of Screens', Pew
   Research Center, 28 July 2020, https://www.pewresearch.org/
   internet/2020/07/28/parenting-children-in-the-age-of-screens
   (Accessed 12 March 2021).

8. *Enabling the Next Generation to Become World Ready, Not Just Exam Ready,* Future Perfect Education Commission, 2020, https://www.edcommission.org.uk/wp-content/uploads/2020/08/ed-commission-final-report.pdf (Accessed 12 March 2021).

9. Ebrahimi, Farhad. 'Why Should It Take a Pandemic to Bring Out the Best in Philanthropy?', *Inside Philanthropy,* https://www.insidephilanthropy.com/home/2020/3/30/transformative-philanthropy-in-the-time-of-covid-19-why-should-it-take-a-global-pandemic-to-bring-out-the-best-in-us (Accessed 12 March 2021).

10. https://www.goodreads.com/quotes/7746746-every-crisis-actual-or-impending-needs-to-be-viewed-as (Accessed 12 March 2021).

11. Ibarra, Herminia, *Working Identity: Unconventional Strategies for Reinventing Your Career* (Harvard Business School Press, 2003).

Index

Abraham, Reuben 64, 65
Abreh, Might Kojo 198
abundance mindset 101, 103,
    122, 137
accumulated advantage 18, 102,
    107
Ackman, Bill 11, 103
Adecco Group Foundation 79,
    286
Africa 54, 202–5, 237–8, 243
Agarwal, Ashok 164
Agassi, Andre 126
Ahmed, Abiy 237, 243, 248
Ai Feng 278
Ainsworth, Mary 167
'AJ' 152–4, 155–6, 157, 158, 177
Amansa Capital 190
anxiety 20, 186, 189
Ashoka 213–14
attachment theory 167–8,
    217–18, 300
Autonomy 6, 7, 10, 11, 130
  at work 68–72, 87–8
  citizenship and 234, 236,
    250–3, 263–7, 271
  and cost of inaction 282
  definition of 31
  'guided Autonomy' 69–72, 251
  parenting and 202–8, 216–21
  in relationships 159–63, 172–3,
    176
  talent and 110–17, 128–31, 136
  work and 32, 49–58, 68–72

Bao 123, 124
Barrett, Mark 259

Becker, Boris 127
Bénabou, Roland 43
Benchmark 121–2
Bentley, Tom 232, 266
Bercow, John 239
Berenjak 124
Berson, Sasha 145
Besley, Timothy 233, 234
Béteille, Tara 40
Bewtra, Vineet 223
Biden, Joe 231
Bill and Melinda Gates Founda-
    tion 56
Black Lives Matter 19, 78, 242
Blair, Tony 234, 249
Blockbuster 261–2
Bodgas, Meredith 162
Bogg, Grace Lee 293
Bowen, Renee 235
Bowers, Chris 104
Bowlby, John 167, 217
Bratton, William 49–50
Brazil, education in 104–5
Brexit 238–40, 243, 247–8, 266
Bridge International Academies
    54–5
Brookings Institution 146, 149
Brown, Gordon 11, 72, 234
BUILD 130, 293–4
burnout 17, 47–8
Bush, George W 57
business education 36–7
Buurtzorg 69

C-SPAN 250
Caddick, Karen 47

Cambridge University 98, 99, 100–1, 105, 113, 222
Canongate 53
capitalism 22, 245–6
Carnegie, Dale 275
Chandra, Vikram 64–5
Charan, Ram 255
charitable foundations 112
'Charles' 37–8, 59–60
Chayatte, Michelle Renee 164
Cheung, Elaine 160
The Children's Society 20
China 59–60, 277–81, 282
Choudhury, Prithwiraj 44–5
Christensen, Clayton 36, 206, 207
Chrysler 60–1
Chua, Amy 201–2, 241–2
Citizen Assemblies 267
citizenship 21–2, 230–73
Clarke, Samantha 297, 298, 299
climate change 21, 264–5, 266, 271
Clinton, Bill 11, 98
cognitive diversity 79
Cold War (1985–1991) 244
college sports system 133–4
competition 76, 109
The Conduit 62–3
Connaught Hotel 62–3
Cooper, Jamie 269
Coumau, Francois 297–8
Covid-19 23, 35, 255, 277–81, 282, 292–3
  education and 105, 198
  lockdowns 184–5, 252, 260, 261, 262, 263–4, 289
  overinvestment in hygiene factors 43–4
  remote working 44–5, 85–6
  women and childcare 161

Coyle, Daniel 134
Crehan, Lucy 79–80
crime rates 49–51
Csikszentmihalyi, Mihaly 196

Dabbous, Ollie 46
Dalai Lama 20, 201, 213
Darwin, Charles 108, 136
Das, Jishnu 194–5
dating, online 19, 152–8, 176, 177
Deaton, Sir Angus 246, 247
Deci, Edward 10
Dell 206
Deming, David 98–9
democracy 22, 244, 250
Democratic National Congress 53
demotivation 9, 14, 15, 20, 39, 41
Dighero, Robert 131–2
diversity 79, 117, 136
divorce 143–8, 162, 166, 171, 291
Djokovic, Novak 94–5, 96
Doepke, Matthias 190–1
Doerr, John 121
Dost 192, 193
downsides, managing against 289–92, 294, 297–8
Draper, Bill 11
Dreze, Jean 245
Drummond, Steve 51–2
Duncan, James 208
Dunning, Victoria 293
Dweck, Carol 13, 103, 178, 212

Eblis 62–3
Ebrahimi, Farhad 293
The Economist 74–6, 105–6, 243, 262, 267
Edmondson, Jeff 267
education 198, 258, 265, 287, 291–2

academic selectivity 98–101, 102, 107
Autonomy in 54–8, 69–72
children's engagement with 197–201
citizenship 269–70
higher education 98–101, 102–3
Mastery in 73–4, 79–83, 86
nurturing talent in 100–2, 103, 104–6
parenting and 197–213
pay 39–43
principal agent theory 113–17
Purpose and 38
snowplough parenting 189–90, 197–8
Education Commission 11, 72–3, 291
empathy 213–15
The English Patient (film) 29
entrepreneurship 118, 128, 223
Epstein, David 59, 113
Escallón, Cristina 168–9
Ethiopia 45, 237–8, 243
Evans, David 40, 200

Facebook 226
Family Independence Initiative 292
family life 159–60
fear 169
Federer, Roger 59, 93–5, 96, 97, 104, 125, 127, 128, 136
Feickert, Rebecca 133
Feinberg, Mike 206
Ferraro, Anthony 208
Finkel, Eli 150, 151–2, 159–60
Finland 79–80, 246–7
Ford Foundation 130, 131, 293
France 46–7, 118, 143–7

Franklin, Daniel 74–6
Fukuyama, Francis 22, 244–5

Galloway, Scott 98
Gates, Bill 54, 56, 257
gender inequality, income and 19, 87
Ghatak, Maitreesh 233, 234
Gibran, Kahil 187, 218
Gilbert, Richard 259
Gingrich, Newt 251
Ginott, Haim 187
Giridharadas, Anand 113
Gladwell, Malcolm 18, 49–50, 58, 102, 107
Goldman Sachs 36, 298
Golinkoff and Hirsch-Pesak 193–4
Google 79
Gore, Al 219
Gottman, John 173, 174
Grant, Adam 27, 84, 160, 197
Gratton, Professor Linda 48
Gross-Loh, Christine 189
growth mindset 13, 103, 178, 212
Guilfoyle, Simon 51
Gupta, Dr Ravindra (Ravi) 30–1, 33, 89

Haidt, Jonathan 157
Hamilton, Alexander 240–1, 272
Hamm, Mia 127
Hanauer, Nick 258–9
Hansen, Cynthia 79, 286
happiness 195–6, 246–7
Harari, Yuval Noah 227, 261
Harbour, Claire 299–300
Hardman, Isabel 254–5, 268–9
Harkness, Sara 190
Harlow, Harry 9
Harris, Kamala 40

Harvard Business School (HBS)
36, 44, 80
Harvard Graduate School of
Education 213–14
Harvard University 98, 113
Heath, Chip 70
Heath, Dan 70, 258
Heckman, James 265
Heffernan, Margaret 108–9
Heller, Rachel 168
Henderson, Paul 100–1, 105, 137
Herzberg, Frederick 9–10, 39,
40–1
HighScope Indonesia 211
Hilton, Steve 200–1
Hingorani, Pritika 65–6
Hirsch, Afua 270
HIV/AIDS 30–1, 89
Hoffer, Eric 91
Homeless World Cup 110
Honig, Dan 250, 251–2
Hoppers 123, 124
Hunt, Jeremy 34
Hussein, Saddam 100
hygiene factors 16, 31–2, 33, 244
education 98, 198, 202
money as 246, 262
overinvestment in 43–4
parenting 227
relationships 19, 150, 151, 155
work and 36, 41, 43–4, 49, 61,
85, 155

Ibarra, Professor Herminia 299
iCivics 270
IDFC Institute 64, 65, 66
inaction 74, 282–3, 294, 295
incentives 14, 43, 111–12, 137
income 85, 246
GDP 266
guaranteed basic 257–62

and happiness 246–7
inequality in 19, 87, 112
performance-based pay 42–3
politicians' 234–5
teachers' 39–41
India 1–7, 10–11, 15, 54, 302
civil service in 77
education in 40, 113–14, 205
entrepreneurship in 118–21
income in 259–60
parenting in 192–3, 226
policing in 64–6
relationships in 152, 177–8
socialism in 245
Indian Institute for Technology
(IIT) 98, 113–14, 120–1
Indonesia 115, 191, 194, 201,
210–11, 226–7
infertility 164–5
informal sector 45
Inland Revenue Service (IRS) 216
INSEAD 80, 222, 235, 299
International Labour
Organization 45
Ipsos 161, 233

Japan, education in 116–17
Jay, John 93, 240–1
Jensen, Michael 111, 112
JKS 122–4
Judge, Emma 63

Kahneman, Daniel 246, 247
Kalauserang, Jimmy Peter 210–11
Kalet, Adina 35, 286
Kennedy, John F 63, 240, 242,
248, 254
Kenrick, Douglas 154
Kern Institute for the
Transformation of Medical
Education 35–6, 286–7

Kets de Vries, Manfred 235
Keynes, John Maynard 13
Khan, Asma 170–1, 295
Khan, Mushtaq 170–1, 295
Khosla, Vinod 128–9
Khosla Ventures 128, 129–30, 131
Kim, Su Yeong 202
King, Martin Luther 242
Kings Fund 35
KIPP (Knowledge is Power Programme) 206, 213
Kleiner Perkins 121, 128
Knight, Lord Jim 234, 243, 256
Kodak 261–2
Kohn, Alfie 42, 198
Koko 288
Kopp, Wendy 216, 296
Krishnamoorthy, Rajesh 302–3
Krishnamurthy, Kavitha 124–7

Lai, Dr Shengjie 280
Laloux, Frederic 68–9
Lammy, David 243
Lau, Charles Q 171
Lawn Tennis Association (LTA) 289–90
Laws, David 236, 252
Lazear, Edward 96
Le Page, Michael 108
leadership, transitions 81–3
'learning to learn' 134–5
Leavitt, Steven 50
L'Economie du couple (film) 144
Lemann Foundation 104–5
Levine, Amir 168
Li, Norman 154
Li Wenliang, Dr 278, 279–80, 281, 282
Libreria 64
life: an intrinsic life 276–303

life expectancy 48
life-satisfaction 20
life scripts 106–7
work-life balance 46–9
London Patient 29–31, 89
Loyola 81–3
Lubell, David 284–5
Lucey, Anne-Marie 162, 166
Lukianoff, Greg 157
Lyle's 123
Lythcott-Haims, Julie 192, 194, 209

Ma, Yifang 105–6
McCallum, Doug 89
Macdonald, Sir Alasdair 132–3
McKinsey 19, 36, 82, 83, 113, 227, 298
Macron, President 118
Madison, James 240–1
Mahesh, Shripriya 105
Mandela, Nelson 253–4
The Manifest 156
Marinova, Polina 121
Markovits, Daniel 102
Marr, Andrew 75–6
marriage 144–50, 159
Marriage Story (Netflix) 144, 240
Marteau, Theresa 43
Maslow, Abraham 9
Mastery 6, 7, 10, 11
  at work 58–60, 63, 72–83, 86, 88
  citizenship and 253–6, 267–71
  definition of 31
  parenting and 208–9, 221–6
  in relationships 164–7, 173–5, 176
  and talent 104, 118, 119, 121–2, 132–5, 136
Matthews, Amy 298

May, Shannon 54
May, Theresa 239
Meckling, William 111, 112
medical professions 33, 34–5
Menzies Institute for Medical
  Research 196–7
meritocracy 101–3, 107, 138
military 41, 66–8
Millennium Development Goals
  115–16
minority groups 19, 76, 78, 107
Mo, Cecilia 235
Modi, Narendra 118
Moilanen, Kristin 207–8
Moncaster, Cameron 63
Morgan, Baroness Sally 234, 243,
  268
Morpeth School 132–3
Mucha, Laura 146
Mudde and Kaltwasser 241
Mukherjee, Satyam 105–6
Mulgund, Aditi 164
Mullainathan, Sendhil 258
Mumsnet 64, 226
Murphy, Nora A 259
Murray, Sir Andy 112
Murthy, Vivek 288
myelin 134

Namulinda, Brenda 205
Narayanaswamy, Pradeepa 164,
  165–6, 177, 178
narcissism 235–6, 252
NASA Space Center 63
National Education Union 55, 56
National Health Service (NHS)
  33–5, 48, 69
National Public Radio 51–2
National Tuition Service (NTS)
  287
Neha 1–2, 4

New Amsterdam 35
New York Times 30, 175, 197
Newkirk, David 135
NMIMS's School of Business
  118–20
No Child Left Behind 57, 200
non-profit organizations 282–3
nursing, burnout of staff 35

Obama, Barack 53, 57, 98, 102,
  242
O'Connor, Sandra Day 270
OECD 291
Office of National Statistics 148
OFSTED 55, 56, 132, 186, 199,
  200
Ohio State University 156
Ondaatje, Michael 29
opportunity, intrinsic 284–9,
  294–5
Opportunity Insights 102
Ortiz-Ospina, Esteban 147
Otika, Brenda Akite 203–4
Owen, Jo 295, 296
own-label parenting 225

Palo Alto 185, 188–9, 190, 225–6
parenting 182–227
  and Autonomy 202–8, 216–21
  helicopter parenting 20, 172,
    184, 186, 187–8, 189, 191,
    207–8, 209, 221, 272
  Mastery and 21, 208–9, 221–6
  purpose of 20–2, 187–202,
    210–16, 227
  snowplough parenting 189–90,
    192, 197–9, 221
  tiger parenting 201–2, 226, 241
Parikh, Amee 189–90
Passion Capital 131–2
Peel, Robert 64

peer pressure 226
Peery Foundation 130
Pereira, Camila 104–5
Perel, Esther 151
Pew Research Center 157
philanthropy 112–15, 130, 287, 292–3
Pink, Daniel H 10, 79
Pinker, Steven 218
Pintus, Walter 62–3
Play Bigger 60, 77
policing 49–51, 64–6
politicians 231–44, 248–56, 264, 268–71, 272, 296
populism 241, 247
poverty 245, 258, 260
principal-agent theory 111–17
Pritchett, Lant 56
Promberger, Marianne 43
Proulx, Christine 149
publishing industry 52–4, 74–6
Purpose 6, 7, 10, 11, 15, 38
  citizenship and 233, 234, 236, 237–50, 253, 254, 257–63, 270, 271, 272
  definition of 31
  parenting and 187–202, 210–16, 227
  reframing 61–8
  in relationships 37, 150–8, 167–72, 176
  and talent 108, 109–10, 124, 136
  work and 31–2, 33, 34–46, 47, 49, 61–8, 72, 84–6, 87, 88–9
Purvis, Jeanette 156
Putnam, Robert 159, 285

quality time 174

race, income inequality 19
Race To the Top 57
Ramaphosa, Cyril 254
Rauch, Jonathan 251–2
Ravitch, Diane 57–8
Rawls, John 103
Reed-Fitzke, Kayla 208
Reeves, Richard 145–6, 149
Reich, Kathy 293
relationships 19–20, 142–78, 291
  Autonomy in 159–63, 172–3, 176
  Mastery in 164–7, 173–5, 176
  Purpose in 37, 150–8, 167–72, 176
rewards 14, 156
Reynolds, Brian 133
Rezvani, Selena 76, 77–9, 86, 119
Robinson, Ken 197
Rogers, Carl 169
role-modelling 223–5
Romer, Paul 99
Rosen, Sherwin 96
Rosenfeld, Michael 152
Roser, Max 147
Rossiter, Jack 198
rote learning 15
Roth, Avery 295, 297
Russell, Bertrand 195–6
Ryan, Richard 10, 37, 41–2, 43, 71, 160, 173, 216–17

Sabarwal, Shwetlena 43
Sachs, Jonathan 158
Sacred Games (Netflix series) 64–5, 66
Saga 47, 49
Sandel, Michael J 102
scarcity mindset 96, 101
Schleicher, Andreas 291–3
Scoville, Heather 108

Second Home 63–4
self-actualization factors 151
self-advocation 78–9, 86
Sen, Amartya 245
Seran, Dr Nappinnai 152
Sethi, Jyotin 123, 124
sex 151
Shackelford, Schmitt and Buss
   154–5
Shah, Harshal 118–19, 120, 122
Sharma, Krishna 193
Shell, Ellen Ruppel 37–8
Sheth, Sneha 192–3, 205, 226
Shusterman, Melissa 296
Sims, Sam 39
Sinek, Simon 263
Singapore 79–80, 209, 221, 267
Singh, Gaurav 113, 114, 120, 303
Slemen, David 287
Sng, Oliver 154
social media 20, 21, 175, 176–7,
   183, 249–50, 252, 288
socialism 245
South Africa 254
Spero Ventures 105, 288
sport, talent in 93–5, 96–7, 104,
   109–10
Sportscotland 110
Sreekumar, Rajiv 151
Stepka, Allison 259
steps, taking small 292–4,
   298–300
Stern, Lord 265
STiR Education 2–7, 10–12,
   14–15, 42–3, 69–70, 71, 72, 87,
   103, 200, 220, 223, 251, 258,
   262, 296, 298
Stone, Jim 257
Strive Together 267
Subramanian, Arvind 259–60
success 17–18, 88, 92–138

survival of the fittest 108
Sweden 47–8, 49
Swedish Social Insurance Agency
   48

Tabichi, Peter 39–40
Taiwan 49
talent 17–18, 19, 91, 92–138
   Autonomy of 110–17, 128–31,
    136
   and Mastery 118, 119, 121–2,
    132–5, 136
   nurturers of 100–7, 109–10,
    117–18, 120–37, 161–2, 301
   and Purpose 108, 109–10, 136,
    124
Teach First 296
Teach For America 216, 296
Teach for India 216
teaching see education
Teaching Leaders 80–1
Teal organizations 68–9
technology 287–8
Tehusijarana, Rosita 191, 194,
   224, 226–7
ThoughtCo 108
321 Education Foundation 113,
   114
Thurman, Howard 141
time diaries 74
Tinder 152–3, 156
Tirole, Jean 43
Tough, Paul 199
Trey Athletics 133–4
Trump, Donald 242
Turnock, Lieutenant Colonel
   Steve 41, 67–8
Tyson, Mike 223

Uber 102
Uganda, parenting in 202–5

UNICEF 145
Unilever 63, 77
Uniqlo 93–4
United Nations 42, 246
University of Life 12
University of Minnesota 159
University of Southern California 189
USA 249
  Covid-19 279
  education in 206, 208
  happiness in 246–7
  marriage in 149
  parenting in 219–20
  politics in 250–1
Uzzi, Brian 105–6

The Varkey Foundation 39–40

Walsh, Boehm and Lyubomirsky 196
wealth inequality 102–3
Welch, Jack 76
Welcoming America 284–6
Welcoming International 284, 285
Wellcome Trust 30
Weston, Dr Kathy 288
What Works Centre for Homelessness 283
white identity politics 242–3
Whitty, Professor Chris 281
Widerquist, Karl 261
Williamson, Lucy 291
Wimbledon 95, 96–7, 125, 127, 132
winner takes all approach 97–8, 102, 103, 110, 138, 162, 232, 287
Wojcicki, Esther 201–2, 219–20

women: discrimination against 76, 77, 78
  recognition of talent 19
  work and 19–20, 161–3
Wong, Michael James 175
work 28–89
  Autonomy at 32, 49–58, 68–72, 87–8
  demotivation at 39
  effect of on women's lives 161–3
  hygiene factors 31–2, 33, 36, 43–4, 49, 61, 85, 155
  Mastery at 58–60, 63, 72–83, 86, 88
  Purpose at 16, 31–2, 33, 34–46, 47, 49, 61–8, 72, 84–6, 87, 88–9
  vs retirement 47
  work-life balance 17, 46–9
Working Mother (magazine) 162
Worku, Dianne 259
World Bank 40, 43, 115, 234, 245, 260
World Health Organization (WHO) 165, 278–9
Wuhan 277–9, 281, 282, 299

Yale University 102–3
Yang, Andrew 257
Young, Mel 110

'Zayna' 143–5, 146, 147, 171, 174
Zuckerberg, Mark 54
Zuma, Jacob 254

About the Author

Sharath Jeevan is one of the world's leading experts on reigniting our inner drive (intrinsic motivation). He founded and led STiR Education – arguably the world's largest intrinsic motivation initiative. STiR reignited the motivation of more than 200,000 teachers, 35,000 schools and 7 million children in emerging countries.

Sharath is currently Executive Chairman of Intrinsic Labs, which supports organizations all around the world to solve deep motivational challenges, from governments to leading UK universities and high-profile corporations. His work has been featured in *The New York Times*, *The Economist*, NPR, CNN, CNBC, *The Hindustan Times* and *The Times of India*. An accomplished speaker, Sharath has addressed large audiences at the Royal Festival Hall in London, Lego Ideas Festival in Denmark, TEDX Shiv Nadar Conference in Delhi and WISE Summit in Qatar, to name just a few.

Sharath holds degrees from Cambridge University, Oxford University and INSEAD. He was awarded an Honorary Doctorate for his contributions to the field of intrinsic motivation and was invited to serve on the high-level steering group of the Education Commission, the pre-eminent global think tank founded by former British Prime Minister Gordon Brown.

Sharath lives in London with his wife and two young boys.

Visit intrinsic-labs.com to find out more about Sharath and his work.